D1186774

The Unexplained

THE ULTIMATE GATEWAY TO THE WORLD OF THE UNKNOWN

The Unexplained

THE ULTIMATE GATEWAY TO THE WORLD OF THE UNKNOWN

Edited by

John and Anne Spencer

SIMON & SCHUSTER

A VIACOM COMPANY

First published in Great Britain by Simon & Schuster Ltd, 1997
A Viacom company

Copyright © First Information Group plc,1997

Produced by Good Publishing

This book is copyright under the Berne Convention.
No reproduction without permission.
All rights reserved.

1 3 5 7 9 10 8 6 4 2

Simon & Schuster Ltd
West Garden Place, Kendal Street, London W2 2AQ

Simon & Schuster Australia
Sydney

A CIP catalogue record for this book is available from the British Library

ISBN 0-684-81985-6

Contents

Introduction

Since civilisation began we have searched for a greater knowledge of ourselves and our planet. As our wisdom has grown, we have pushed back the boundaries of the unknown, solving many of the mysteries that confounded our ancestors. A belief has emerged that science and rationality can, and will, eventually reveal the truths behind our existence. But today, our understanding is far from complete. We even appear to have lost some of the great powers of early civilisations.

Our planet remains strange, and the closer we look, the more it seems beyond our laws of science and nature. This is a world we should not ignore: the world of The Unexplained - rain creatures falling from the sky, timeslips, hauntings and ghostly experiences, spontaneous combustion. Much of the phenomena that has been reported in the past continues today - repeated visitations from UFOs, alien abductions, monsters and beasts that elude capture. There are unknown powers that science cannot account for, even under close investigation - mind over matter, telepathic abilities, convincing near-death experience.

Clearly, we have much to learn about ourselves and the world around us. Examine the evidence. Explore the world of The Unexplained.

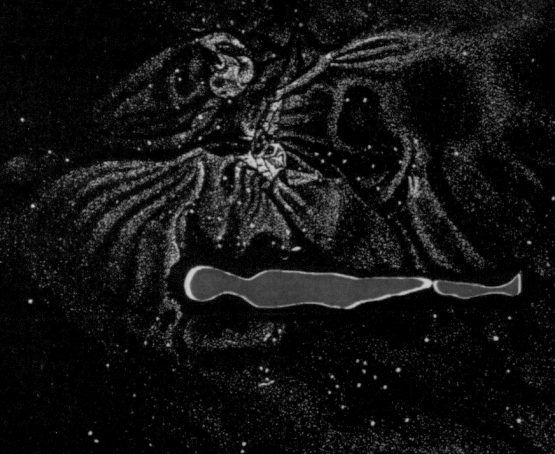

Chapter One

Strange Phenomena

Charles Hoy Fort, widely regarded as the father of modern phenomenalism, was once described as 'a sane man in a mad world'. The expression 'mad world' is sometimes used to refer to its inhabitants and their actions; but Fort's research led him to the conclusion that it was the planet itself which was strange, so numerous were its mysteries that could not be explained by science.

A descendant of Dutch immigrants, Fort was born in Albany, New York, in 1874. He spent his lifetime researching countless curious events - or 'unnature', as he called such phenomena - in the New York Public Library and the British Museum Library. His philosophy was to accept such events at face value, even if that meant discarding scientific orthodoxy. In fact, Fort was highly sceptical of scientific explanations, which he believed could sometimes be guilty of ignoring the evidence and rejecting the inexplicable. It was this rejection that led him to refer to unexplained phenomena as 'the realm of the damned'.

Fort presented the fruits of his exhaustive research in several published works. In one book alone he documented 40,000 incidents that could not be explained by the laws of nature. And 'the realm of the damned' was certainly diverse: sea ships sailing through the skies; aerial battles involving spectral armies; spiritual auras appearing before clairvoyants; fire-balls, spontaneous combustion, amazing coincidences and much else besides.

Fort's primary aim was not to seek explanations for such extraordinary occurrences, but simply to affirm their existence, provide all the evidence and leave the readers to make their own judgments. That is not to say, however, that Fort did not have his own theories regarding these phenomena. In fact, when contrasted with the plodding persistence of science, Fort's ideas were audaciously far-fetched and often brilliantly inspired. For example, when he read of strange yellow oil falling from the heavens, his reaction was not to analyse it, but to propose the existence of spacecraft with leaking engines flying between Venus and Mars. There was no solid evidence that such spacecraft existed, and yet his outlandish theory struck a chord with popular imagination. After Charles Fort, it was difficult NOT to imagine that there might be such things as UFOs.

The realm of the unexplained is, of course, fluid in nature. Occurrences regarded as mysterious and unnatural in one era can become widely understood in another as scientists push back the boundaries of knowledge. Meteors streaking through the skies fall into such a category. But other extraordinary happenings remain more doggedly resistant to the best efforts of science. Hordes of frogs raining down from the skies, for example, are as much a mystery today as they were in Fort's lifetime.

Opposite page: Artist's impression of an astral body floating in the cosmos

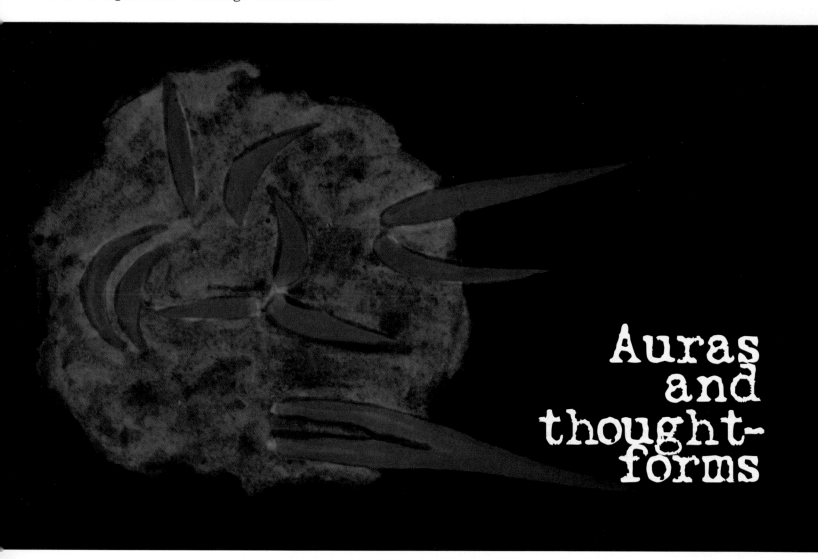

Auras and thought-forms

Above: Images of anger - a thought-form

The Spirit World And Astral Travel   For thousands of years people have believed the human body and spirit to be separable. At the core of many religions is the conviction that after death the soul moves into the spirit world. But is the separation of body and soul simply a question of faith? Or can the human spirit become a distinct, observable entity? Many clairvoyants are convinced that it is possible for the living to actually see or even visit the astral world; it is a phenomenon termed 'astral travel' or 'sky-walking'.

In the late 1860s, an American, Edwin Babbitt, was determined to see the astral plane for himself and report to others what he saw. After months of practice, his persistence was rewarded and he described the experience: 'At last I was able to see those glories of light and colour which no tongue can describe or intellect conceive of, unless they have seen.....And later, when I opened my eyes upon the sky and earth.....they seemed almost colourless and dim.'

Babbitt said he couldn't possibly have imagined the beauty he saw on his astral travels; but according to the 19th century clairvoyant Charles Leadbeater, the exquisite images on the astral plane are created by our very thoughts: 'Every thought gives rise to a set of correlated vibrations in the matter of the astral body, accompanied with a marvellous play of colour, like that of a waterfall as the sunlight strikes.'

Leadbeater called these images 'thought-forms', and his book on the subject had a revolutionary effect on the course of modern art. Leadbeater himself employed professional artists to paint his astral visions, and there are an increasing number of psychic artists today who claim to draw their inspiration from the spirit world. Many writers and musicians, too, have sought to convey the beauty of the astral plane.

Since the 1850s, a succession of pioneering scientists have searched for ways of revealing and using the human aura for practical purposes. A breakthrough was achieved with the invention of aura photography in 1939. Russian scientist Semyon Kirlian, having accidentally received a sparking shock from an electrical device, went on to develop what he saw as a means of capturing the image of an aura on photographic paper. Kirlian photography has produced images of both plant and animal material, and, although still considered controversial within conventional medical practice, it is now used by many doctors to detect diseases such as cancer.

Examples of the Soul

In 1918, the writer Ernest Hemingway was wounded by a mortar blast. He later told a friend he felt his spirit leaving his body at that time, and wrote of the experience in his novel A Farewell To Arms: 'I tried to breathe but my breath would not come....I felt myself forced bodily out of myself and out and out and out and all the time bodily in the wind. I went out swiftly, all of myself, and knew I was dead and that it had all been a mistake to think you had just died. Then I floated, and instead of going on, I felt myself slide back. I breathed and I was back.'

When William Blake was 29, he watched the death of his younger brother and reported seeing 'the released spirit ascend heavenwards, clapping for joy'.

The Astral Plane

The word 'astral' comes from the Greek word meaning 'starry'. Clairvoyants say that we all have an 'astral body' - a 'star body' - which exists on a different plane to our physical world. Those who can see this body say it is luminescent and charged with ever-changing colours: a colourful cluster of twinkling stars.

The astral body is said to encase the physical one like a sheath. But when the physical body falls asleep, or loses consciousness, mystics believe that the spirit can slip away to swim in the realm of the stars. Unfortunately, most people only recall these experiences as strange, confused dreams. Clairvoyants believe, however, that we can discipline the spirit - by meditation and other exercises - to practise this body-free flight consciously, and afterwards recall the experience vividly.

Astral Thought-forms

Among the many mysterious things which clairvoyants can see on the astral plane are the images created by human thought. Charles Leadbeater called these 'thought-forms'. Leadbeater was accustomed to observing auras and other psychic entities, and felt the need to communicate what he saw to those less privileged than himself.

In a remarkable series of experiments conducted in London at the end of the 19th century, Leadbeater attempted to record these astral thought-forms. Working with a group of artists who were interested in the occult, he described the forms he could see on the higher plane so that they could paint them. For the first time, something of the nature of the hidden world was revealed to those who had not been trained to see it.

One such image shows the thought-forms created when one mixed anger with jealousy - emotions indicated by red slashes and a green cloud respectively. These contrast dramatically with thoughts which are well-meaning or contented. Serene blue tends to predominate in such calm thought patterns, and the forms are usually more geometric.

Above: The soul leaves the body of a dying girl

Below: Ernest Hemingway felt his spirit leave his body

Origins of Abstract Art

When the Russian-born artist Vasily Kandinsky first saw the astral music forms in Charles Leadbeater's book, he was so fascinated that he decided to incorporate the ideas into his own work. Whether Kandinsky learned to see astral forms for himself is not clear; but what is certain is that his interest in the subject led him to produce, around 1910, what some regard as the very first abstract paintings.

Kandinsky had a profound influence on the painter Paul Klee, and subsequently a whole generation of artists. It may therefore be true that the roots of modern abstract art can be traced back to two clairvoyants' experiments with astral forms.

Auras and Science History

Clairvoyants are not alone in claiming to have seen auras. Some doctors and scientists, who are accustomed to making

Above: Nikola Tesla described an electro-magnetic fluid similar to von Reichenbach's zodic fluid

Below: A Kirlian photograph recording the interplay of biogenetic energies on the surface of a leaf

careful observations, have also described these phenomena.

In the 1840s, the German chemist Baron Carl von Reichenbach was one of the first scientists to represent auras in graphic form. After studying animal magnetism, he claimed to have discovered a new force - 'Od' - the intermediate between electricity, magnetism, heat and light. According to von Reichenbach, this force was detectable only by especially sensitive people. The emanations could best be seen as a glow around magnets and some gemstones, but they could also be perceived around human beings. He called these 'odic fluids'.

After von Reichenbach's experiments, many other scientists and doctors tried to put his discoveries to practical use. The extraordinary Croatian-American Nikola Tesla (1856-1943) described an electro-magnetic force remarkably similar to the 'odic fluid' in his work with transformers, dynamos and electricity.

In the 1930s, the English scientist George de la Warr claimed that there is an electronic web around the human body. He constructed a machine to identify subtle radiations from human beings and objects. This 'radionics box' was used for diagnostic and healing purposes.

Kirlian Technology

In 1939, the Russian engineer Semyon Kirlian was adjusting an electrical device when his hand accidentally got too close to a live electrode. The electric shock and visible flash which resulted interested him, and he repeated the incident, this time including light-sensitive paper. When the photograph was developed, he saw streamer-like emanations from the image of his fingers. Kirlian and his wife went on to produce hundreds of such images, and many came to believe that this photographic technique was showing what psychics had seen for themselves - the aura.

The basic device used in Kirlian photography is quite simple. A light-box is connected to a transforming generator to create an electrical discharge of up to 30,000 volts. This discharge is transferred on to a surface with an object resting on light-sensitive paper. The photograph records the interplay of biogenetic energies on the surfaces of objects or parts of the body - usually the hands. This originates in negative form and is rephotographed to reverse the image.

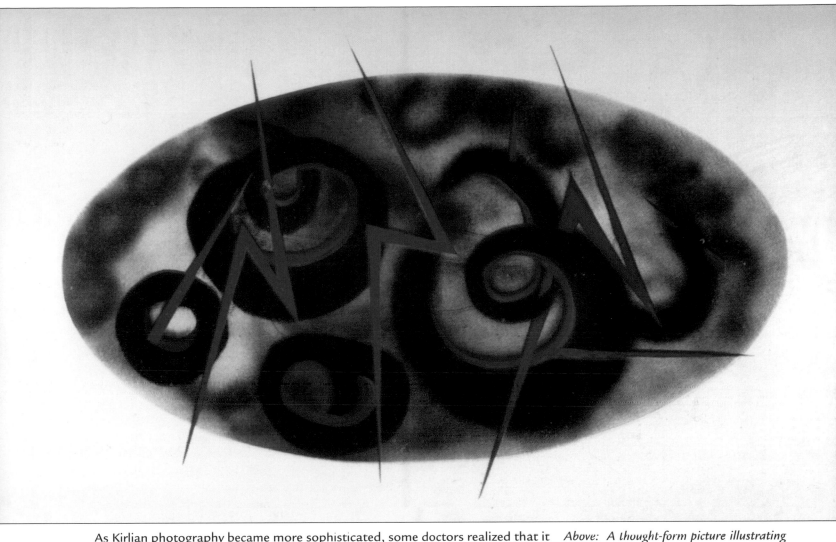

Above: A thought-form picture illustrating
anger, from Charles Leadbeater's book
Man Visible and Invisible

As Kirlian photography became more sophisticated, some doctors realized that it could record the body energies which reflect our general state of health. As a result, some medical practitioners began to use this technique for diagnostic purposes, even though its mechanism remained unexplained. In Athens, the psychiatrist Dr Marangoni-Adamenko has used Kirlian photography to diagnose psychological disorders; in the USA, Dr Alfred Benjamin uses it for the early detection of cancer; and at Madras University, Dr Ramesh Singh Chouhan and Dr Srinivas Bathula have researched into Kirlian images of the fingertips and have also found the technique invaluable in detecting cancer. Some medical centres use macro lenses to show the response of blood or plasma to voltage-sensitive liquid crystals. Although Kirlian photography has its advocates, its use in conventional medicine remains controversial.

Auras The aura marks the interface between the physical and spiritual planes. It really belongs to the realm beyond the veil, and so is usually hidden from sight, but sometimes it can appear as a luminescence around people, animals and plants, and even minerals. According to clairvoyants, human auras are the most beautiful and complex of all.

Auras were often depicted in medieval Christian art. The halo, the glory and the nimbus are different representations of auras, indicating that a person is holy or has direct access to the spiritual world. The more spiritual a person is, the stronger and more splendid the aura. While the aura of an ordinary person may radiate only a few inches from the physical body, that of an initiate may extend to several feet. Since Buddha is believed to have been spiritually perfect, his aura was said to be several miles wide.

Mysterious Fires

Fire and lightning, although awesome in power and spectacular in nature, might appear somewhat misplaced in being categorised as strange phenomena. Surely it was in the Middle Ages when such events were regarded as unnatural, even portentous, and they have long since been comprehensively explained? While it is true that science has supplied a lot of the answers regarding such phenomena, and they may no longer be seen with such ominous import, there are many particular manifestations which remain shrouded in mystery. Fire-balls, lightning tattoos and Spontaneous Human Combustion fall into this category; all are well documented and continue to baffle the scientific world. Accounts of incidents such as these are powerful enough in their own right, but their impact is made even greater by our instinctive fear of fire.

Underground Lightning
To early man, lightning came from the hands of the Gods themselves. Although we are now closer to understanding the scientific nature of lightning, there are many aspects which still defy explanation. One such example is its ability to penetrate deep into the earth.

On July 5, 1855, lightning struck coalminers a thousand feet below the ground at Himmelsfrith, Germany: 'Some of us felt a blow upon the back, while others were struck about the arms and legs. It appeared as if we were all shaken together by some great invisible hand, which seemed to come out of the ground, the roof and the sides of the galleries at one and the same time. In the darkness, we began to blame each other, and a fight would have broken out had it not become clear that something strange was happening.'

Lightning Tattoos
Lightning has also been known to burn 'shadows' of what it has travelled through onto objects or skin. People sheltering under trees when lightning has struck have been branded with images of branches.

In 1825, a sailor aboard the ship Buon-Servo, which was anchored in the Adriatic, was killed by lightning. He had been sitting below the mast when he was struck, and his body was subsequently inspected by a doctor. He found a long dark narrow line, stretching from the neck to the small of the back. Mysteriously, near his groin was tattooed a perfect image of a horseshoe. This was an exact copy of the horseshoe which was nailed to the foremast of the ship as an amulet to ward off evil spirits.

Above: Ball Lightning

Carbon Copies

In 1752, lightning struck the church in Antrasme, France. Hitting the tower first, it left a trail of burn marks down the aisle, as a clergyman explained: 'It melted the gilding of the picture-frames, blackened the faces of the saints, and made its exit from the church by burning two round holes through the floor of the chapel.'

The damage was repaired, the pictures repainted and reframed, and the holes in the chapel floor filled with cement. But then, 14 years later, the church tower was struck again. The lightning hit the same point on the tower, left a similar snail-trail of burns in the church, damaged the same pictures, and left through two holes in the floor which precisely matched the exit points 14 years earlier.

Human Conductors

Although the saying has it that lightning never strikes the same spot twice, there is evidence to show that it is attracted to particular places. Stranger still, certain people seem to have a dangerous affinity with lightning, having been struck on numerous occasions against incalculable odds.

According to 'Fate' magazine (May 1952), during World War 1, Major Summerford was wounded by lightning in Flanders, Belgium. The bolt knocked him off his horse and paralysed him from the waist down. He retired to Vancouver, Canada, where he took up fishing. In 1924, he was with three angling friends when lightning hit the tree they were sitting by. On this occasion, Summerford's right side was paralysed. He recovered sufficiently to be able to take walks in Vancouver park, where, in 1930, he was struck yet again, and this time paralysed permanently. He died two years later, but in a weird postscript to the misfortune that befell him in his lifetime, Summerford's tombstone was shattered by lightning in 1934.

The Guinness Book of Records (1996) states that Roy C Sullivan was struck by lightning seven times. The ex-Park Ranger from Virginia was first hit in 1942, losing his big toenail. He was struck a further six times between 1969 and 1977, sustaining various injuries in the process. Sadly, having survived all these close calls, Sullivan committed suicide in 1983 after being rejected in love.

Above: A sailor sitting below the mast was killed by lightning. On his body, near his groin, was tattooed an exact copy of the horseshoe nailed to the foremast

Below: Lightning over Johannesburg, 1991. To early man, lightning came from the Gods themselves

*Above: Comet -
the origin of the mythical Firedrake?
Below: In 1561,
the inhabitants of Nuremberg witnessed
an incredible sky vision*

Wild Electricity

Even in the harnessed form of a domestic power supply, electricity doesn't always behave in expected ways. On February 14, 1990, in the Italian village of San Gottardo, the electrical power system appeared to go completely out of control. One inhabitant saw that the fusebox outside his house was burning. A new one was fitted, but this also burned through. Then a succession of mysterious events began to plague the village: car indicators flashed and engines started, apparently on their own; television sets switched themselves on and off; a pair of ski boots, an armchair and a wheelchair caught fire; and observers reported car lights melting 'in front of their eyes' and bursting into flames.

People began to complain of headaches and skin inflammations which would not respond to treatment. Family members started taking turns to sleep, so that there was always someone awake to ensure that their houses did not burn down.

Some people blamed these incidents on neighbours, while others said it was the work of the Devil himself. Certainly the local emergency services were baffled, and the little mountain village was finally invaded by an army of special investigators. But they fared no better, and no explanation for these extraordinary events was ever found.

Sky Fires

There have been many reports of strange fires in the sky which could never be associated with lightning. In medieval times, balls of fire seen in the sky were believed to come from firebreathing monsters roaming above the Earth. Mythical creatures such as the 'Firedrake' came from a band of fire between the Earth and the Moon, and were capable of bursting free to wreak havoc. This myth was still current in the 16th century, when two of the most famous sky fires were seen: at Nuremberg, in Germany, and Basel, in Switzerland.

In 1561, the inhabitants of Nuremberg witnessed an incredible sight in the sky overhead: 'At sunrise, blood-red fire-globes were seen moving rapidly in the skies above

Left: Above the town of Basel in 1566, large black balls were seen in the sky, moving with great speed

Below: Dr. Sestier observed a display of globular fire which brought down trees and damaged houses

the city. The skies also displayed moving, blood-coloured crosses, and two cylinders. Suddenly, it was as though all these strange objects began to fight. Soon it seemed to the onlookers that the entire skies were on fire.'

Five years later, a similar phenomenon was seen above the town of Basel: 'Many large black balls were seen in the sky, moving with great speed. They would turn towards each other, as though fighting. One or two of them became blood-red, and became like fire.'

On these two famous occasions no one was hurt; but fire-balls can be deadly, and continue to be reported, despite the general scientific view that they don't even exist.

Fire-balls or Meteors?

Fire-balls are often dismissed as being no more mysterious than meteors. However, when meteors burst from outer space into the Earth's atmosphere, they usually disintegrate through friction with the air.

'The World of Wonders' (1893) explains how, in 1885, two doctors in Fonvielle, France, witnessed the same event but interpreted it in completely different ways. One doctor thought he had seen meteors, the other claimed that this was impossible: 'Dr Gardino saw many globes of fire hovering on all sides. They floated at a slight distance above the ground, before exploding to cause all kinds of damage.'

Dr Sestier, who observed the same display of globular fire, called them meteors. He noted that this fiery display killed a man who was asleep in his bed, and struck several animals. It also brought down a number of trees and damaged houses.

Spook-lights

'Spook-lights' - mysterious lights with no apparent energy source - were once thought to be the work of evil fairies. The Will o' the Wisp, for instance, was believed to lure travellers over marshes and hidden pools to their doom.

Above: Will o'the Wisp was believed to lure travellers to their doom

Below: John Heymer concluded that Spontaneous Human Combustion is caused by gas-fuelled flame within the body

Today we no longer believe in these mischievous spirits; but investigators in Norway have now shown that 'spook-lights' might actually be directed by some form of intelligence.

So many strange lights have been seen in the remote farming district of Hessdalen, in Norway, that it has become a place of pilgrimage for scientists and amateur enthusiasts hoping to record and measure them. Erling Strand made a remarkable discovery when he led one such project in the early 1980s. When he directed a laser beam at one of the lights, it started flashing twice as fast, indicating that it was reacting to the stimulus.

Spontaneous Human Combustion

Perhaps the most terrifying mystery concerning fire is Spontaneous Human Combustion, where humans have inexplicably exploded into flames. The source of the fire appears to be internal rather than external, and the body is usually almost entirely consumed by the flames, while the surroundings remain untouched, except for thick deposits of soot.

In 1951, in St Petersburg, Florida, the charred remains of 67-year-old Mary Reeser were found in her apartment under mystifying circumstances. Her body had almost completely disintegrated: it had been reduced to a burnt skull, a few spinal bones, and one foot, which was still wearing a black satin slipper. The surrounding area, meanwhile, was largely untouched. Arson experts, pathologists and the FBI were all called in, but the cause of the fire could not be established. The coroner finally recorded a verdict of accidental death, but it remains unexplained to this day: a classic case of Spontaneous Human Combustion.

This phenomenon was widely recognised in the 19th century too. For example, on February 19, 1888, the remains of a soldier were found in a hayloft in Colchester, England. Although his body had been burnt to a crisp, the wood adjacent to it was only slightly charred, while the hay all around was unscathed.

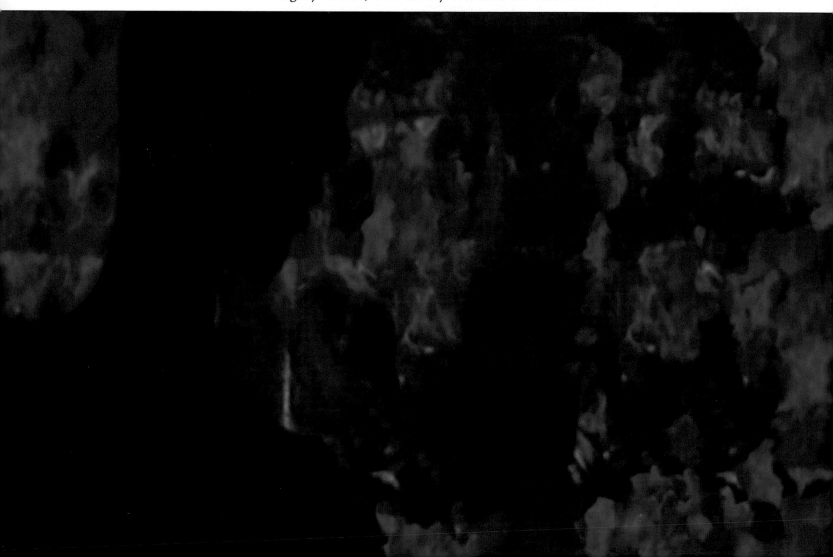

Left: Clearing up after the charred remains of Mary Reeser were found in her apartment

Below: Mary Reeser's death remains a mystery to this day - a classic case of Spontaneous Human Combustion

The finding of burnt remains must often lead to a suspicion of foul play, but there have been instances when people have burst into flames in public. In 1938, a girl died after suddenly catching fire in a ballroom in Chelmsford, England; and in 1980, another English girl burst into flames at a disco in Darlington. Had these victims of spontaneous combustion consumed huge amounts of alcohol? Were they wearing flammable clothing? No explanation can be found to account for the intense heat needed to reduce bones to mere ashes.

A few people are known to have survived Spontaneous Human Combustion. One such person was Jack Angel, who fell asleep in November 1974 and woke four days later to find his right hand burnt black. He also had burn marks on his chest, legs and back but, amazingly, felt no pain. Angel went outside, where he collapsed and was taken to hospital. His hand had to be amputated and was described as having burnt from inside out. His bed and his motor-home were untouched by fire.

On October 9, 1980, Jeanne Winchester was a passenger in a car in Florida when she burst into yellow flames. The driver of the vehicle quickly put the fire out, but she had already suffered severe burns. Jeanne had no memory of the fire, which is characteristic of many cases of spontaneous combustion; the victims, if found alive, are rarely able to recall what happened.

One of the most committed investigators into the phenomenon of spontaneous combustion is the retired British detective John Heymer. In 1995, Heymer came to the conclusion that the intense heat which causes spontaneous combustion is gas-fuelled flame that comes from within the body. This is the only plausible explanation for the high temperatures attained in some localized areas.

Some of the most important clues which led to this conclusion came from a case which occurred on September 13, 1967. On this occasion, the fireman reached the scene in time to observe a blue flame still issuing with considerable force from a slit in the victim's abdomen. It must be assumed that the man was still alive when the flames had begun to consume him, for in his agony he had bitten deep into the wooden post of the stair-well into which he had fallen.

Although the theory regarding gas-fuelled flames is the most plausible explanation of Spontaneous Human Combustion, exactly how and why it occurs remains a mystery.

Coincidences

In the autumn of 1994, a 60-year-old Dutchman, Cor Stoop, took a pleasure cruise in the North Sea. Unfortunately, he became seasick during the trip, and if that were not bad enough, his illness caused him to lose his false teeth overboard. Three months later, a fisherman caught a cod with a pair of false teeth inside it. After hearing this story on the radio, Mr Stoop was reunited with his teeth.

Coincidences often appear meaningless, or perhaps the work of some 'cosmic joker'. But in 'The Book of the Damned', Charles Fort wrote of the interconnectedness of things; he believed that no event is completely without meaning, a point which he graphically illustrated: 'Not a bottle of catsup can fall from a tenement-house fire-escape in Harlem without....affecting the price of pyjamas in Jersey City.'

Until recently, coincidences weren't considered a proper subject for study; but the extraordinary nature of some of the documented examples have changed all that. Stories that seem far too uncanny to have occurred simply by chance have exercised some of the greatest minds of the 20th century; and their investigations and deliberations have spawned a startling range of theories on the subject.

Coincidence Theories Albert Einstein, Carl Jung and Arthur Koestler were among those fascinated by coincidences. According to Jung, who teamed up with Nobel prize winner Wolfgang Pauli, coincidences are connected not by cause but by meaning. He believed that everything that takes place at a particular moment in time shares the qualities of that moment, and all those events are therefore linked. To explain his theory he coined the word 'synchronicity', which he defined as 'the

Above: Twins separated at birth and reunited years later often discover extraordinary similarities between them

simultaneous occurrence of two meaningfully but not causally connected events'. Jung believed that sometimes, so-called 'coincidences' were 'connected so meaningfully that their "chance" concurrence would represent a degree of improbability that would have to be expressed by an astronomical figure'. Jung thought that we should open up our minds and lives to synchronicity, and cited examples indicating how often coincidences seem to help us:

A woman owned a lucky sixpence that was engraved with her initials. She lost it one day and was distraught - until she went into a shop and received the coin in her change.

A great bishop was ousted from power and forced to return to the humble life of a monk. In despair he threw his ring of office into a lake. A week later, the monks had fish for dinner, and when it was cut open, the ring was found inside. As a result, the ex-bishop was triumphantly restored to office.

These are the most satisfying kinds of coincidence, making us believe that there is some powerful, benevolent force shaping our lives. Whether we try to do good or evil, we know as little about the long-term consequences of our actions as the fish did when it swallowed the bishop's ring.

The biologist Paul Kammerer believed that there was a fundamental principle in the universe which tended towards unity: a force of attraction comparable to gravity. But whereas gravity acts on all mass without discrimination, Kammerer's universal force acts selectively, bringing similar things together in space and time. According to Kammerer, the study of what he called 'seriality' would change the destiny of mankind, since it is 'ubiquitous and continuous in life, nature and the cosmos'. Einstein once remarked that Kammerer's theory was 'by no means absurd'.

In the early years of the 20th century, Kammerer collected exactly one hundred examples of coincidences. Most were trivial, with only one or two layers of coincidence, but some were remarkable. His 10th case concerned two young German soldiers who, in 1915, were separately admitted to the same military hospital in Bohemia. They had never met before. It transpired that both had been born in Silesia 19 years earlier, both were suffering from pneumonia, both were volunteers in the Transport Corps, and both were called Franz Richter - making at least six 'parameters' of coincidence.

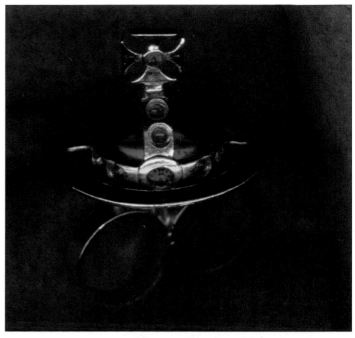

Above: A bishop who threw his ring of office into a lake was served it up in a fish a week later

Below left: Albert Einstein was fascinated by coincidences

Below right: Carl Jung believed that coincidences are connected not by cause but by meaning

Above: Two Mr Melchisadecs coincide over a Nova at the Royal Observatory in Edinburgh

Below: Emile Deschamps is served up a coincidence on a plate

Star Turn

Many people have experienced the infuriating situation in which two versions of the same events differ, and both parties are convinced that theirs is the correct account. If recourse to an unimpeachable source is possible, the matter can usually be settled one way or the other. But just occasionally, perhaps it is possible for both parties to be proved right.

Scottish astronomer Professor Archie Roy received a phone call one day from a stranger with an unusual name: Mr Melchisadec. The stranger wished to claim the discovery of a new star - perhaps a nova. Professor Roy told him to contact the Royal Observatory at Edinburgh. Roy himself then rang a colleague at the university to pass on the news. 'I've just been talking to a Mr Melchisadec on the phone about a nova,' said Professor Roy.

'You can't have been,' his colleague replied. 'Mr Melchisadec has been here for the past half hour, talking to me about a nova, and he hasn't phoned anyone.'

After some argument and confusion, it emerged that there were two Mr Melchisadecs, who were not related and did not know each other. They had indeed been talking at the same time - one about a new star, and the other about a 'Nova' computer.

Just Desserts

One of the oldest and most absurd stories in which coincidence figures prominently concerns the French poet Emile Deschamps and a traditional English dessert - plum pudding.

As a schoolboy, Deschamps was given a slice of plum pudding by a friend of his parents, Monsieur de Fortgibu. He had never tasted it before and it left a great impression on him. Ten years later, he was passing a restaurant in Paris when he noticed a delicious-looking plum pudding inside. He went in to try it, only to discover that the last slice had just been ordered by an elderly gentleman sitting in the corner. It was Monsieur de Fortgibu, whom Deschamps had not seen in those intervening years.

Many more years passed, in which Deschamps saw neither Monsieur de Fortgibu nor another piece of plum pudding. Then he was invited to a dinner party, where he was told that the pudding in question would be served. Deschamps promptly amused the other guests with his story about the earlier coincidence, and concluded by saying: 'All we need now is Monsieur de Fortgibu'. At that moment, the door opened and in walked a frail old gentleman. Monsieur de Fortgibu had been invited to a different dinner party and had come to the wrong address.

Killing Joke

In the film 'The World According to Garp', Robin Williams buys a house which a plane has crashed into, because he is sure that nothing bad will ever happen there again. Clearly he had never heard of the cosmic joker.

In Bermuda, a man was knocked off his moped and killed by a taxi. Exactly a year later, his brother was riding the same moped when the same taxi came down the same street carrying the same passenger, who was not a regular taxi user. Again they collided, and again the rider was killed.

In 1784, Daniel Spicer of Leyden, Massachusetts, died following an attack in which he was shot twice. Three years later, Daniel's brother was wearing the same coat when he too was the victim of an attack and died from two bullet wounds. It was found that the bullets had passed exactly through the same two holes.

These gruesome coincidences cannot compare with events that took place in Tokyo in 1657, however. A kimono had belonged in turn to three teenage girls, each of whom had died before it could be worn. A priest was called in to burn the unlucky garment; but as he was doing so, a wind blew up and fanned the flames out of control. The resulting fire destroyed three-quarters of the city and killed 100,000 people.

Parallel Lives

There are many accounts of identical twins being separated at birth and reunited many years later to discover extraordinary similarities between them, down to the tiniest details of their lives. One of the most remarkable concerns identical twin boys, who were adopted by different families shortly after their birth in 1940.

Almost 40 years later, they were reunited and found that they had both been christened James. Each had married a woman named Linda and had a son - one named James Alan, the other James Allan. Each had then divorced and married a woman called Betty. And both had a dog named Toy.

Biological factors may explain some similarities between twins, even those that are separated. But what of people who are not related, yet seem to have parallel lives? This was the case with a Mr Armstrong and a Mr Riesneren, two complete strangers who met one day. They found that as well as looking similar, they shared the same birth date. Their paths crossed one further time in more tragic circumstances: their cars collided with each other and both men were killed.

The Newspaper Spy

In 1944, the German High Command were probably too busy to sit around doing the Daily Telegraph crossword puzzle. But if they had, they might have discovered the top-secret code names for the Allied invasion of Europe. Clues which appeared at the time included:

This bush is a centre of nursery revolutions - (8)

Britannia and he hold to the same thing - (7)

Some big-wig like this has stolen some of it at times - (8)

'Mulberry', the answer to the first clue, was the code name for the artificial harbours used for beachhead supply. 'Neptune', the second answer, was the code word for naval plans. And 'Overlord', the third, was the name given to the entire operation. Other code names, such as 'Omaha' and 'Utah', also cropped up in the puzzles.

Military intelligence raided the Telegraph's offices, expecting to find a German spy; instead they found a bewildered schoolteacher who had been compiling the puzzle for the previous 20 years and had no idea about the breach of security.

History shows that Germany reaped no benefit from such an extraordinary coincidence, nor was it the only one of its kind as far as World War 2 was concerned. For just two weeks before the bombing of Pearl Harbour, two advertisements for a new dice game appeared in the 'New Yorker'. Under the slogan 'Achtung' - 'Warning' - 'Alerte' was a picture of two dice, showing the numbers 12, 7, 5 and 0. The attack on Pearl Harbour took place on December 7, at 5.00am. Once again it was just coincidence - but this time, no one noticed until after the attack.

Missing Words

In 1973, the British actor Anthony Hopkins was signed to star in a film version of a novel by George Feifer - 'The Girl from Petrovka'. He scoured all the bookshops in London's Charing Cross Road for a copy of the book, but could not find one. Eventually he went to Leicester Square underground station to catch a train home - and found a copy of the book lying on a bench.

Later, he met George Feifer, who confessed that even he didn't have a copy of his own book. He had lent his personal annotated copy to a friend in London, and it had been stolen from his car. 'Is this the one?' Hopkins

Above: A kimono caused the death of 100,000 people

Below: Charing Cross Road bookshops failed to produce a copy of The Girl from Petrovka *for actor Anthony Hopkins who, that same day, found the author's own copy lying on a bench*

enquired, 'with the notes scribbled in the margin?' It was indeed the author's own copy.

The French astronomer Camille Flammarion was writing a chapter about the wind for his book 'The Atmosphere', when a gust blew the loose pages out of his window. A few days later, he was astonished to receive proofs of the missing chapter from his publisher. It transpired that the pages had been found by the publisher's messenger, who had gathered them up and taken them to be typeset in the usual way.

Coincidence or Second Sight?

Where does one draw the line between coincidence and clairvoyance? Can all cases of 'precognition' actually be put down to coincidence?

When King Louis XV1 of France was a young boy, an astrologer warned him to be on his guard on the 21st day of every month. The boy was terrified, and thereafter refused to do any important business on that day. However, although he tried to regulate his own life, he found that he could not control events. On June 21, 1791, he and Marie Antoinette were arrested at Varennes as they tried to escape from the Revolution. On September 21, 1792, France abolished the monarchy. And on January 21, 1793, Louis XV1 was beheaded. Had the astrologer really been able to see into the future, he might have given King Louis some more useful advice.

Above: Louis XVI was warned to be on his guard on the 21st day of every month

Below: There are many stories about those who decide not to catch an ill-fated flight

Fashionably Late

Stories abound of people who, for some reason, failed to catch a certain plane which then crashed, killing everyone on board. The good fortune of those who missed their flight must, of course, be balanced against the ill-luck of those who did not. But on March 1, 1950, a series of chance events caused delays which were to benefit all.

The incident occurred in the town of Beatrice, Nebraska, where a church choir's practice had been scheduled to start at 7.20 on the evening in question. But, extraordinarily, everyone involved was running late: the minister's wife was having problems pressing her daughter's dress; two choristers wanted to listen to a particular radio programme; another young girl was desperately trying to finish her maths homework; one family's car wouldn't start. Everyone had a different reason for being late, the consequence being that no one was in or near the church when, at 7.25 pm, it was completely destroyed by a gas explosion.

Sorry, Right Number

In the British comedy show 'Monty Python's Flying Circus', a man who is in the middle of nowhere suddenly finds that his bicycle needs

fixing. He pushes it to the next village to be informed by a local that there is just a single shop. Absurdly, it turns out to be a bicycle repair shop.

The author of Jonathan Livingston Seagull, Richard Bach, had an even greater stroke of luck when his rare 1929 biplane broke a strut as it came in to land in a remote part of the American Midwest. Only eight such planes had ever been built, and repairing it seemed an impossibility.

A man then appeared on the scene, saying that he had a pile of old machinery and an assortment of parts. Bach was naturally pessimistic, but, amazingly, the component needed was there, just ten feet from where they were standing. As Bach wrote later, the odds against this happening were 'so high that coincidence was a foolish answer'.

In 1967, an English policeman named

Peter Moscardi told a friend that the number of his police station had changed to 40166. In fact, he'd got the number wrong, but neither person realised the mistake until Constable Moscardi was on patrol duty a few days later. He went to investigate a factory which had been inexplicably left open, with its lights blazing. As he looked around, the phone started ringing and Moscardi answered it on impulse. On the other end was his friend, who was trying to call him at the police station on the 'wrong' number - 40166.

Above: Flying over a particular field, aerial photographer of crop circles, F C Taylor, thought how neat it would be to have a crop circle in the shape of a Celtic cross. The following day he discovered just such a circle had appeared

Wish Fulfilment

In his book on *Daimonic Reality*, Patrick Harpur describes how as a little boy he was desperate for a fishing-rod. After weeks of doing odd jobs and saving his money, he was still half a crown short of the amount needed.

One day he was sitting on a grass verge, wondering if he would ever have enough for his intended purchase. As he did so, he idly began prising weeds out of the ground with his fingers. One weed was particularly stubborn, but when Harpur finally managed to pull it up, he found a half-crown coin, green with age, caught up in its roots.

Harpur believes that coincidences often contain an element of wish fulfilment. To support his theory, Harpur relates the story of an aerial photographer of crop circles, F C Taylor, who was flying over a field one day, thinking about a recent quintuplet of circles. How neat it would be, he thought, if the five circles could be joined together by a ring, to form a sort of Celtic cross. Flying over the same field the following day, he discovered that such a ring had appeared.

Sky Visions

Many people automatically associate unexplained phenomena in the skies with UFOs or alien activity of some kind. However, not all reports of strange visions overhead involve cigar-shaped flying craft. Indeed, many such visions appear recognisably terrestrial, mundane even, in form; mundane, that is, when observed on the Earth's surface. But when people have claimed to see such things as armies doing battle in the heavens, then these occurrences are no less bizarre than the archetypal flying saucer.

Many witnesses have reported seeing huge spectral armies in the sky, even great battles taking place in the air. Such stories have prompted different explanations. Perhaps a battle or event was so dreadful that it has left an imprint on the astral plane, to be played out over and over again in the heavens; or perhaps the visions appeared as predictions of impending defeat.

Even if one rejects the suggestion that sky visions predict the future, they can certainly be said to have influenced it. In 312 AD, a fiery cross seen in the sky may have altered the whole course of history. For if Emperor Constantine hadn't seen this vision, which occurred on the eve of battle, Christianity might never have become one of the world's major religions.

Astral Imprints

In 1642, during the English Civil War, sky battles were said to have taken place above two battlefields: Naseby and Edgehill. At Naseby, the battle was observed annually for about a century afterwards. The ghostly Edgehill battles were replayed over a number of weekends and were extraordinarily vivid.

Edgehill was the first important battle of the Civil War. It resulted in the deaths of 2,000 men, and seems to have left an imprint on the astral plane. Just two months after the battle, people saw ghostly re-enactments in the skies, accompanied by the crash of gunfire and the sound of the cavalry. When news of this battle in the sky reached Charles 1, he ordered an investigation. The reporting officer, Colonel Sir Lewis Kirk, went to Edgehill and saw the spectral battle himself. To his astonishment, he was able to recognise comrades of his among the phantom warriors, some of whom were living and others already dead.

Aerial Armageddon

On a single day in 1646, also during the Civil War, a succession of strange apparitions was heard as well as seen above Cambridge and Norfolk: 'A Navie or Fleet of Ships under Sayle. A Ball of wild-Fire rolling up and downe. Three men strugling with one another, one having a Sword in his hand....Extraordinary beating of Drumes in the ayre, & a Piller of Cloud ascending up from the earth like a spire-Steeple, being opposed by a Speare or Lance downwards.'

The most famous sky vision of modern times occurred near the Portuguese village of Fatima in 1917. Three children believed that they saw 'a lady of Heaven' in the clouds. Although the vision was a peaceful one, it later warned the children that humankind was in danger of destroying itself. Decades later, this seems to have been a forewarning of the nuclear arms race. Perhaps, with the end of the Cold War, this danger has at last been averted.

Astral Armageddon

Violent sky visions are most often seen at times of political or religious crisis. At the height of the Reformation in 16th century Europe, the German writer Grunbeck described one such vision: 'The heavens themselves opened, and a great army of mounted warriors, their horses armoured for battle, leapt through the crowds towards the sun.'

Also in the 16th century, Ambroise Pare, the great French doctor and friend of Nostradamus, described another sky vision, one that was: '....so horrible that common people died in the street from fear. It was a blood-covered comet, and I could see the shapes of a curved arm holding a large sword, ready to strike. At the end of the blade were three stars, and to the sides could be seen axes, knives and swords.'

Custer's Last Stand

If General Custer had taken notice of a mysterious sky vision, his regiment might have been saved. According to the writer Fairfax Downey, when Custer rode with the 7th US Cavalry against the Sioux indians in May 1876, an aerial vision seemed to predict their fate. As they rode out of Fort Abraham Lincoln, the residents watching the departure saw half the regiment rise up and vanish into the skies. Just one month later, on June 25, the Battle of the Little Big Horn took place. In this famous encounter, where the Indians were led by Sitting Bull and Crazy Horse, almost half of Custer's 600-strong regiment were massacred.

Trench Angels

In 1914, during World War 1, it is believed that a spectral army saved British troops at Mons. This is one soldier's account of what happened: 'Yes, I saw the vision. But it was not Saint George with his bowmen, as the newspapers said. The army was not like any ordinary army; it was like a film projected on the skies, and flooded with light. Perhaps they were

Above: The most famous sky vision of modern time occurred near the village of Fatima in Portugal

Below: Custer's fate seemed to have been predicted by a sky vision

Above: A spectral army saved British troops at Mons in 1914

Below: Emperor Constantine saw a vision of a cross of light in the sky

angels. I do not know. They were not ordinary men. They were carrying swords, not guns. I remember at the time wondering what those poor swords could do against those terrible machine guns. When the vision appeared, the Germans were charging us with their fixed bayonets, and we were sure that we were going to die. But somehow (there were no words spoken) the vision urged us on. We took new courage and fought back. Yet I do not think that the Germans retreated from us, but from the vision in the skies, which their machine guns could not harm.'

'By This Sign, Conquer'

In 312 AD, Constantine's army was camped at the Milvian Bridge, near Rome. While deciding whether or not to invade the city, Constantine had a vision. He saw a cross of light burning above the midday sun. The cross was inscribed with the words 'By this sign, conquer'. Constantine took it as a sign that he should invade Rome, and his army marched upon the city and seized it.

Later, he professed that this vision had converted him from his pagan religion to Christianity. He ordered that the widespread persecution of Christians should cease, and declared that Christianity should become the official religion of the Roman Empire.

Ships in the Sky

'She was a real ship. Square-rigged, though ghostly, like. She would come from the sea mists and sail over the hill, her keel all but scraping the Logan Rock......'

This is one of many accounts of flying ships. People believed in such things long before airships or aircraft were invented. Often they were regarded with the same mixture of fear and hope that UFOs inspire in many people today.

Over a thousand years ago, a mob of angry Frenchmen claimed to have captured four aliens after they landed in a flying boat. Permission was sought from their archbishop to stone the prisoners to death, for they had had enough of ships coming down from the clouds to 'bear away the fruits of the earth'. The archbishop refused to believe their story on that occasion; but visions of flying ships have continued right up to the present day. Such visions have been interpreted in a variety of ways and as both good and bad omens: for example, they have sometimes been said to predict a death, yet they have also been known to lead to buried treasure.

Ghostly Crews

In Scotland, when a senior member of the Clan Campbell dies, an ancient ghostly vessel is said to appear on Loch Fyne, by Inveraray. According to the Duke of Argyll, after the death of Lord Archibald Campbell in 1913, the galley appeared in the loch and then headed over the land to the sanctuary of St Columba.

There are two remarkable things about this story. One is that the vision was seen not just by local people, but also by an English tourist, who exclaimed: 'Look at that funny airship!' The other extraordinary feature is that the three-man crew of the galley was clearly visible.

In June 1959, another phantom crew was seen, this time over Papua New Guinea. The witnesses consisted of the entire staff and inmates of an Anglican Mission. The spectral ship was described as circular, with a superstructure like the bridge of a boat, and when Father Gill and his flock waved to the crew, they politely waved back. This vision took place at the time of a huge wave of UFO sightings in Papua New Guinea.

Phantom Anchors   Stories of phantom boats, with their anchors trailing, have recurred for hundreds of years, and the details of such stories are often strikingly similar.

The first such reported sighting dates from around 956 AD, and is said to have occurred in the borough of Cloera, England. According to the story, a sky ship's anchor became caught on the porch of a church, and one of the phantom sailors climbed down the rope to free it. The onlookers wanted to seize him, but the bishop prevented them and the sailor escaped unharmed - leaving behind the anchor as a souvenir of their visit.

250 years later, people were coming out of Mass from a church in Bristol, England, when they heard a cry in the air and saw a cloud-ship with its anchor caught on a tombstone. Once again, one of the sky-sailors came down the rope to free it, but this one was not so fortunate. For, according to reports, the congregation grabbed hold of him and he suffocated in the earth's atmosphere; whereupon the rest of the crew cut the cable and sailed away.

Above: In Scotland an ancient ghostly vessel appears on the death of a senior member of the Clan Campbell

Below: Many people claim to have witnessed visions of entire cities in the sky

Sky Cities   Perhaps the grandest scale on which visions in the sky have occurred is where people have witnessed entire cities in the heavens. In 1840, an image of a 'distant land with wonderful white buildings' was seen from the island of Sanday, off the Scottish coast. It was observed again in 1857, when it lasted for three hours. Local people believed that it was the crystal and pearl city of the mysterious 'Fin Folk'.

People often claim to recognise the sky cities they see, which tends to support the theory that what they are in fact observing are reflections of actual places transmitted over extraordinary distances.

In Alaska, there is a traditional belief that the city of Bristol, England becomes visible every year between June 21 and July 10. This phenomenon is said to have been regularly observed by the Alaskan Indians, even before white settlement took place. In 1887, the explorer Willoughby claimed to have photographed the city in the sky. The picture certainly shows Bristol, but whether it was taken from Alaska remains open to question.

Other visitors to Alaska have claimed to have seen the aerial city. One party from Canada could not agree on whether it looked like Toronto, Montreal or Beijing, but finally decided that it was more like 'some ancient city in the past'.

Above: A vision of Christ caught on camera?

Below: The face of Jesus in the clouds?

Photographic Proof?

One might expect that any photographs of sky visions that exist might shed light on this mysterious phenomenon; often, however, such evidence has a habit of creating more mysteries than it solves.

Many photographs have been taken which appear to show the face of Jesus Christ in the sky. 'The most famous picture we have ever printed', declared The Sunday People on November 13, 1977, when it published a picture that was said to be of the face of Christ. The newspaper later received 30,000 letters asking for a copy of the photograph.

There is no agreement regarding the picture's provenance. The earliest story seems to be that it was taken by a Seattle woman, Mildred Swanson, on July 15, 1920. This version of events, which was published in Fate magazine in July 1955, has it that the picture was taken while Mrs Swanson was photographing her daughter. At one point she put her camera down on the grass, and the shutter mysteriously 'clicked itself'. When the film was developed, a Christ-like image, supposedly making a gesture of blessing, was superimposed over the flowers.

But there are many other stories explaining the same picture from all over the world. A man in China claims to have heard a voice which said 'Take a photograph'. He pointed his camera into the air and the resulting image converted him to Christianity. Then there is the story of a Bristol girl, who tripped and clicked her camera as she fell. Other versions say that the face appeared in the clouds over New Bedford, or in a snow-covered hedge in Sheffield, Yorkshire, or, in one case, that the picture was taken by someone trying to photograph a UFO in the Swiss Alps, but the face of Christ got in the way!

Jesus in Korea

Another famous incident involving the image of Christ occurred in Korea, and is also shrouded in mystery. This version of what happened is recounted by a US Air Force veteran: 'I heard it was taken by this airman in Korea, during the worst part of the war. He was taking snaps of our guys and the commies in combat, and didn't see the face in the clouds until after the film was developed. I guess those back home found the picture a whizz. When the local rag published it, their whole Sunday edition ran out. In my opinion, these two planes don't seem to be fighting each other, yet the picture sure is strange.'

The name of the airman who took the picture has never been supplied. A copy of the original print was said to have been sent by a neighbour of the airman's family in Chicago to his brother in Ashland, Illinois; but neither the family nor the brother in Ashland have ever been traced. This illustrates a secondary enigma which commonly surrounds such baffling photographs: not only is the subject matter contentious, but it often proves difficult to locate the people who actually took the pictures. Forteans have coined an expression for this: F.O.A.F. - from a 'Friend of a Friend'.

The Face of Christ in Space?
Images of Christ are not an exclusively terrestrial phenomenon. When the Hubble space telescope took pictures of the Eagle Nebula on April 1, 1995, some people claimed it revealed the face of Christ.

Lenticulars
Lenticulars are lens-shaped clouds which resemble flying saucers. Of a thousand supposed 'UFO' pictures in a private archive in Britain, at least half a dozen are really lenticulars.

Sometimes, however, the images are much more mysterious. When Deputy Sheriff Arthur Strauch took a photograph of a strange cloud on October 21, 1965, he thought it was merely a self-glowing lenticular. But ironically, many experts doubt this explanation and think it more likely that his picture shows a genuine UFO!

Above: The face of Christ in the Eagle Nebula?

Below: Lenticular clouds can be mistaken for UFOs and UFOs can be mistaken for lenticulars!

Strange Rains

Above: Manna from heaven

Unlike most unexplained phenomena, strange rains at first seem not so much frightening as absurd. The idea of hordes of fish or frogs mysteriously falling from the sky seems so surreal that it can surely only be the product of a fertile imagination. However, closer investigation suggests that such bizarre incidents may really have happened; and some of the explanations seem more alarming than the events themselves.

Reports of animals dropping from the sky date back 2,000 years. The Greek historian Athenaeus referred to a shower of fish that lasted for three days, and a cascade of frogs so serious that roads became blocked, people couldn't open their front doors and the town stank for weeks.

Since then, falls of fish and amphibians have been reported on hundreds of occasions; in Australasia alone there were over fifty recorded incidents between 1879 and 1971 - more than one every two years. Usually the creatures involved are small, but there is one account of a bull falling from the heavens; thankfully, this appears to have been an isolated example of the phenomenon.

Rains of strange objects falling from the heavens are not confined to living creatures, however. People have been pelted by coins, stones and even huge blocks of ice. One of the most unlikely missiles was a silver notecase containing thirteen pages of a notebook; unfortunately, the pages were blank.

So numerous and diverse are the reported incidents which can be categorised as 'strange rains', that a special word has been coined to describe them: 'fafrotskies'.

When the Israelites encountered the most famous example of this phenomenon - the fall of manna in the wilderness - they believed it came from God. Today, we prefer more rational explanations; but what Charles Fort described as 'the uninspired persistence of the scientific' still hasn't explained where most fafrotskies come from.

Charles Fort had his own theory to explain rains of strange objects: he called it the 'Super-Sargasso Sea' - a sea suspended in the sky, waiting to disgorge its contents onto the earth. This theory has the great virtue of being impossible to disprove; but even if one is sceptical about this or any suggested explanation, the fact remains that there is an impressive bank of first-hand accounts relating to the phenomenon of 'strange rains'.

Buckets of Fish

One of the best documented showers of fish happened in the small Welsh town of Mountain Ash in 1859: 'The roofs of some houses were covered with them....They were from an inch to three inches in length, and fell during a heavy shower of rain and storm of wind.

'I was getting out a piece of timber, when I was startled by something falling all over me - down my neck, on my head and on my back. On putting my hand down my neck, I was surprised to find they were little fish. By this time, I saw the whole ground was covered with them. I took off my hat, the brim of which was full of them. They were jumping all about. My mates and I might have gathered bucketsful of them.'

Scientists who investigated this bizarre incident could come up with no explanation, and dismissed events at Mountain Ash as a prank played by practical jokers.

Naked in the Rain

RAF officer Ron Spencer had a similar experience when he was serving in India. He used to like going out into the monsoon rains to wash himself, but on one occasion his natural shower took a strange turn: 'I was in quite a lather when things started to hit me, and looking round, I could see myriads of small wriggling shapes on the ground and thousands being swept off the roofs, along channels and into the paddy fields. They were small sardine-sized fish. Needless to say, very shortly after the heavy storm none were left. Scavengers had gobbled them up.

Plague of Frogs

When stories of showers of frogs are reported, the usual explanation is that these creatures simply emerge from their hiding places during rainstorms, and people only imagine that they have fallen from the skies. But many accounts contradict this theory.

In County Durham in 1887, Edward Cook saw a storm approaching and took shelter with his horse and cart beneath the gables of a house. He described what happened next thus: 'In a few minutes, large drops of rain began to fall, and with them, to my astonishment, scores of small frogs, about the size of a man's thumbnail, jumping about in all directions.'

When Cook found several of the tiny creatures on his cart, he knew that they must have fallen with the rain.

Joe Alpin had a similar encounter during World War 2. He was stationed at Alton Towers in Staffordshire, England, when, one evening, he was driving through the deer park: '.....the sky suddenly darkened...and then the frogs came, millions of them raining out of the sky....They fell all over us. It rained frogs for at least an hour and a quarter.'

Above: Falls of fish are among the most commonly reported strange rains

Below: RAF officer Ron Spencer found himself hit by small fish when out washing in the monsoon rains

Some of Napoleon's soldiers were attacked by a torrent of toads

Reports of this phenomenon are legion. In Sutton Park, Birmingham, England, hundreds of frogs peppered people's umbrellas during a summer shower in 1954. On a golf course in Arkansas, in 1973, players watched as thousands of frogs came down during a rainstorm. At Canet-Plage in France, in 1977, frogs the size of peas were seen bouncing off the bonnets of people's cars. Stranger still, in 1987, pink frogs rained down on towns and villages all over Gloucestershire, England. It was later discovered that the frogs were actually albinos, whose blood showed through their white skin, making them appear pink.

It appears that frogs do not even have to be fully developed to feature in such reports. In 1979, a housewife from Bedford, England, went into her garden and found not just frogs all over her lawn, but also frogspawn hanging from the bushes.

Toads against Napoleon

In 1794, a group of Napoleon's soldiers was subjected to a torrent of small toads so great that they were forced out of the depression where they were hiding. The soldiers made sure that the toads were really raining down from the skies by holding out a handkerchief and catching several of them as they fell.

Almost 2,000 years ago, the Roman historian Plutarch wrote that he 'personally saw a rain of toads' which came down in such quantities that they were seen crawling over the roofs of houses. In Norfolk, England, in the 19th century, an insect-catcher was bombarded by toads, many of which landed in his net; and toads fell for two days at Chalon-sur-Saone, France, in 1922.

Living Proof

When people see tiny creatures dropping from the heavens, often the first reaction is to gather some evidence. In London, in 1960, a schoolboy filled a sweet-box with frogs to show his friends. Adults, on the other hand, are more likely to refer the living proof of their experience to more official bodies. For example, when small seawater fish fell on Kent in 1666 - a year surrounded by fear and superstition - they were sent to London to be examined by magistrates.

In October 1947, a Louisiana man rushed into the offices of the local newspaper brandishing a fish and exclaiming: 'Here's one of 'em. Take a look and then see if you think I'm talking through my hat.' The journalists remained sceptical and published an article ridiculing him - not realising that half the town had also seen the fish raining down. One of those was marine scientist Dr Bajkov, who was having breakfast in a cafe when he witnessed the event. His response was rather more phlegmatic. He rushed outside and collected as many samples as he could, some for scientific analysis and some for the table. Later, he gave his verdict: 'Delicious.'

Strange Missiles

Lynne Connolly was hanging out her washing in Hull, England, in October 1975, when she felt a tap on her head. She discovered a small silver notecase in her hair. Engraved on it were the letters JB or TB, SE, C8, a six-pointed star and the word 'Klaipeda' - which, by coincidence, was the name of the Baltic town where sheets of black 'marsh paper' fell in the 17th century.

People have also been hit by falling eggs, peas, broad beans, maize - even a storm of hazelnuts which on one occasion descended from a clear blue sky. At Ruislip, in Greater London, in 1942, clods of earth seemed to fall slowly and gracefully from above. And in 1979, a Southampton man witnessed a fall of millions of mustard and cress seeds. As with most falls, only one kind of object came down at a time - in this case, the cress seeds fell first, with the mustard seeds following 45 minutes later.

Angel Hair

Angel hair is perhaps the most mysterious of sky-falls. Reports describe it as web-like filaments of white silky material in strands of anything up to 50 feet long. It can also be very strong, as the captain of the ship Roxburgh Castle found in an incident that took place in 1962. He noticed white filaments over the railings of his vessel, with small cocoons of the same material still floating down from the sky. When the captain tried to pull the strands away, he could scarcely break them; but within minutes this strange material had disappeared.

A scientist who has subjected angel hair to analysis describes his findings regarding this phenomenon: 'My research has shown that angel hair is very unstable, and that it degrades in oxygen. Shortly after falling on the ground, it usually disappears. A few specimens have been preserved, when, shortly after falling, they have been sealed in air-tight containers. Analysis has shown that its structure contains silicon, magnesium, calcium and boron. The strands in our laboratories are therefore not alien to the earth, yet they are very strange indeed. I have not seen anything quite like this substance. I cannot say whether it comes from UFOs.'

Waterspouts and Whirlwinds

Currently, the most popular theory is that both creatures and objects are picked up by freak winds and waterspouts, carried aloft, then deposited on the earth again when the strength of the wind declines. However, whirlwinds are generally very messy and unselective, picking up everything in their path and scattering it in all directions - which is inconsistent with the pattern of most strange rains. Moreover, the whirlwind theory does not explain why such incidents are sometimes seen on clear days, or continue for long periods in one particular place.

An incident which occurred in 1936 also calls this theory into question. Major J Hedgepath of the US Army reported a fall of fish in that year, the details of which he gave to 'Science' magazine: 'I witnessed a brief rainfall of fish, one of the specimens of which was identified as the tench, which is common only to the fresh waters of Europe.'

Since Major Hedgepath observed this fall while in the western Pacific island of Guam, it is difficult to believe that a waterspout could have had anything to do with it.

UFOs and Other Craft

Some people believe that terrestrial or alien craft might be responsible for some of the strange rains that have occurred. UFO watchers believe that angel hair may be the exhaust residue from alien craft. Most falls of ice, on the other hand, are said to come from aeroplanes. When a block of ice fell through the roof of a house in the north of England in 1981, police scientists found that it contained coffee and sugar, and concluded that it must have fallen from a jumbo jet.

But ice falls can't always originate from aeroplanes, as Arthur C Clarke points out: 'We must look for another explanation in the case of the 20-foot-diameter block that fell on an estate in Scotland....Boeing 747s were not very common at the time of the report: 1849.'

Clarke's own theory is that such ice meteorites come from outer space.

Marsh Paper

In 1687, huge flakes of a black fibrous material fell near the town of Klaipeda, on the Baltic Sea. The material was damp, tore like paper and smelt of rotten seaweed, although the smell disappeared when it was dry. Some of the sheets of this marsh paper were as big as tabletops, but even larger pieces fell in Silesia in 1839, when a similar phenomenon occurred. A writer in the Edinburgh Review said that he had a portion of a sheet measuring 200 square feet. He stated that it was like cotton felt, and that clothing could have been made from it.

Above: Angel hair is perhaps the most mysterious of sky falls

Below: Tornadoes and other freak winds are thought to provide an explanation for strange rains

A scientific analysis was undertaken, the results of which declared that the marsh paper 'was found to consist partly of vegetable matter - chiefly Conferva crispata - and partly of about 29 species of infusoria.'

These findings did not impress Charles Fort, however, who said: 'We see again that, though nothing has identity of its own, anything can be 'identified' as anything.....(That) everything seemingly found out is doomed to be subverted - by more powerful microscopes...always (with) the illusion of the final.'

Fort had shown once again how sometimes an explanation can merely provoke more questions.

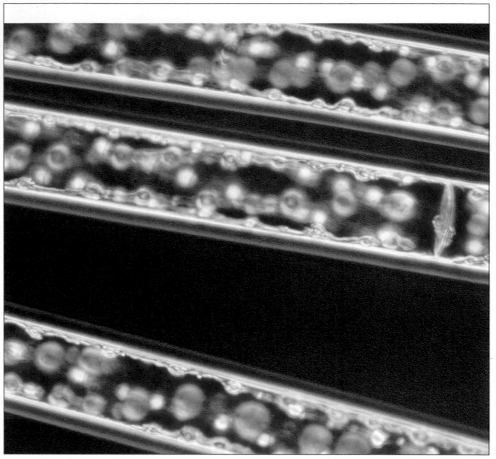

Seaweed (above left), algae (above right) and frogs (right) have all been reported as falling from the sky

1921

SHOWER OF FROGS.

THOUSANDS OF SMALL HOPPERS FALL AT GIBRALTAR.

During a recent thunderstorm at Gibraltar a shower of frogs fell on the North Front.

Thousands of these small hopping creatures, unusual at the Rock, may be seen in the hedges (says Reuter), and have aroused much curiosity.

Some seven years ago a similar phenomenon occurred, and later a shower of sand covered everything with a pink deposit.

Scientific Wisdom

Many theories have been suggested in an attempt to shed light on the phenomenon of strange rains. Of these, the earliest explanations now seem laughable. In 1584, Reginald Scot, author of The Discoverie of Witchcraft, wrote: 'It is certain that some creatures are self-born, and have no need of parents. For example.....those frogs which come from nowhere. These are carried on the rain. These creatures grow themselves, and are born in showers....We call these creatures "temporaries".

John Lewis, who was one of the main witnesses to the events at Mountain Ash, sent some of the fish that fell to earth to London Zoo for examination. Scientists immediately began to pour scorn on his story. J E Gray, of the British Museum, told the Zoological Magazine: 'On reading the evidence, it appears to me most probably to be only a practical joke of the mates of John Lewis, who seem to have thrown a pailful of water with the fish in it over him.'

Dr Gray's verdict flew in the face of the fact that the incident, far from being isolated and involving a handful of people, was witnessed by many and involved thousands of fish falling over a wide area.

In the last century, it was believed that solar evaporation carried up the spawn of frogs and toads from the water of the marshes. The spawn would survive in the vapour of the clouds and develop into mature frogs and toads, which would then fall to earth like rain.

Above: 1958 cover of 'Fate' magazine recording a strange rain in Sutton Park, Birmingham

The Nonsense of Logic

A mysterious rain of coal and bricks in the streets of Kilburn, London, in 1877, inspired arguments that travelled half way round the world. A meteorologist named Symons believed he had the answer: 'The fall consisted of brick, soot, unburned coal and cinders. It is therefore my proposal that lightning flashed down the chimney of a neighbouring house and fused some of the brick in it.'

Unfortunately, that failed to explain how it came to be outside, and the paranormal investigator Charles Fort was unimpressed: 'Methinks if a red-hot stove should drop from a cloud into Broadway, someone would find that at about the time of the occurrence, a moving van had passed, and that the moving men had tired of the stove, or something - (and) that it had not been really red-hot, but had been rouged instead of blackened by some absent-minded housekeeper.'

Super-Sargasso Sea

Charles Fort himself had several theories to explain strange falls from the heavens. His most imaginative idea was the concept of what he called the 'Super-Sargasso Sea'. Just as the Sargasso Sea in the North Atlantic is supposed to be full of shipwrecks and all manner of objects caught up in its gulfweed, so the 'Super-Sargasso Sea' might be a repository for terrestrial and extra-terrestrial matter high above the earth's surface. Sometimes the sea would suck things up; at other times it would spew them back down to earth.

Fort also came up with the theory of 'teleportation' - a force capable of transporting objects from place to place without traversing the intervening distance. He claimed that this power was once more active than it is now, and had unfortunately become a pale and erratic shadow of its former self.

Chapter Two

Beyond Science

Throughout history, science and religion have been hugely influential in shaping mankind's perception of the world. But in expressing their different ways of understanding the universe and the role of human beings within it, scientific knowledge and religious belief have often come into conflict.

Distrust between science and religion can be traced back 400 years, when the Italian scientist Giordano Bruno was burnt at the stake for suggesting that the universe was infinite and that our world might not be the only one. Science has since proved Bruno to be right; the earth is not at the centre of the universe and, far from ruling the planets, we may, in fact, be ruled by them. Scientists are only now beginning to realize how many aspects of our lives are influenced by the moon, planets and cosmos as a whole, from the weather to the way we feel on a particular day. Could it be that the ancient astrologers, whose art has so often been dismissed as superstitious nonsense, actually knew more than today's scientists about how the planets affect our lives?

Over the years, many scientists have tried to debunk supposed miracles and provide logical explanations for mystical experiences. At the first mention of the word 'paranormal' members of the scientific community rush to investigate. Sometimes their research proves fruitful, but occasionally, their best efforts yield no logical answer and the mystery merely deepens.

In the last century, the great English scientist William Crookes was called in to investigate the claims of the Scottish spiritualist D D Home regarding levitation. Crookes not only failed to find a rational explanation for this phenomenon, but in the process he made the complete transition from sceptic to convert. A more recent example of events which have baffled the scientific world is Uri Geller's ability to bend metal using psychokinetic powers. Even after decades of scrutiny, no one has yet been able to provide a satisfactory explanation for such extraordinary occurrences.

When the American doctor Raymond Moody published a book on the subject of near-death experiences in 1975, the scientific establishment ranged against him to refute his ideas. However, many people have experienced what they are convinced is a glimpse of heaven, and under rigorously controlled conditions can even recall past lives.

Since the 1960s, western scientists have been studying the effects of meditation on the body and mind. Their investigations have shown that the mind can indeed control the body; and this has led to the development of an advanced technique known as biofeedback, which is being used to treat medical and psychological disorders. Perhaps the scientific world is beginning to realise that it has something to learn from the study of ancient mysteries.

Left: Firewalking is practised in many parts of the world

Powers of the Mind

Investigators of the unexplained don't always need to go to the ends of the earth in pursuit of their subject matter. The workings of the human mind are still little understood, despite being the focus of extensive research over a long period of time. And if there is still much that is not known about the everyday functions of the brain, even less is understood about its mystifying powers which manifest themselves in many forms.

In 1967, a professor at the University of Chicago hypnotized a subject named Don in front of her students. When she told him to 'be three years old', he broke into fluent Japanese and continued speaking the language for about twenty minutes. It emerged later that during World War 2, Don's family had been living in California, where a large number of Japanese prisoners were held. The fact that Don could, under hypnosis, recall a language he hadn't spoken for 22 years may not of itself be startling; but Don's earlier encounter with Japanese had been when he was just two years old. Somehow it had remained with him, in a part of his brain which he didn't know existed and which could be unlocked only under hypnosis.

The mechanisms at work during hypnosis are poorly understood, and perhaps for that reason, the relationship between hypnotism and science remains an uneasy one. It is only recently that psychologists such as Charles Tart have tried to establish a theoretical basis for hypnotism, examining such things as its effects on brain chemistry, and placing levels of hypnotic susceptibility within a wider psychological profile.

But even if hypnosis is not yet on a firm scientific footing, its effects can certainly be clearly demonstrated. Its application as a form of entertainment is well known, but on a more serious level, hypnosis can be used to alleviate pain, relieve symptoms of mental illness, assist in solving crimes and unravel past events hidden in the unconscious part of the brain. As far as research into the paranormal is concerned, hypnosis is an invaluable investigative tool, albeit a source of mystery in its own right.

Some investigators believe in the existence of mental powers which extend beyond the five senses, transcending the constraints of space and time. One theory is that our brain is a 'super-conscious' computer capable of receiving signals which are not only geographically distant, but which can emanate from the past and the future.

Visions which cross the boundaries of time seem best explained by the existence of a parallel universe. This would allow the possibility of movement through time warps to glimpse past and future events. However, this theory raises the issue of the classic time paradox: if the future has already happened, how is it possible to change it?

As yet, no one has been able to induce what is known as extrasensory perception in a systematic way, but some researchers believe that hypnosis can be used to unlock these extraordinary mental powers.

Above: Mesmer achieved spectacular cures for what would be recognised today as illnesses of the mind

Below: Mark Chapman was said to be in a trance when he shot John Lennon

Mesmerism

The name of Dr F A Mesmer (1734-1815) has become eponymous with hypnotic states. An Austrian physician, Mesmer developed techniques which caused a sensation in Vienna in the 1770s. He believed that there was an invisible fluid in the body - animal magnetism - which could be activated by any magnetized object. Obstacles which impeded the flow of this fluid through the body resulted in disease, but these blockages could be removed by what Mesmer called 'crises' - trance-like states often ending in delirium or convulsions. According to Mesmer, during the healing process, animal magnetism flowed through the healer and into the patient.

Using equipment such as baths of iron filings, Mesmer achieved spectacular cures for what would be recognised today as illnesses of the mind. There was, almost inevitably, widespread scepticism regarding Mesmer's theories, and many people made fun of him. Mozart, in his opera Cosi fan Tutte, presented his own thinly-disguised jibe in the character Dr Fatalis with his giant magnet.

When he was accused of fraud, Mesmer moved to Paris, where he was investigated by a commission of scientists that included Benjamin Franklin. Although Mesmer was unable to provide any scientific basis for his results, his success rate continued to amaze.

Hypnosis

In the 1840s, the Scotsman James Braid realized that no complex or gimmicky apparatus was needed to induce what he called 'neurohypnosis'; patients could be hypnotized by staring into a bright light, or merely by suggestion.

With the discovery of chloroform in 1848, surgeons lost interest in using hypnosis on patients during operations. It was reintroduced in the 1880s by Jean-Martin Charcot, who was Sigmund Freud's mentor. Charcot used hypnosis to treat hysterical illnesses, although he also seems to have used it for his personal amusement, making patients bark like dogs or flap their arms like wings. His experiments led him to an important discovery: that subjects cannot be made to do things against their will. A graphic illustration of this fact occurred when Charcot put a beautiful young woman into a trance in front of a group of students. He was then suddenly called away, whereupon an assistant took over and told the woman to remove her clothes. She immediately opened her eyes, emerged from the trance and slapped the assistant's face.

Crime and Justice

It is now commonplace for detectives to use hypnosis as a means of helping victims and witnesses to recall events more vividly. In New York, in 1982, this technique was used to good effect when two women witnessed a fatal shooting. Under hypnosis, one of the women was able to remember the tiniest details about the gunman, right down to the type of spectacle frames he had been wearing.

Hypnosis also enhanced the powers of recall of a bus driver in Israel whose vehicle was blown up by a terrorist bomb. When interviewed, he had been unable to give any useful information, but under hypnosis, he remembered a youth who had boarded the bus carrying a parcel. He even recalled that the youth's palms had been sweating when he was handed his change. With a detailed description to go on, the police quickly made an arrest and a confession soon followed.

Above: Victor Korchnoi claimed he was 'telehypnotized' to lose the 1978 World Chess Championships

Below: Nine year old Eryl Mai Jones from Aberfan dreamed 'something black had come down all over' her school just the day before it was covered by a mountain of coal waste

An intriguing question which has often been posed is whether a person could be induced to commit a crime whilst under hypnosis. Although Charcot's research indicated that subjects cannot be made to act against their will, there is a theory that Mark Chapman was in a trance when he shot John Lennon. The fact that he committed the murder so calmly, and afterwards simply sat down and waited to be arrested may lend support to this theory.

Telepathic Hypnosis

While the scientific establishment was still struggling to accept the existence of hypnotism, an even more startling possibility became evident: telepathic hypnosis.

In 1845, the Russian hypnotist Pashkov demonstrated that he was able to hypnotize a patient 300 miles away. Later, a Dutch doctor named Gilbert noticed that he could hypnotize a woman by placing pressure on her hand - but only if he concentrated. This led him to wonder what would happen if he applied the concentration, but without the physical contact. He discovered that concentration alone was sufficient to hypnotize her. And one of Dr Gilbert's colleagues, Pierre Janet, found that he could summon the woman by hypnotizing her from the other side of the city.

At the 1978 world chess championships between Soviet defector Victor Korchnoi and Anatoly Karpov, Korchnoi claimed he was 'telehypnotized' to lose the match. The Soviets would certainly have been eager to see Korchnoi defeated, but it is unlikely that telehypnosis had any effect on the outcome. And although implications of telepathic hypnosis would be earth-shattering, there is still no proof that it is possible.

Precognition

In October 1966, one of the worst civil disasters in British history occurred in the small coalmining town of Aberfan, in Wales. A mountain of coal waste slid down the side of a valley and submerged the local junior school, killing 116 children and 28 adults.

As the news broke, it emerged that many people believed they had foreseen the tragedy. The most heartbreaking prediction came from nine-year-old Eryl Mai Jones, who told her mother: 'Mummy, you must listen to my dream. I dreamed I went to school and there was no school there. Something black had come down all over it.' Eryl Mai Jones was one of those buried alive in her school the following day.

So many people professed that they had foreseen the tragedy that a special bureau was set up. People were encouraged to write down their premonitions at the time, rather than articulating them after the event had happened.

After several months, two individuals in particular were found to be making predictions that were uncannily accurate on a regular basis. They were called in to be interviewed, but almost at once their ability vanished. As one of the investigators concluded: 'Premonition is literally a flash of intuition. I'm afraid that with every single person that looked interesting, the same thing happened - they lost it when they started to think they were good at it.'

Changing the Future

A young man was about to return home following a visit to Hobart, Tasmania, when his mother warned him that she'd had a premonition that he was about to have an accident. Halfway home he remembered his mother's words and slowed down to 25mph. Moments later, the car skidded on a patch of ice and ended in a ditch. He was unhurt, but knew that things could have been much more serious had he not heeded his mother's words.

Remote Viewing

In the mid-19th century, Frenchman Alexis Didier was at the theatre one night when he agreed to go onstage and be hypnotized. He created such a sensation that his employer gave up his business to become his manager, and Didier rose to stardom.

Didier had the uncanny power of 'remote viewing'. His abilities were put to the test one day by a sceptic named Seguier, who challenged Didier to describe his whereabouts at two o'clock that afternoon. 'In your study,' came the reply. 'It is cluttered with papers, twists of tobacco, drawings, and little machines. There is a pretty little bell on your desk.' Seguier said he had never had such a bell, and went home, believing his scepticism to have been vindicated. But when he arrived, he found that his wife had bought him a bell and placed it on his desk that very afternoon.

The Soul of Things

Psychometry is the ability to detect an object's history, and the emotions of those who have handled it, by psychic means. In the 1940s, a London psychometrist was handed a sealed parcel and asked to describe its contents. After some concentration, he said that it contained two bowls which had been glazed by a Chinese craftsman. When he went on to say that he could see the studio where the bowls were being made, and the studio contained two modern kerosene lamps, the owner of the parcel lost interest. For although the parcel did indeed contain two Chinese bowls, they were valuable 300-year-old antiques, and the description of their being made in a studio containing kerosene lamps could not therefore be accurate.

But two years later, the supposed Ming bowls were examined by an expert, who declared them to be forgeries, dating from the early 20th century. The psychometrist had been proved right.

If psychometry does exist, it seems to indicate that everything that has ever happened is somehow on record, and certain exceptional individuals are able to gain access to that information.

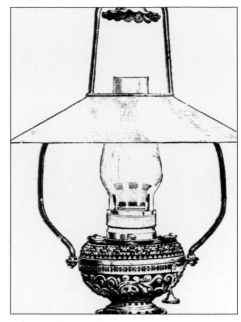

Above: Two antique vases were discovered to be forgeries by a psychometrist who could tell that they had been made in a twentieth century studio lit by kerosene lamps

Below: Parapsychologist J B Rhine designed a set of cards to test telepathic abilities

Telepathy

Telepathy, which is defined as 'communication between two minds without the use of the known senses', is the one aspect of ESP which lends itself most readily to scientific experimentation. It ought to be possible to definitively prove or disprove the existence of such powers by scientific means; but in spite of many such attempts over recent decades, categorical statements regarding telepathy remain elusive.

In the 1930s, the American parapsychologist J B Rhine devised a famous series of tests which he believed proved the existence of telepathy conclusively. He used a pack of 25 specially designed cards, each with one of five symbols on one side. In the experiment the tester concentrated on each card in turn, while the subject tried to identify the unseen symbols.

The early results of Rhine's experiments were startling. One student correctly identified all 25 cards, against odds of 2,000,000 to 1. But critics identified flaws in his test procedures. Subjects may have been able to recognise the markings on the back of the cards; and some openly admitted that they had cheated. These 'Zener' cards are still sold today, through the Society for Psychical Research, but they do carry a warning: 'If held at a certain angle and in certain light, the symbols can be perceived through the back of the card'.

Rhine continued his experiments for 50 years, right up until his death. He himself remained uncertain as to whether his tests demonstrated telepathy, clairvoyance or telepathic clairvoyance. The interpretation of his results was further complicated by the occurrence of a 'displacement effect', where subjects were able to guess the previous or next card with remarkable accuracy. Despite any shortcomings in the methods he employed, Rhine at the very least was responsible for establishing a framework which influenced subsequent research.

In 1971, two experiments took place which were remarkably ambitious in scale: one involved thousands of people attending a rock concert, while the other was conducted from outer space.

After visiting the 'dream laboratory' at the State University of New York, the rock group The Grateful Dead decided to involve their fans in a mass experiment during a forthcoming tour. At six successive concerts a picture of a psychic named Malcolm Bessent was briefly projected to the audience. This was followed by another picture, which the audience had to try to transmit to Bessent, who was sleeping in the 'dream laboratory' some 50 miles away. When Bessent awoke, he would describe his dreams. It was found that on four of the six occasions, what Bessent saw in his dreams bore a significant resemblance to the picture the audience had sought to project.

The experiment that astronaut Edgar Mitchell conducted aboard Apollo 14 took place without NASA's knowledge. Prior to the flight, he had arranged with four friends that he would concentrate on sequences of 25 random numbers, which they would attempt to receive 150,000 miles away. Only two of the four recipients scored above what might have been expected by chance, and this only moderately so.

Telepathy Between Twins

Of all the documented examples of telepathic communication, some of the most powerful and dramatic have occurred between twins.

The lead singer of an English pop group, Boy's Wonder, described an incident in his childhood when he suddenly knew that his identical twin was in trouble. He rushed to the local rubbish dump and made straight for an old refrigerator. His brother had climbed inside for a game and become trapped inside.

Perhaps even more intriguing are the situations where the communicative process has included a physical manifestation. Christine Young, from South Yorkshire, England, claims to have experienced labour pains when her twin sister was giving birth to a baby son. A more extreme form of this phenomenon concerned twin sisters in the State Mental Hospital, South Carolina. Although they were separated within the institution, the sisters still appeared to be able to communicate. And when one of the sisters died, her twin seems not only to have sensed the loss, but to have willed herself to die just moments later. The two were also found lying in identical positions.

Telepathy between twins is often extremely strong and urgent - even violent

Mental Radio

Various theories have been suggested to explain how telepathy might work. The writer and philosopher Arthur Koestler believed there might be a mental version of the subatomic phenomenon of 'action at a distance'. Rupert Sheldrake asserted that we may share a 'morphic field', akin to a radio frequency, allowing thoughts to be transferred between minds which are attuned to each other.

Two people who would probably have subscribed to the 'mental radio' theory were the Australian explorer Sir Hubert Wilkins and a writer he met just before embarking on an expedition to the Arctic in 1937. They discovered that they shared an interest in telepathy, and the writer, a man named Sherman, enthused about the possibilities it held: 'Wouldn't it be great if the minds of some humans could be developed to such a point that all you'd have to do, if.....your radio went out of commission, would be to sit and think of your latitude and longitude (and) transmit that information to a human receiver.'

With Wilkins about to go off exploring the Arctic wastes, the two men had the perfect opportunity to conduct their own experiment, and agreed that they would try to remain in mental contact. Sherman soon found that he was able to envisage Wilkins' movements and surroundings with extraordinary accuracy. On one occasion he was astonished to 'see' Wilkins at a formal ball, wearing an evening dress suit. He knew that Wilkins had not taken such a suit with him, and had not planned to attend any functions of this kind. He subsequently discovered, however, that his vision had been correct in every particular. Wilkins had been forced to land at Regina, Saskatchewan, where the governor of the province had invited him to attend a ball and lent him suitable evening wear for the occasion.

Other people who tried to maintain more conventional links with Wilkins had often found it impossible to establish radio contact; the 'mental radio' had proved to be a much more reliable instrument of communication.

From the Arctic wastes (above) Sir Hubert Wilkins (below) maintained a 'mental radio' link with a writer named Sherman

Mind Over Matter

In 1934, the parapsychologist J B Rhine was visited by a compulsive gambler who declared that he was able to use his willpower to influence the way the dice fell on the gaming tables. Rhine was fascinated and embarked on a series of experiments in which dozens of people spent long periods of time trying to roll sixes. Unfortunately, these experiments were badly conducted and proved little; and the gambler went on his way, leaving it a matter of conjecture as to whether he possessed powers which did enable him to grow rich at the gaming tables; but the story does illustrate the phenomenon of psychokinesis - the ability to affect the material world using the power of the mind.

Over the years an extraordinary range of psychokinetic powers have been demonstrated, from the potentially useful, such as dowsing for water, to the bizarre and cruel, such as willing a heart to stop beating. But many feats of 'mind over matter' are performed simply for the purposes of entertainment, and none has been harnessed successfully for practical application.

As psychokinesis is by definition a spectacular phenomenon, magicians and illusionists have long sought to incorporate it into their acts. The American James Randi, himself a stage magician, is one of the most persistent debunkers of alleged paranormal powers. He warns against being seduced by performances which can be extremely slick and sophisticated: 'Scientists are the people least qualified to detect chicanery. They're the easiest to fool of all. If you want to catch a burglar, you go to a burglar, not to a scientist. If you want to catch a magician, go to a magician.'

While the appetites of impresarios and television producers for feats involving mind over matter may trivialise the subject, entertainment as a vehicle for psychokinesis does bring certain benefits. Those who claim to possess psychokinetic powers are - quite literally - put under the spotlight. There is a constant demand for new and more spectacular manifestations of such powers, both to amaze the public and confound the scientists, while trickery is becoming increasingly difficult to disguise.

Above: Levitation as entertainment

Raging Horn

In 1925, the Englishman F W Warrick was called in to investigate the activities of a medium named Mrs Deane. He kept a 'seance diary' of his observations, which included the phenomenon of telekinesis:

March 10: The table jumped right over the wire netting, landing near me. The trumpet, which had a detector on it, rose into the air (and) touched my right-hand neighbour.

April 27: The trumpet, in response to my request that it should hit us all, did so. One could see it flying about all over the table.

May 4: This evening there were some large lights under the table. The trumpet rose in the air and hit several sitters, giving me a resounding blow on the top of my head.

May 11: During the sitting I put out my hands to feel for the table. I could not find it; the others then put their hands forth and we discovered that the table had been removed noiselessly from within the wire fence, and without touching anyone. It was found between me and the camera.

Exploding With Anger

'Exteriorization' is the word used to describe mental energy which erupts and causes objects to move or make a noise. A dramatic example of this occurred when the psychologists Sigmund Freud and Carl Jung were arguing one day about psychic research. Freud, who was sitting at his desk, was being difficult and causing Jung to lose his temper. Jung could feel his anger rising until, suddenly, the force was released and, simultaneously, an explosive sound issued from Freud's bookcase.

'There!' declared Jung. 'That is an example of the so-called catalytic exteriorization phenomenon.'

Freud dismissed the idea, which made Jung angrier still, and a second sound was heard. This time Freud was won over.

However, the matter did not rest there. For the explosive sounds occurred again later, by which time Jung had left. This opens up three possibilities, two intriguing and one prosaic. Was Jung's explosive energy still present in the room? Had Freud himself been angered sufficiently to induce the catalytic exteriorization phenomenon? Or could there simply have been something wrong with the bookcase?

Above: Monica Tejada, 15, concentrates to bend a metal strip inside a sealed container

Below: In 1934, J B Rhine attempted to investigate a gambler's claim that he could use willpower to influence the fall of a dice

Above: Dowsing is one of the oldest paranormal skills

Below: Escapologist Harry Houdini was an ardent campaigner against hoaxers who tried to claim paranormal skills

Striking It Rich

One of the oldest of the paranormal skills is dowsing - the ability to locate water and minerals underground. Ancient Egyptian paintings show people with forked dowsing sticks, and in the Middle Ages this method was used to find coal. It has even been used to search for missing persons and murderers, but its principal application is in locating water and oil. Successful dowsers can detect these precious commodities where scientific methods are useless. And in the United States, some exponents of the art charge thousands of dollars per day to people hoping to find oil on their land.

In Edwards County, Illinois, USA, the principal of the local high school was approached by a dowser named Clayton McDowell, who claimed to have found oil on the school's land. The principal was bemused, but the school was desperate for funds and he gave McDowell permission to investigate further. Oil was soon gushing out at a rate of over a hundred barrels a day.

This incident reveals another aspect of the phenomenon: that dowsers do not necessarily have to walk over a particular piece of land in order to pick up signals from it. For Clayton McDowell's dowsing is all done from behind the wheel of a car. He holds the dowsing rod while a passenger takes charge of the steering wheel.

The legendary spoon-bender Uri Geller employs a somewhat different technique, and one which is even more remote from the territory under investigation than McDowell's. Geller uses a pendulum to dowse over maps, and when the pendulum indicates the presence of oil, he flies over the area in question in a light aircraft. He determines the precise location of the oil psychically.

A Minefield for Dowsers

During World War 1, dowsers helped to locate landmines and unexploded bombs for the military. In 1970, the British Ministry of Defence set up an experiment to ascertain whether or not dowsing had any part to play in modern military thinking. Seven people, all of whom claimed to be skilled dowsers, were given the task of seeking out 20 defused mines which were buried over an area of 400 acres. The results were unimpressive, to say the least; the dowsers performed even worse than a control group of volunteers who had made random guesses. The Ministry then made 400 holes in a tract of land and buried landmines in 160 of them. Once again the dowsers were set to work, but again the results were disappointing.

Evidence related to dowsing is thus mixed: while experiments carried out under rigorously controlled conditions, such as the above, seem to suggest a success rate no greater than would be obtained by chance, certain individuals have undoubtedly grown rich after discovering oil in this unorthodox way.

Behind The Iron Curtain

In the former Soviet Union and other Eastern Bloc countries, telekinesis was accepted as a scientific phenomenon and investigated officially by the Soviet Academy of Sciences. Between the 1940s and the 1970s, the phenomenon was not only well documented, but photographic and film evidence was also gathered. The claims of many individuals and the techniques employed received validation as a result of this research.

Although some western scientists have cast doubt on the objectivity of the methods used, and suggested that some of the most impressive results may have been obtained fraudulently, the Soviet Academy certainly amassed a bank of material on the subject of telekinesis which has yet to be surpassed.

The biggest star to emerge from this period was a housewife named Nina Kulagina, who repeatedly demonstrated under laboratory conditions the ability to move objects across tables - even when they were placed under glass and in a vacuum. In one of the most impressive displays of her telekinetic powers she separated the white and yolk of an egg without making any physical contact, a feat which was captured on film.

Cloudbursting

Dr Rolf Alexander, a New Zealander, claimed that he could dissolve clouds simply by looking at them. He maintained that his cloudbursting skills used a 'new kind of energy by which the human mind can act at a distance'. Alexander travelled the world, giving displays of cloudbursting which impressed some observers more than others:

'It may not come during the life of Rolf Alexander, but sometime he will be referred to in the mental and physical sciences as are Einstein and Pasteur in their respective fields.'

'I really find it very difficult not to believe, startling and improbable though it may seem, and almost in spite of myself, that Dr Alexander can disintegrate clouds.'

'Apparently, he only "works" with fair weather cumulus, and clouds of this type usually disappear in 15-20 minutes anyway. If we assume that Dr Alexander is sincere and honest but misguided, then the simplest explanation is that when alone, he has discovered that clouds of this type at which he looks intently disappear, and concludes that he has been responsible for the dissolution of the cloud.'

The Rope Trick

In January 1919, the British newspaper The Daily Mail published the following letter from the editor of the Magic Circle:

Sir, For at least 500 years the rope trick has been an Indian fable. No conjuror who has visited India in quest of the trick has ever seen it. When our King went to India, as Prince of Wales, in 1902, that country was scoured to find a performer who could do it; Lord Lonsdale offered £10,000 for a sight of it. The reward is still unclaimed.

In that same year, however, some British soldiers described seeing the feat performed. One of those present recounts what happened: 'We had been only two days in Ferzapore when there came one morning into the barrack square an old Hindu. He had a little basket, a long thick rope thrown across his shoulder, and two young lads with him. The old man suddenly threw one end of the rope up into the air, and it remained taut and firm, standing up from his hand as if pulled tight by an invisible arm in the sky. We clearly saw the end of the rope up there above. Then one of the lads swarmed hand over hand up the rope till he reached the top. How was it done? Two score of us East Surreys saw it all. But it was a marvel to us, and is yet.'

Many theories have been put forward to explain the rope trick: some have suggested that the rope is supported by fine wires, others that it is really a sheep's vertebrae covered in cord. But there is still no definitive explanation, and the rope trick remains an enigma, a classic of its kind.

There is no definitive explanation of the Indian Rope Trick

Mental Murder

Kulagina gave one of the most bizarre and gruesome demonstrations of her powers when she stopped a frog's heart from beating just by concentrating on it. This might be regarded as cruel and pointless enough when it involves a frog, but what if a human being is the intended victim?

A circus performer who was sacked for drunkenness waged a subtle but deadly vendetta against his former employer over a 13-year period. Each year, on the same day, he sent the circus owner a birthday card, but with the word 'birthday' crossed out and 'deathday' scrawled in. Inside the card there was just a date and the man's signature. As the appointed 'deathday' grew closer, the circus owner became increasingly terrified. Finally, he summoned his children and announced that he had just one week to live. A doctor was called, who examined him and declared that he was in perfect health. Yet he did indeed die on the predicted day. He had undoubtedly been killed by the power of the mind - but was it the mind of the embittered ex-employee, or that of the circus owner himself?

Thoughtography

Thoughtography is the ability to imprint thoughts directly onto camera film. The world's most famous exponent of thoughtography was an American named Ted Serios, who first came to prominence in the 1950s as a subject in hypnosis demonstrations. It was in one such hypnotic trance that he claimed to have met the spirit of the pirate Jean Lafitte on the astral plane. He further claimed that he had been told the whereabouts of some treasure buried in Florida. The intense amount of publicity that the story generated allowed someone else to beat Serios to the prize. He tried to repeat the feat, but had difficulty describing exact locations. Eventually one of his partners lost patience, handed him a camera and told him to take a picture of the image in his mind. The result was the first thoughtograph.

For a few years in the mid-1960s, Serios seemed to be able to imprint his thoughts directly onto Polaroid film, simply by pointing a camera at his face. People would suggest a subject and Serios would try to produce an image of that subject using the power of thought.

In the frenzy that Serios created around himself at the critical moment, it was often difficult to see exactly what was happening; and he also insisted on holding what he called a 'gizmo' - a small tube covered at one end with transparent material - while the pictures were being produced.

Ted Serios had enough successes to convince many of his paranormal powers; and those more sceptical never saw him exposed as a fraud. On the other hand, he never allowed anyone to examine his gizmo, and eventually his thoughtographic skills deserted him.

Above: Nina Kulagina separated the white and yolk of an egg without making any physical contact

Below: Psychokinetically bent spoons

The Guru-buster

Until his death in 1978, Dr Abraham Kovoor was Sri Lanka's foremost investigator of strange phenomena. He was determined to root out superstition in his country, and he even offered a reward of 100,000 rupees to any magician who could perform 'any one of the 23 items of miracles mentioned in my permanent challenge under fraud-proof conditions'. In 15 years no one agreed to be subjected to Kovoor's scrutiny.

Kovoor was not only a debunker of the tricks of others, he had remarkable powers of his own. In 1965, he was called in to investigate a 'poltergeist' which had been plaguing a family for three months, throwing bottles and tins, hiding keys and money, and putting dirt in the rice. Kovoor met the family: an elderly couple, their son and daughter, and the daughter's three girls, aged 13, 8 and 4. As soon as he set eyes on them, Kovoor realised that it was the 13-year-old who was responsible for the mischievous goings-on. Her 'facial expressions betrayed her', according to Kovoor, who duly questioned the girl and elicited a confession. He prescribed a course of hypnosis for the girl and told her family to treat her with extra love in the future. The 'poltergeist' never reappeared.

Mind Over Metal

Uri Geller has become world famous through his apparent ability to bend keys and cutlery just by touching them. His method involves holding the object in question between the tips of his fingers. Then, as he concentrates, the object begins to bend, although there is no perceivable external force at work. Geller claims that he need not even touch the metal: he can produce the same effect simply by the power of thought.

His strange abilities became apparent at an early age. When he was just five, the hands of a watch he was wearing began to revolve wildly; and in a Tel Aviv coffee-shop he would cause consternation by twisting spoons merely by staring at them.

Geller has also claimed that he can transmit his powers to other people. In 1983, on a West German television show, he encouraged viewers to concentrate on any broken watches they had. Many notable successes resulted: one man in Freiburg 'repaired' his own watch, which had been smashed in battle during World War 2 and had not worked for 40 years.

Ever the showman, Geller decorated the exterior of a Cadillac with over 5,000 bent spoons - though he admits that only about 1,000 of them were distorted using his mental abilities. Some of the cutlery used was apparently once owned or used by such modern shamans as Rasputin, Houdini, Jimi Hendrix, Picasso, Andy Warhol, and the father of mesmerism, Franz Anton Mesmer.

Spiritualism's Greatest Star
Daniel Douglas Home was born in Scotland in 1833. In the 1840s he was sent to the USA to live with an aunt, but she became so alarmed at the strange noises and other phenomena associated with his presence that she threw him out.

Home quickly became spiritualism's greatest star, and was also feted for his spectacular feats of levitation. He levitated publicly on more than a hundred occasions, and moved pianos at will while tied up in a chair. He was also able to make other people levitate, as the wife of Sir William Crookes found. Crookes was a top scientist who had been asked to debunk Home's amazing claims.

When Crookes conceded that Home's powers were genuine, his professional colleagues were outraged. What Home was doing, they insisted, was scientifically impossible. Crookes replied: 'I never said it was possible, I only said it was true.'

One of Home's most sensational feats was to appear to float out of a third-storey window, returning through the window of another room. However, the fact that he instructed observers not to leave their seats during this display of his powers might suggest a clever piece of trickery, such as an ingenious system of ropes and connecting doors, or even hypnosis.

"My God! It's All Coming True!"
The levitator D D Home, the thoughtographer Ted Serios, the spoon-bender Uri Geller: none has ever been exposed as a charlatan, although many harbour doubts.

In 1974, the science fiction writer Arthur C Clarke and the philosopher Arthur Koestler were among those who sought to investigate Uri Geller's powers. This is from Geller's own account of what happened: 'I sensed that I wasn't really getting through to Arthur C Clarke. (So) I asked him to hold his key out in his own hand and watch very carefully, so that he would know that I wasn't substituting another key, or taking it away from his hand, or putting pressure on it.

'Within moments his key was bending....Arthur Clarke seemed to have lost all his scepticism. He said something like, "My God! It's all coming true!"'

Clarke's own version of events is very different. He maintains that Geller did take his key and did place it on a firm metal surface while stroking it.

The great American debunker James Randi is another who has professed himself sceptical of Geller's powers, going so far as to accuse him of fraud. Although he was sued as a result, Randi continues to offer special prizes in the field of parapsychology - for example, for 'the "psychic" performer who fools the greatest number of people with the least effort'. The awards - bent spoons mounted in perspex - are called Uris, and winners are notified telepathically.

Arthur Koestler, however, was more impressed by Geller; and when he died, he left half a million pounds in his will for the study of parapsychology at a British university.

Above: Uri Geller claimed he could transmit his powers to other people

Below: Science fiction writer Arthur C Clarke investigated Geller's powers

SET AND HORUS POURING UOT LIFE OVER SETI I.

Beyond the body

The suggestion that we have a spiritual as well as a physical being is a concept widely associated with religion; but scientists and psychologists have become increasingly interested in this idea, investigating such phenomena as out-of-body experiences, past lives and - perhaps the strongest basis for our belief in another world - dreams.

Dream Diaries   Many people keep a pencil and paper by their bed in order to record their dreams before they fade from the memory. This idea is not new. In fact, some of the first journals ever kept were largely 'dream diaries' - a recognition that one's dream life may be more important than one's waking existence.

Queen Elizabeth 1's astrologer, Dr John Dee, recorded some particularly strange dreams. On December 9, 1579, for example, he wrote:

'My wife dreamed that one came to her and touched her, saying: "Mistress Dee, you are conceived of child, whose name must be Zacharias; be of good chere, he shall do well." '

And three years later he noted:

'Saterday night I dremed that I was deade, and afterward my bowels wer taken out I walked and talked with...the Lord Thresorer who was com to my house to burn my bokes when I was dead.'

None of these things actually came true, showing that the true meaning of dreams lies beneath their surface level.

Above: Most religions, ancient and modern, believe we have a spiritual being as well as a physical one

Symbols and Meanings

There is a difference between ordinary dreams, whose contents come from our everyday lives, and what the Ancient Greeks called 'big dreams'. According to the Swiss psychologist Carl Jung, dreams of the latter type come from a collective unconscious and contain images that we all share.

Jung believed that dreams were the most reliable indicators of people's inner minds. He himself once had a vivid dream about killing the mythical German hero Siegfried, which he interpreted as a sign to reject his ego. He was inspired to turn away from mainstream psychology, moving instead towards what might be called 'pseudoscience'.

Much has been written on the subject of interpreting particular images that occur in dreams: a unicorn, for example, means that you will receive an official letter; a raven is said to signify bad news. However, one of the purposes of dreams is to take aspects of our waking lives and turn them into images which are not instantly open to interpretation. Not only might the wrong meaning be ascribed to such images, but it could even be a mistake to drag them out into the open. The writer on the 'Otherworld', Patrick Harpur, has said that Jung may have been wrong to try and force the unconscious contents of dreams to become conscious: 'No wonder we forget dreams....No wonder they come with difficulty, with distortion. It is our turn, perhaps, to abandon our egoistic daylight world and go to where they are, in the dark....For dreaming may be the only method of initiation left to us: each night brings a "little death" by which we acclimatize to the Otherworld, rehearsing the journey that all souls have to take in the end.'

The writer Laurens van der Post was a friend of Jung's, the two drawn together by a shared interest in dreams. As a child, van der Post was infuriated by the way adults poured scorn on his descriptions of dreams, dismissing them with the stock response, 'But it was only a dream'. He regarded the Biblical dream of Jacob and the ladder as the greatest of all. He wrote: 'For the first time, a dialogue becomes possible between God and Man. Further, the dream seems to imply that the creator has delegated some of his own infinite power to the created.'

But dreams may be open to different interpretations, and one particular illustration of such ambiguity was to have profound ramifications for the 20th century. During World War 1, Adolf Hitler was asleep in a trench at the German front line, when he dreamed 'that he was about to be engulfed in an upheaval of earth and mud'. He broke out of his nightmare and ran out into the night. Moments later a shell landed and all his sleeping comrades were killed.

For Hitler this was a sign that his life had special meaning: Providence had saved him for a greater purpose. But according to van der Post, 'upheaval of earth and mud' could apply equally well to the chaos that Hitler later brought to the rest of the world, and which did finally engulf him.

Dreams and Precognition

The idea that dreams can reveal the future is as fascinating as it is mysterious. Laurens van der Post had first-hand experience of precognition when, one night in 1961, Jung appeared to him in a dream. The image was of Jung waving goodbye and saying 'I'll be seeing you' from his garden in the

Above: Dr John Dee, Queen Elizabeth I's astrologer, kept a dream diary

Below: The Biblical story of Jacob's dream suggests a dialogue between God and man

Above left: Victorian hypnotists discovered memories of past lives in their subjects

Above right: Nineteenth century Grafton Street, Dublin, where Bridey Murphy is supposed to have lived

Below: Dorothy Eady believed she had lived in Egypt 3,000 years previously

Swiss Alps. Van der Post awoke to discover that his friend had just died in Switzerland.

Robert Morris junior was known as 'the financier of the American Revolution'. He was a signatory to the Declaration of Independence, and founded the Bank of North America. His biography reveals how his father, Robert Morris senior, met a bizarre end, which he had foreseen in a dream.

Morris snr. was due to meet a Captain Mathews and his crew when they arrived at harbour in Maryland. On the night before the arrival of the ship, however, he dreamed that he would die as a result of a salvo fired in his honour. At first he refused to go on board; and so, to reassure him, Captain Mathews promised that no salute would be fired. Later, when Morris was enjoying the party on the ship, Mathews said that the crew were upset at not being able to fire the customary salute. 'Very well,' Morris replied, 'but do not fire until I or someone else gives the signal.'

Back on deck, just as Morris was ready to be taken ashore, a fly settled on his nose and he brushed it away. The gunner took this for the signal he had been waiting for and fired the salute. The wadding struck Morris's elbow, breaking the bone, and he died a few days later from the resulting infection.

Past Lives Many religions believe that the spirit is immortal and passes through a succession of perishable bodies. Ancient Egyptians, Australian aborigines, Hinduism, Buddhism: these are some of the cultures and beliefs which subscribe to the idea of reincarnation. It does not form part of any of the mainstream Christian religions, and yet in Europe and North America too, about 20 per cent of adults believe in multiple existences.

Since Victorian times, a flood of stories relating to past lives has appeared. In a celebrated case in the 1950s, a young woman from Wisconsin apparently regressed to a previous existence under hypnosis. She was able to describe her life as a woman called Bridey Murphy living in 19th century Dublin with astonishing clarity. Names of shops and places were authenticated and old maps supported her description of the neighbourhood.

Children's Memories
Children might be expected to have more vivid memories of previous lives than adults, since they are nearer in time to the former existence and their minds are less cluttered by the everyday concerns of their present one.

In the last century, a nine-year-old Japanese boy named Katsugoro told his sister about his previous life in another village. He described the village with great accuracy, though he had never been there, and said that until the age of four he had been able to remember everything, not just about his past life, but also his death, burial, between-lives state and rebirth.

Most children who talk of previous lives do so between the ages of two and five years. The memories occur either spontaneously or as a result of some physical trauma.

In 1907, an English girl named Dorothy Eady fell downstairs and was initially pronounced dead. She recovered, but began having strange dreams about a temple and garden. She complained to her parents that she was not 'home'. Later she came to believe that she had lived in Egypt 3,000 years previously, as the mistress of a pharaoh, and had committed suicide after becoming pregnant. She had been visiting the pharaoh in out-of-body trips to the afterworld, and eventually went to actually live in Egypt, near the temple she had first seen in her vision as a young girl. She died in 1981, convinced to the end that she would be reunited with her former lover in the world beyond.

Above: Salvador Dali regarded dreams as a crucial source of inspiration

Below: Can memories be carried in our DNA?

Inspiration and Creativity
Dreams can be a fertile source of creativity, both for the expressive arts and for more practical applications. William Blake and Salvador Dali regarded dreams as a crucial source of inspiration; and the inventor Elias Howe literally 'dreamed up' the idea of the sewing machine. The idea for the story Dr Jekyll and Mr Hyde came to Robert Louis Stevenson in a dream, and Paul McCartney has described how the tune of one of the most popular songs of all time, 'Yesterday', came to him in the same way.

Inspirational ideas are particularly accessible during the intermediate stages between waking and sleep. What is known as the 'hypnagogic' state occurs as one descends into the first stage of sleep and the subconscious mind takes over. Fleeting images appear, as well as sounds and voices. The 'hypnapompic' state comes at the end of the sleep cycle. The imagery in these states is not the same as dream imagery, but it can be just as instructive in terms of self-understanding, and can also provide answers to questions and problems from our everyday lives.

Genetic Memory?
In 1957, two young sisters were walking home from church when a car mounted a pavement and killed them. When their mother became pregnant again, her husband was convinced that their daughters were going to be restored to them in a new incarnation. Twin girls duly arrived in 1958.

It was not long before the twins started demonstrating knowledge that they could not possibly have acquired by themselves. The family had moved from the neighbourhood within months of their being born; but on returning three years later, the twins seemed to know where everything was. They could point out their former home, and knew where the school and playground were before they were in view.

These memories did slowly fade, but there was one final uncanny twist. Although the twins weren't usually allowed to play with their dead sisters' toys, they did eventually manage to get hold of two particular dolls. To their parents' amazement, they gave the dolls exactly the same names that their sisters had before them.

Human or Non-Human Forms?

Reincarnation does not have to manifest itself in exclusively human form. In Africa, many tribes believe it is more common to be reincarnated as animals, plants and monsters than as humans. Ancient Egyptians believed that a soul could spend 3,000 years perfecting itself in various animal forms before returning to a human body. Buddhists and Hindus believe that all forms of life undergo a variety of incarnations; and some early Christians believed that 'unworthy' human souls were reincarnated as wild beasts.

The American psychologist Helen Wambach used hypnosis to regress over a thousand subjects to previous lives. She collected data about race, sex and class, and found - realistically - that most people had not been kings or pharaohs in their earlier existences; the overwhelming majority had lived in the lower strata of society. But none could recall previous incarnations as dogs, rocks or different types of grass!

Near-Death Experiences

Our consciousness is said to leave the body just before death, and case histories of the 'near-death experience' seem to bear this out. Here, an eight-year-old describes what happened when he almost drowned: 'All I remember was my hair getting stuck in the drain and then blacking out. The next thing I knew, I floated out of my body. I could see myself under the water but I wasn't afraid. All of a sudden I started going up a tunnel, and before I could think about it, I found myself in heaven. I knew it was heaven because everything was bright and everyone was cheerful. A nice man asked me if I wanted to stay there. I thought about staying....But I said, "I want to be with my family." Then I got to come back.'

Above: Ancient Egyptians believed that a soul could spend 3,000 years perfecting itself in various animal forms before returning to a human body

56

Death of a General

An officer serving with the Indian Army once had a vivid experience suggesting that he had existed in a previous incarnation. The incident led Major McDonough to conclude that he had been at the spot where Alexander the Great's army had camped 2,000 years before: 'I reached a ridge which overlooked a precipitous drop into a densely wooded valley.....Suddenly, I found myself down in the valley, amid a large number of Ancient Greek soldiers...In the centre of the valley were three altars. But what attracted me most was a group of men at the head of the valley, looking up at something.....I went over and found that it was a newly cut inscription in Greek on the dressed surface of the rock, commemorating the death of one of Alexander the Great's generals. Now I never studied Greek, but I was able to read the inscription clearly and understand it. There was a tense atmosphere of sorrow in the vicinity.

'A sudden blank and I was back in my place on the ridge, still gazing into the valley....I determined....to explore it with the help of Indian coolies....The whole place was densely covered in rank vegetation and jungle growth....I headed for the place where the rock-cut inscription was, and after much labour....I exposed what was once a dressed surface, with traces of Greek letters.'

Carl Jung (above) had a near-death experience in which he saw a number of images, including a Hindu sitting in the lotus position (below) next to a temple

Over My Dead Body

In 1944, a British soldier lost consciousness after being accidentally electrocuted. When he came round, he discovered that he had been declared clinically dead, and that everything he'd observed must have really happened: 'Suddenly....I was looking down on myself lying in the grass - with the smoke wreathing up from my fingers as the flesh was burnt away....

'Although there seemed to be a gentle force pulling me away, I was so intrigued that I resisted. A few moments later, a 'blood wagon' raced up and.....an M.O. got out.....As he bent over I saw he had a bald patch on top....He thumped my chest....then filled a syringe and plunged it in....Up above I winced then and laughed - of course, I couldn't feel it! Then he listened again, shook his head and put the blanket over my face. I shouted to him, 'Hey, I'm up here - I'm not dead!'....I didn't want my body to go without me so the 'cord' shortened and I slammed back into my body - and blackness again.'

A Glimpse of Heaven

Carl Jung himself had a near-death experience, which affected him profoundly. It happened in 1944, when he was in hospital recovering from a heart attack. A nurse in attendance reported seeing a bright halo of light around him, a phenomenon she had observed many times around dying patients.

Jung felt he was floating high above the world - about a thousand miles into outer space - and able to see from the Mediterranean to the Himalayas. Then he saw a huge stone temple, next to which a Hindu was sitting in the lotus position. As he aproached the temple, he felt that he was about to understand the meaning of life. But before he could enter, the doctor who was treating him appeared before him in the guise of an Ancient Roman healer. His doctor told him to return to earth, and Jung did so, but with great resentment.

Jung obviously drew on this experience when he wrote later to a friend who was herself dying of cancer: 'Death is the hardest thing from the outside. But once inside you taste of such completeness and peace and fulfilment that you don't want to return.'

A Universal Experience?

Raymond Moody, whose book 'Life After Life' created a sensation when it was published in 1975, wrote that almost all near-death experiences follow a similar pattern. The patient sees his or her corpse, travels down a dark tunnel and arrives in a place of great peace. Dead relatives and friends appear, and a powerful being asks the new arrival to evaluate his or her life. The major events of that life are played back, and then a symbolic barrier is reached - the border between earthly life and the life beyond. No one who has had a near-death experience has ever reported going through this barrier; instead, the spirit returns to earth.

A large-scale survey of medical practitioners in the USA and India, however, has revealed many significant differences between cultures and faiths. Hindus did not see Jesus, and no Christian reported seeing Hindu deities. Americans were likely to see their mother, whereas Indians seldom saw any females at all. And while Americans were often happy to see their dead relatives, Indians tended to fight against each step of the journey.

The Dying Brain

Scientists are by no means convinced that near-death experiences are exclusively concerned with the soul and its transition to another world. Indeed, recent research suggests an explanation which is more physical than spiritual. According to the scientists, the dark tunnel leading towards the light is a physical effect of the brain being starved of oxygen. This lack of oxygen causes cells in the cortex to be stimulated, producing the image of a bright light at the 'end of the tunnel'. If the whole cortex were to become so stimulated that all the cells 'fired' quickly, the whole area would appear to be light; in fact, one would seem to have 'entered' the light.

Sensory deprivation is known to induce hallucinations, which can be pleasurable even in terrible circumstances. Two miners who were trapped underground for six days described seeing strange lights, doorways, radiant women and a beautiful garden.

The peaceful and euphoric feelings described by most 'returnees' may also have a physical origin. A massive release of endorphins from the brain could produce such feelings. These chemicals have a narcotic effect, and their ability to cause electrical seizures in parts of the brain could produce visions of the kind described by those who have had near-death experiences.

Opposite page: An artist's impression of heaven - the light at the end of the tunnel'

Below: Scientists have suggested a physical rather than a spiritual explanation for near-death experiences

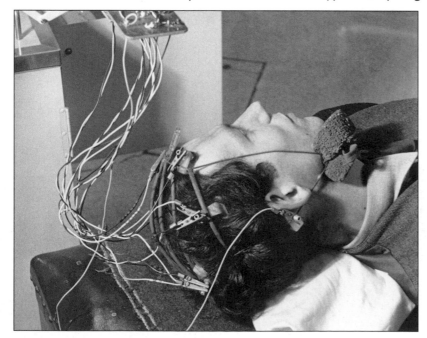

Total Recall

The commonest way of regressing people to their previous lives is through hypnosis; but this technique must be employed with great caution, as the case of Blanche Poynings illustrates.

Under hypnosis, a young Englishwoman was found to have astonishing recall of the life of a medieval lady called Blanche Poynings, who was said to have lived during the reign of Richard II. Her case was investigated by the British Society for Psychical Research, who were astounded by her ability to recall the tiniest details, such as the different types of bread that were eaten by different classes of people.

Finally, one of the investigators asked: 'How can we confirm what you are telling us?'

'Read his will,' came the reply.

'Where is it?'

'Museum. On parchment.'

'How can we get at it?'

'There is a book...."Countess Maud" by Emily Holt.'

Emily Holt's historical novel "Countess Maud" turned out to contain all the details of the woman's supposed previous life. Hypnosis hadn't proved the existence of reincarnation on this occasion; it had merely demonstrated the mind's extraordinary capacity for recall.

Lives Transformed   Most people who have had a near-death experience reject the explanations offered by the scientists. They invariably insist that the tunnel was real, that they have seen heaven and that their lives can never be the same again.

One newly-wed woman was in a coma for four days following a car accident. During that time, she wondered whether to live or die. She examined every aspect of her life - from her unhappy childhood to her pleasanter more recent memories - and was finally able to put the negative experiences behind her and return to consciousness.

With many others also reporting that near-death experiences made them re-evaluate their lives, at least one conclusion can be drawn: that irrespective of whether they are factual or illusory, such experiences can have a profound effect on people's lives in terms of changing attitudes and perspectives.

Mind and Body

Just as the power of the mind may be used to influence the physical world around us, so many people believe that the mind can also exercise control over the body itself. The key to such control is an understanding of the body's own energies, the life force itself.

Belief in the existence of a life force transcends both culture and time. For example, many may be aware of the ancient Chinese concept of 'yin' and 'yang', where the body's energies are seen as either masculine or feminine; but they may be perhaps less familiar with Wilhelm Reich's theory regarding a vital omnipresent energy which he called 'orgone'. Reich's ideas were developed in the USA as recently as fifty years ago.

The techniques for harnessing the life force and exercising control over the body are diverse. It is well known that Eastern mystics teach that the power is derived from meditation and spirituality. But once again, modern technology has provided its own alternative. 'Biofeedback' systems involve relaying sophisticated bodily readings back to a subject, who then seeks to control these readings by the power of thought.

The objective of gaining control over the body is often to benefit oneself or others. Yoga is frequently used to ease the stresses of daily life; fire-walking, which is still practised widely, is an act of religious devotion; and some psychic surgeons have performed prodigious feats of healing. But in some cultures gaining control is more associated with pushing the body to its limits. In Malaysia, for example, young males periodically 'go amok', as it is called, demonstrating seemingly impossible feats of strength and endangering both themselves and others in the process. Afterwards they have no recollection of these seizures. Similarly, it is said that before battle, Viking warriors, or 'berserkers', were able to rouse themselves to a state of superhuman vigour and imperviousness to pain. The words 'amok' and 'berserk' have entered the English language as a result, but, ironically, because of their association with acts of aggression, these words have come to indicate loss of control rather than gaining it.

The relationship between mind and body, and in particular, the way in which the power of the mind can assert itself over the physical being, is obviously something we are a long way from understanding. At the moment, we are simply left with the manifestations of these powers.

Above: The power of crystals have been said to soothe both body and mind

Breath of Life

In traditional Hindu teaching, the breath of life - or prana - is the essence of all motion, force and power, not just in people but also in the entire cosmos. Through yoga the body builds up a store of prana, and its flow can be controlled by rhythmic breathing. The right nostril is said to be positive and represents the sun, while the left nostril is negative and represents the moon. Health and vitality can be enhanced by maintaining a balance in one's breathing. In Hawaii the life force is known as mana. It flows through the body from the subconscious to the superconscious level, and can also be manipulated by breathing exercises. The Chinese talk of qi, which also means breath. It is received through food, air and the general environment, but the ability to absorb it declines with age. The Japanese later adopted this idea, relating it especially to levels of courage.

All these beliefs might be regarded as mere superstition, but so many remarkable powers seem to stem from them that they cannot be so easily dismissed.

Yogic Powers

Western scientists once believed that mind and body were separate entities. The Russian behaviourist Ivan Pavlov, in his famous experiments with salivating dogs, proved that this was not the case. What Pavlov called the 'conditioned reflex' showed clearly that the mind can influence many functions of the body through an unseen and unexplained mechanism. We now know that our bodies have an unconscious or 'autonomic' nervous system, which regulates such things as heartbeat, pulse, glandular secretions and brainwave activity. This system is partially controlled by our minds, and simply by closing our eyes and breathing deeply, brainwave activity drops markedly. It is thought that many yogic powers or siddhis work by controlling the autonomic system through breathing techniques and other meditative exercises. Hindu and Buddhist yogis themselves teach that one can attain control over the body through concentration and spiritual development.

Above: In Europe the ability to levitate was once considered a mark of saintliness

Below: The Natural Law Party claim that crime and disease can be reduced by the power of yogic flying

For Hindus these miraculous powers include levitation, invisibility and knowing the moment one will die. In Buddhist yoga the 'wondrous gifts' include the ability to fly, to preserve one's youth and to see the gods. Practising these powers is not encouraged, because they lead away from the true path of enlightenment, but controlled breathing and meditation remain crucial to the Buddhist and Hindu faiths.

In the 1960s and 1970s, scientists in the west persuaded some yogis to demonstrate their powers under laboratory conditions. The scientists measured a variety of autonomic responses, and discovered that the yogis were able to exert a strong influence on their brain activity and skin resistance readings, confirming that they did indeed possess a highly-developed level of mental control over their bodies.

'Vote For Me; I'll Set You Free'

In England in 1994, an unusual political party - whose sponsors included Beatle George Harrison - attempted to win power in the European elections. The aims of the Natural Law Party were ambitious: 'to bring an end to conflict in the field of politics and make government free from problems'. Their key attraction was a kind of levitation called yogic flying.

The Party maintained that 7,000 experts practising yogic flying would 'reduce crime dramatically' and 'eliminate 50 per cent of all disease within three years'. As proof of their claims, a photograph was published showing two experts in the first stage of yogic flying. A graph was also produced, showing the Maharishi effect on crime reduction. The caption ran: 'The crime rate in Merseyside has fallen by 60 per cent compared with national trends, when a group of yogic flyers was set up nearby'. These yogic powers and their associated claims regarding social benefits had little impact on the voters, however. Out of 400 candidates, not a single one was elected.

Above: St Teresa of Avila's experiences of levitation were often so violent her sister nuns had to hold her down

Below: Rolling Thunder, a modern day shaman who became spiritual adviser to many celebrities

'Put Me Down, God!'

In Europe, the ability to levitate was once considered a mark of saintliness. Over 200 saints are said to have been able to raise their bodies into the air, either consciously or unconsciously.

One such was the 16th century Spanish saint, Teresa of Avila. Her experiences were sometimes so violent that her sisters had to hold her down, and she herself would exclaim: 'Put me down, God!'

In 1591, levitation was also a source of embarrassment to a French girl called Francoise Fontaine: 'When I was 12 years old, I was lifted before the altar on three separate occasions. The third time, I was carried through the air with my head downwards. I was not frightened, but rather ashamed because my clothes fell over my body.'

50 years later, the Spanish ambassador to Rome expressed his amazement on seeing a man levitate: 'He swooped upwards through the church door, over the heads of the worshippers towards the altar about 80 yards away....The Pope saw it and was absolutely astonished.'

Churches seem to be a favourite place for acts of levitation to occur. In the 19th century, the Abbe Petit described his terror at being propelled upwards towards the altar, because 'I had no wish to fly'. A German nun, on the other hand, who was 'frequently lifted up onto sculpted ornaments high in the church', declared that she was not in the least afraid, for she believed that her guardian angel was always with her.

The Christian church began to be suspicious of levitation. How could they be sure that this power really came from God? After all, it was believed that witches were also able to fly, and their power was said to come from the Devil. An incident which occurred in 1906 may have borne out these suspicions. In that year a 16-year-old South African girl started levitating uncontrollably, to a height of five feet off the ground. The only way she could be brought down was to sprinkle her with holy water, suggesting that demonic possession was responsible.

The Universal Shaman

The word 'shaman' is applied to a person in a tribe or group who is believed to be in communication with the gods and the spirit world, and who has had mystical powers bestowed upon him. These powers include the ability to heal, which is why, among native Americans, the shaman is known as the medicine man.

One of the most famous shamans from this culture was Rolling Thunder, who was born in 1915. He was instantly recognised as a future medicine man and received special training to prepare him for his destined role. This included spending long periods in isolation, during which he learned to communicate with animals and plants.

One of his first patients was an old woman who seemed to be on the brink of death. After a night-long singing session with Rolling Thunder, however, she made a miraculous recovery. He later became a spiritual adviser to celebrities such as Muhammad Ali, The Grateful Dead and Bob Dylan, who acknowledged his mentor in his Rolling Thunder Revue.

Biofeedback

Biofeedback is sometimes called 'electronic yoga' because it combines modern technology with mystical states of consciousness. This process involves the electronic measurement of various physiological processes, such as heartbeat and body temperature. The information is then amplified and fed back to the subject, who seeks to influence these readings purely by the power of thought.

It was in 1958 when a researcher named Joe Kamiya added a relay circuit to an electro-encephalogram (EEG) machine, so that a tone sounded whenever the subject's brainwaves were in a relaxed state. Subjects quickly learned that they could control this tone, and both the processes and the results were found to be similar to those of yoga.

Hand-held biofeedback units, which monitor skin moisture, are now available for personal use, but with practice, many people find that they can dispose of the electronic equipment and control their physiological responses using concentration alone.

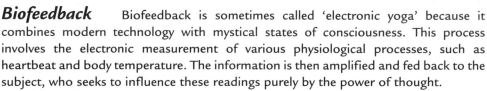

Fire and Magic

Fire-walking, which is still practised in many parts of the world, probably originated in the East. The great Greek magician Apollonius, an early exponent of this amazing skill, acquired his powers when he travelled to India in the first century AD. His miracles were said to rival those of Christ, and his fame went before him, perhaps in part due to his own efforts in self-publicity: 'I am not like ordinary men. I have the power to walk through flames without being burned.'

In Burma in the 1920s, an Englishman managed to capture firewalking on cine-film by bribing a priest. 'Those who aren't pure enough will burn,' the priest commented darkly as he allowed the man into the temple where the fire-walking would take place. Inside, there was a pit of flaming coals generating so much heat that he could scarcely bear it, despite the fact that he was partially protected by a bamboo screen. He observed that even the coal-rakers had to keep turning their heads away to avoid being burned.

The fire-walkers prayed to the firegod to make their hearts pure, then proceeded to walk through the burning coals. They were then whipped three times on the back, which apparently formed part of the ritual, but seemed to emerge from both ordeals relatively unscathed.

This phenomenon was also witnessed by a neutral observer in 1994, when photographer Charles Walker was in a remote village in Sri Lanka: 'The fire pit was about twelve feet long and filled with burning cinders. The assistant threw on brushwood to bring the flames to waist height. It became so hot that I had to move my tripod back and fix a long-focus lens on my camera. Even at that distance I was still afraid that the heat and sparks might damage my equipment.

'The fire-walkers didn't seem to feel the heat. They walked with great dignity and quite slowly through the flames. I watched in amazement, wondering why their clothes did not catch fire. At times I could not see the lower parts of their bodies because of the flames. The parts which were visible vibrated and danced in the heat currents, so that they looked more like coloured spectres than men.

'I had watched them carefully while I was setting up my equipment. They built a small table-shrine clear of the heat and prayed before doing the walk. They were protected by something, but what that something is I have no idea.'

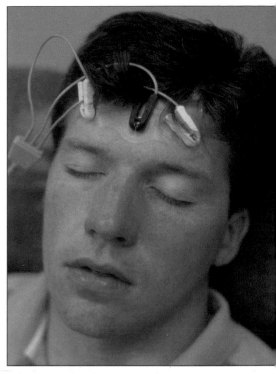

Above: Biofeedback electrodes attached to a man's forehead

Below: Ritual firewalking in Kandy, Sri Lanka

Pure Souls or Hard Soles?

The investigator Carlo Fonseka was determined to discover how people could walk through fire without getting burned. He too went to Sri Lanka, where he witnessed many fire-walking ceremonies, but instead of merely recording the events in words and pictures, Fonseka adopted a more scientific approach. He measured the coal-pits and timed the walkers, and discovered that, on average, the participants were on the coals for just three seconds, in which time they had taken ten steps - an average of just 0.3 seconds per step. He also found that the fire-walkers were accustomed to going around barefoot and the soles of their feet were very hard, compared with those who usually wore shoes. And the thicker the skin on the soles of the feet, Fonseka reasoned, the more they would be able to withstand the heat of the coals. Finally, he sought to demonstrate that fire-walking had no spiritual dimension, nothing to do with the purity of the soul, moral conduct or abstinence from alcohol, meat and sex. As proof of this, Fonseka encouraged a group of fire-walkers to eat pork cutlets washed down with swigs of alcohol. This flouting of strict religious convention had absolutely no effect on their ability to walk over the coals unharmed.

Despite Fonseka's findings, things can and do go terribly wrong. The burns unit of the Kataragama

Above: Carlo Fonseka sought to demonstrate firewalking had nothing to do with ritual or the purity of the soul

Hospital, which is situated at Sri Lanka's holiest shrine, regularly has to treat people whose fire-walking attempts have come to grief. In Tahiti, one western volunteer was not brave enough to go through the coals barefoot, so he kept his shoes on. His feet survived the ordeal intact, but the intensity of the heat caused the skin on his face to peel a few days later. Some have fared even worse. The American investigator Max Freedom Long witnessed one fire-walking ritual in which one man died and two others sustained severe injuries.

Sexually Charged Atmosphere

Wilhelm Reich was a student of Sigmund Freud, the father of psychoanalysis. In the 1930s, Reich cast a new perspective on the concept of the life force when he claimed to have discovered a different kind of vital energy. He called it 'orgone' and believed it was both omnipresent in the earth's atmosphere and also a biological energy source in human beings. In particular, it was produced in concentrated form by sexual activity.

Reich declared that the ability to achieve sexual climax was an essential attribute of a healthy person; but for those who lacked this ability it was possible to 'charge' their bodies with orgone by placing them in a multi-layered box covered with organic and inorganic material. This device, which Reich called an 'orgone accumulator', would increase vitality and improve health.

Reich claimed positive results when he put his ideas to the test on cancer patients, but the US Food and Drug Administration carried out its own research and decided that the claims for the orgone accumulator were worthless. Reich was forbidden to use or sell the device, or even to use the word 'orgone' in his books. Reich refused, saying that federal inspectors had no business interfering in matters of natural science. He was jailed for contempt of court, his orgone accumulators were destroyed and his books were burned. Wilhelm Reich died in prison in 1957.

Energy Below the Earth

Although Reich's orgone accumulator was developed primarily to cure his patients, the implications of the device and the theories which underpinned it went much further. Reich's device was designed to trap the energy which gives life, and through which magnetic and gravitational forces can operate. Its construction was similar to the hidden chambers set deep below many megalithic sites and ancient monuments. What these chambers were used for has never been adequately explained, although many suggestions have been put forward, including religious ceremonies, habitation, storage, burial, even as a repository for rubbish. Were these chamber mounds in fact orgone accumulators, with the stone circles acting as control centres? And was the stored energy put to practical use by those who understood its power?

Power From Crystals

Crystals have been used since ancient times both for good luck and for their therapeutic powers. Quartz crystals are formed when molten silica deep in the earth moves towards the surface, where it cools. When rubbed, they generate an electrical current, and they can also receive, amplify, convert and focus energy. For this reason, many people believe that they can focus the universal life force and harmonize the body's vital energies.

Although there is no scientific evidence that crystals have paranormal properties, many maintain that they emit vibrations undetectable by ordinary means. They are said to relieve mental and emotional tension if held, and to bring peace and harmony to the environment. There are reports indicating that the use of crystals is beneficial to patients suffering from Parkinson's disease, arthritis, chronic back pain and even blindness; but they remain strictly in the domain of alternative medicine. In fact, some mainstream medical groups believe a reliance on crystals is inherently dangerous and have banned their use.

Peak Experience

The psychologist Abraham Maslow coined the term 'peak experience' to describe those sudden moments of intense happiness, affirmation or revelation that can happen to anyone at any time. Here a woman describes a peak experience she had while listening to a Beethoven quartet, Opus 312: 'Suddenly this vast horizon opened up to me. And suddenly I knew that time, past, present and future were all one, and that I was God, and yet at the same time was only the minutest grain of sand. I can remember thinking "How incredible - how can you be both things at once?" And I also saw that the entire universe is on a grid system - I actually saw the grid stretching out into infinity - that every thought, every deed, every word, anything that happened, was not accidental. Everything in the universe was interconnected: every time you meet someone, it's not a chance meeting - there's a purpose for that meeting, it all ties up with everything else in the universe. And that experience changed my life.'

Psychic Surgery

The popular view of psychic healers is of people who claim they can effect cures from a distance, or perhaps by the laying on of hands. There are some, however, who do not shrink from much messier work.

In the Philippines and Brazil, psychic surgeons appear to slice patients open with their fingers, remove pieces of tissue, then close the 'incision' without a stitch. Much blood is shed in the process but the patients, who remain fully conscious throughout, are said to feel no pain. The surgeons claim to use paranormal powers or be guided by spirit helpers.

The evidence from the medical outcomes is mixed. Some patients suffering from apparently incurable diseases insist that they have been cured; but in other cases, the surgeons have merely been performing tricks. What is claimed to be a tumour removed from a patient will often turn out to be a piece of animal flesh that had been concealed up the surgeon's sleeve; and 'kidney stones' are often nothing more than ordinary pebbles. Even where there is no physical evidence of duplicity, it is no guarantee of success; for if a patient complains of not feeling any better, his 'past-life karma' is frequently blamed.

Jose Arigo - Spirit Surgeon

Between 1950 and 1971, the healing feats of a Brazilian peasant known as 'Ze Arigo' made him a national hero. He claimed that he was guided by the spirit of a German physician, Dr Adolphus Fritz, who died in 1918. Using little more than a rusty penknife, Arigo performed a host of surgical procedures, treating up to 300 patients a day. After seeing Arigo carry out a cataract operation, one observer wrote: 'I saw him pick up what looked like a pair of nail scissors. He wiped them on his sports shirt and.....cut straight into the cornea of the patient's eye. She did not flinch, although she was fully conscious. The cataract was out in a matter of seconds.'

No sleight of hand seems to have been involved. In fact, Arigo did not even appear to be aware of what he was doing. Once, when he was shown a film of himself operating, he fainted with shock.

Arigo was jailed twice for practising medicine illegally; but when a team of American doctors investigated him in 1968, they concluded that he was genuinely able to control an unknown form of life energy.

In January 1971, Arigo was killed in a car crash. One might have expected that that would have been the end of Dr Fritz too. But ten years later, it seems he reappeared as medical mentor to another Brazilian; for gynaecologist Edson de Quieroz, claimed that Dr Fritz was now acting as his spirit guide.

Below: Psychic surgery to remove a cataract

Beyond Earth

Of all the mysteries that have faced mankind, the greatest have involved the nature of the universe itself. Paradoxically, however, as our knowledge of what lies beyond our world has increased, more questions have been raised than answered.

The idea of an infinite universe containing many other worlds has been around for over 400 years. This theory has inevitably led people to speculate about the possibility of life on at least some of those other planets. The attempts to find evidence of extra-terrestrial life have been helped by the development of sophisticated equipment such as spaceprobes and huge radio telescopes; which is just as well, for the results continue to be negative and the search becomes ever wider. But negative results so far don't prove that other forms of life don't exist; perhaps they merely indicate that even our most advanced technologies are still hopelessly inadequate.

Perhaps what is needed is a different way of travelling through space and manipulating time. Although ideas such as 'time portals' have long been the stuff of science fiction, they are now the subject of serious research. Professor Stephen Hawking recently shook the scientific world by stating that time travel may one day be a real possibility.

While some scientists turn their thoughts to the outermost reaches of the universe, others are more interested in discovering the extent to which the universe impacts on our daily lives. This idea is a very old one. The study of astrology dates back at least 5,000 years to ancient Babylon. It was practised by the ancient Chinese, Egyptians and Indians, and the Romans learned the art from the ancient Greeks. This makes astrology one of the most widespread and enduring belief systems known to mankind.

With the scientific advances of the 17th century, astrology was relegated to the level of popular superstition; but more recent academic research has shown that the sun, moon and planets can exert an influence on our lives.

It is not just humans who are affected by heavenly bodies; plants, animals and the climate are also sensitive to cosmic rhythms. Earthquakes are often triggered when the earth, moon and sun are in alignment. It is also known that animals have an extraordinary ability to predict earthquakes, sometimes as much as weeks in advance. Is this ability based on detecting and responding to cosmic forces? Perhaps the intensive studies currently being undertaken will one day be able to answer all the questions concerning the nature of the universe and the forces at work within it.

Above: Could black holes provide a pathway to another dimension?

Black Holes

Many people may have heard of black holes through the work of eminent scientists such as Professor Stephen Hawking. At first it might appear that this research is of purely academic interest, but could it lead to an energy supply on an undreamed of scale? Or a revolution in our present thinking regarding movement in space and time?

Black holes are thought to be dead stars that have collapsed under their own weight and become so compact that anything within their grasp is immediately engulfed. Professor Hawking has suggested that matter sucked into black holes might re-emerge instantaneously in another dimension of space altogether.

As a black hole, perhaps containing the mass of 100 million suns, swallows up more material, the theory has it that the energy released would follow the path of least resistance, which would be from its 'poles'. Magnetic fields, atoms and electrons would be emitted into space - indeed, Professor Hawking believes that black holes can emit so much radiation that they can explode. Might there be a way of tapping into this release of energy, or even extracting it direct from black holes themselves?

Above: The study of how the universe impacts on our daily lives is a very old one - 5,000 years ago the ancient Babylonians studied astrology

The Big Crunch

It was Alexander Friedmann who, earlier this century, made the discovery that the universe is expanding. We still do not know exactly how fast this rate of expansion is, or indeed if it will continue. It is possible that at some point in the future the expansion will slow down and stop, and that the universe will then begin to contract again. If that were to happen, the implications would be mind-boggling. For if clusters of galaxies, currently moving apart, started moving closer together again, as they once were, would that be in the future or the past? Some have speculated that in this scenario time would run backwards. Would that mean that we would be 'remembering' the future?

This idea has been taken seriously by astrophysicists, even though it calls into question one of the fundamental laws of physics: the second law of thermodynamics. This states that disorder, or entropy, is always increasing, the implication of which is that all ordered forms of energy in the universe will eventually be destroyed. The consequence of that would be the 'heat death' of the universe. As this law assures a cataclysmic end at some point in the future, perhaps our best hope might lie in the contraction of the universe, which would reverse the process. But it still leaves the intriguing question of whether a contracting universe would cause time to be reversed too.

Time Travel

According to Einstein's theory of relativity, space and time near black holes would behave in ways which run counter to common sense. His theory suggests that if you could hover in orbit just outside a black hole, you would be able to see the entire future of the universe pass by in a matter of seconds.

Einstein's formulation of time as simply another dimension has led astrophysicists to contemplate the theoretical possibility of time travel. It would appear that time is by no means as stable in every part of the galaxy as it is on earth; but to create the conditions in which we could even begin to move in time as we do in space would involve building giant magnets at least the size of our own planet.

'Warp Drive'

Miguel Alcubierre, of the University of Wales, Cardiff, believes that the space-time near a spaceship could be made to expand and contract, producing a 'warp drive'. This would both push a spaceship away from the earth while pulling it into space by the force of space-time itself. This theory requires masses to repel each other, but that is exactly what happened as the universe expanded rapidly after 'big bang'. Scientists are currently looking for what they call the 'exotic matter' which experiences this anti-gravitational force.

Professor Eric Laithwaite believes there is a force which is independent of gravity, anti-gravity, which could aid space travel

Prominent among anti-gravity theorists are Captain Bruce Cathie and Professor Eric Laithwaite. Cathie is an airline pilot who believes that Einstein's last theories hold out the prospect of unlimited energy and space travel. Laithwaite, who designed the high-speed hovertrains used in Germany and Japan, came to believe in the idea of a force independent of gravity after noticing an anomaly in the forces active in a gyroscope. Unfortunately, despite a spectacular demonstration in London where he lifted an enormous weight almost effortlessly with the aid of a spinning gyroscope, tabloid headlines such as 'AntiGravity Prof' tended to debase his achievements, and scepticism on the part of his colleagues led to his ostracism from the scientific community.

Testing Astrology

Astrology is an ancient system of divination using the positions of the sun, moon and planets. These bodies are said to produce cosmic forces which can influence events on earth, and these effects can be determined by mapping out their relative positions.

The early Christians, like most modern scientists, frowned upon astrology as a belief system based on superstition; and it is certainly true that the rationale behind birth-signs can have little validity today, simply because the positions of the stars have changed since it was originally formulated. And yet it would be going too far to say that astrology is purely for the eccentric and the gullible, and has never had a place in serious scientific thought. It was the famous psychologist Hans Eysenck who pointed out that astrology was the forerunner of astronomy; and many of the great astronomers of early modern times were extremely sympathetic towards astrology. The Swiss psychologist Carl Jung often consulted his patients' horoscopes as a method of establishing both their potential and their problems. He believed that astrology united the inner world with the outer one.

Breeding Champions

In 1949, the French psychologist Michel Gauquelin set out to disprove the claims made by the proponents of astrology. Early indications were in his favour, but some curious findings then started to emerge. Examining the horoscopes of almost 600 French physicians, he discovered that a disproportionate number of them had been born when Mars, Jupiter and Saturn were either close to the eastern horizon ('rising') or directly overhead ('culminating'). Similarly, he found that sports champions tended to have been born after the rise and culmination of Mars.

By the mid-1970s, Michel and Francoise Gauquelin had collected a great deal of evidence to show that people excelling in certain fields (e.g. science, literature and sport) tended to have been born with certain planets in certain positions. A sceptical American organisation, the Committee for Scientific Investigation of Claims of the Paranormal, decided to look into these findings, which had also been replicated by other researchers. In the event, they were unable to refute any of the Gauquelins' methods, and became so frustrated that they took to amending the data to produce different results. One member of the Committee finally broke ranks and accused others of falsifying the data, leaving the integrity of the Gauquelins' work intact, which it is to this day.

More recently, computer-designed astrological charts have being subjected to rigorous scientific testing, and if anything, this research tends to support the idea that astrological predictions are not random; for some studies do suggest a greater accuracy from birth charts than could be expected purely by chance.

Plants and the Cosmos

Gardeners have known since time immemorial that certain plants are likely to germinate if planted at certain times of the year or during certain phases of the moon. For example, annuals bearing above-ground crops should be planted during the waxing moon; biennials, perennials and root-crop plants, on the other hand, should be planted when the moon is waning. Pruning and harvesting should also be done during a waning moon.

An experimenter named Frank Brown has carried out tests to see how plants respond when environmental factors are eliminated. He found that even when kept in the dark, and at constant temperature and pressure, his plants continued to follow patterns which bore a close relationship with external factors. He discovered, for instance, that potatoes responded to the precise position of the moon just as strongly as if they were outside in natural conditions.

His results had far-reaching implications. Any natural scientist who had ever conducted an experiment in supposedly 'constant conditions' was now open to the accusation of trying to do the impossible.

Circadian Rhythms

Our lives are influenced by natural cycles, partly due to the earth's rotation but partly due to factors which are still unexplained. Our bodies are regulated by 'circadian' rhythms, which are responsible for producing different chemicals and energy levels at different times of the day. This phenomenon is not, as was formerly thought, simply a question of the presence or absence of sunlight. Experiments have been carried out in which people given watches set deliberately fast or slow extended or contracted their circadian rhythms according to what time they believed it to be. Other experiments, in which people have been quite literally left in the dark, indicate that the circadian rhythm is attuned to a cycle nearer to 28 hours than 24. Unconstrained by external factors, our natural rhythm would see us awake for sixteen hours, asleep for twelve and pushing forward two or three hours through the clock cycle every day. This explains why some people always feel like staying up later at night and getting up later the next day.

Above: Plants are more likely to germinate during certain phases of the moon

Below: Some animals seem to have internal mechanisms for predicting earthquakes

Body temperature also follows a regular circadian pattern. It rises with the sun and continues to do so, along with heart rate, until reaching a peak in early afternoon. It then slowly falls, reaching a trough at around 4 o'clock in the morning. The fact that the body is at its most sluggish at this time has been exploited in many diverse ways. For example, secret police forces around the world have found it to be the best time to interrogate suspects; and it is also the peak time for mothers to give birth, for the body is at its most relaxed.

Predicting Earthquakes

In 1960, one of the worst earthquakes on record occurred in Agadir, Morocco, resulting in the deaths of 15,000 people. Stray animals were observed streaming away from the city before the earthquake struck. Just prior to the great earthquake which hit Tashkent, Central Asia, in 1976, there were widespread reports of animals displaying unusual patterns of behaviour. The Chinese radio network broadcast examples of this phenomenon: 'The Tibetan yak lay sprawling on the ground, the panda was holding his head, screaming, and the swan got up from the water and lay on the ground.'

These stories suggest not only that animals have some kind of internal mechanism for detecting such natural disasters, but that the process at work is far more sophisticated and sensitive than anything produced by science. Then there is the question of exactly what signals the animals are picking up. Are they responding to tiny vibrations in the ground? Or could they be somehow receiving information from much further afield, perhaps from beyond our planet?

Chapter Three

Earth Mysteries

The Pyramids, Stonehenge, ley lines, crop circles: these are just some of the many examples which show that the very earth itself is a vast repository of the mysterious, from the amazing structures scattered across its surface to the energies that somehow seem to be generated within.

Many of these mysteries are the product of ancient civilizations, civilizations which we in the industrialised, technologically advanced world of the late twentieth century invariably describe as 'primitive'. We categorise these past eras as simple, rudimentary, where scientific knowledge was limited and its application even more so.

Perhaps the starkest manifestation of this contrast - and understandably so - is the relationship between people and the earth itself. Early civilizations must have felt a special bond with the earth; they were dependent on its providence, fearing its power both to bless and to take away. There were good reasons for such peoples to worship the sun, moon and earth, for the connection was direct and absolute: a poor harvest could spell death as surely as an invading army.

For mankind today, by contrast, the earthly and cosmic patterns have more to do with science than mysticism. And most of us are fortunate enough not to be at the mercy of the planet's vagaries.

But the more we learn about these so-called 'primitive' civilizations, the more complex the picture becomes. We find staggering feats of design and construction; sites of spiritual significance which also acted as observatories and giant calendars; early types of computer built with astonishing precision. And ancient skills which involve sensitivity to the earth's energies - such as dowsing, and the Chinese art of Feng Shui - are also being rediscovered and re-evaluated. These skills stand in sharp contrast to the indiscriminate ways that 'advanced' societies treat the earth, which environmentalists are warning will have grave consequences.

It is certain that our ancestors attained levels of knowledge, skill and understanding greater than was once thought, but the extent and nature of those powers remain a mystery. The earth has revealed some of her secrets; others have yet to be uncovered.

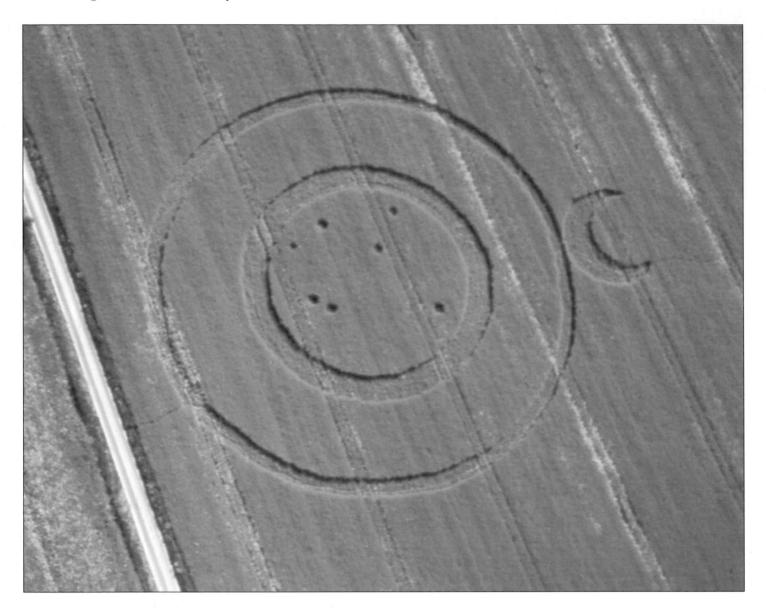

Crop Circles

In August 1980, John Scull, a farmer in Wiltshire, England, made a bizarre discovery in one of his oat fields: a circle, some 60 feet in diameter, of flattened crops. A report in the local press attracted the attention of UFO enthusiasts and it was not long before tales of giant craft landing in the fields of southern England were up and running. Thereafter, each summer brought forth up to fifty new circles, most appearing in the Wiltshire/Hampshire area - an area well known for its ancient mystery sites.

As crop circle fever took hold, so a host of different theories were proposed, and three figures in particular rose to prominence. Pat Delgado and Colin Andrews' involvement began in the mid-1980s. Delgado had worked at the British Missile Testing Range in Australia, and then for NASA at one of their deep-space tracking stations. Andrews was an electrical engineer by training. Delgado and Andrews' theory was that crop circles were an attempt by some form of intelligent life to communicate with us, and that the increasingly complex configurations of the circles were part of a universal pictorial language.

Dr Terence Meaden, on the other hand, put forward a widely publicized theory that nature itself was responsible for the circles. Meaden, who had studied physics at

Above: There is evidence that the phenomenon of crop circles goes back at least 400 years

Oxford University and had developed an interest in meteorology, believed that the circles were formed by unusual atmospheric conditions which generated plasma vortexes, a form of ball lightning.

By 1989, scientists were descending on the area from around the globe, taking innumerable measurements, photographs and recordings. With every year that passed, the images were becoming more complex, more exotic, apparently more 'intelligent'. There was also an explosion of stories involving other unexplained phenomena in the same area: people heard strange crackling electrical noises; dowsing equipment behaved erratically; cameras malfunctioned.

With the researchers still vying with each other for the most convincing theory, crop circles quickly became the focus of huge media attention. Delgado and Andrews were catapulted to celebrity status, and aerial pictures from their best-selling book Circular Evidence were flashed around the world. It was not long before reports of similar crop formations emerged from all parts of the globe. America, Japan, Russia, Australia - as many as forty countries, each with its own extraordinary tale to tell.

In September 1991, however, the bubble looked set to burst. Researchers were devastated when a newspaper reported that two retired artists from Southampton, England, were behind the crop circle phenomenon. This proved to be a slight exaggeration, for although Doug Bower and Dave Chorley admitted that they had been responsible for hundreds of circles, going right back to the mid-1970s, they were certainly not suggesting that they had made all of them.

The pair had even made it clear that other hoaxers were at work when in two of their creations they had written in words across the fields: 'WEARENOTALONE'. The fact that the message read 'WE' rather than 'YOU' should have given the game away, but those who subscribed to the UFO theory seized on it as evidence supporting their case.

Gary and Vivienne Tomlinson found themselves witnesses to the birth of a crop circle

The media were still interested, but from a different angle now. Newspapers started to run 'hoax a circle' competitions, for example. And there was much fun to be had at the expense of the serious researchers, who had claimed to be able to tell the genuine article from the fakes but who were now left with a considerable amount of egg on their faces.

In the following year, however, a hundred circles still formed in the fields, fuelling fresh theories involving government conspiracies, MI5, CIA; it seemed that there was a deliberate attempt to 'kill' the subject off with misinformation, and if there was any meaning in the circles, it was becoming increasingly difficult to detect.

As the fog of confusion has gradually cleared, many researchers have come to agree that around one in ten of the formations - all simple circles - still defy any satisfactory explanation. The existence of first-hand accounts of circles forming tends to support the experts' view that not all of them can be put down to trickery. And the fact that there is evidence of the phenomenon going back some 400 years lends considerable weight to the view of those who say that the crop circle story is far from over.

Birth of a Crop Circle

In August 1991, Gary and Vivienne Tomlinson were out for an evening stroll in Hambledon, England, when they found themselves witnesses to the birth of a crop circle:

Vivienne: 'We were standing on a narrow footpath at the edge of a cornfield, when we saw the corn on our right was moving...There was a mist hovering above and we heard a high-pitched sound. Then we felt a strong wind pushing us from the side and above....It was forcing down on our heads so that we could hardly stand upright, yet my husband's hair was standing on end. It was incredible. Then the whirling air seemed to branch into two and zig-zagged off into the distance. We could still see it, like a light mist or fog, shimmering as it moved...As it disappeared, we were left standing in the circle with the corn flattened all around us....Everything became very still again and we were left with a tingly feeling...It all happened so quickly it seemed like a split second.'

Right: A simple crop circle

Below: This article and illustration confirms crop circles are not a new occurrence

Historical Crop Circles

The fact that crop circles date back long before Bower and Chorley and their fellow hoaxers got to work shows that it would be a mistake to dismiss the entire phenomenon as a late twentieth century joke. The earliest known circle seems to have been in Assen, Holland, in 1590. Then, as now, explanations varied from the scientific to the superstitious.

In the 17th century, a scientist named Robert Plot suggested that the circular patterns might be caused by blasts of descending air, a theory borne out by the Tomlinsons' experience and one which some 20th century researchers have endorsed.

But the following account, also from 17th century England, reveals that some thought a bizarre occurrence called for a bizarre perpetrator - a 'mowing devil'.

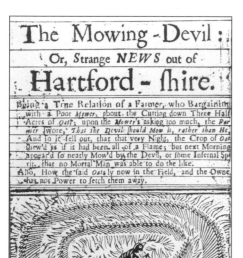

The Mowing Devil: or, Strange News out of Hartfordshire

Being a True Relation of a Farmer, who Bargaining with a Poor Mower, about the Cutting down Three Half Acres of Oats: upon the Mower's asking too much, the Farmer swore That the Devil should Mow it rather than He. And so it fell out, that every night, the Crop of Oat shew'd as if it had been all of a Flame; but next Morning appear'd so neatly mow'd by the Devil or some Infernal Spirit, that no Mortal Man was able to do the like. Also, How the Said Oats ly now in the field, and the Owner has not the Power to fetch them away.

The Tully Tale

One of the earliest crop circle stories of modern times occurred in Tully, Australia, in 1966. On January 19 of that year, tractor driver George Pedley was startled by a strange object rising from a reed lagoon. When he reached the spot where the object had been, he saw that the reed grass had been flattened and swirled in a clockwise direction, making a circle with a diameter of 10 metres.

News of this incident quickly spread, and many investigators of the paranormal descended on the area. Further searches revealed four more circles in the lagoon, the plants having been ripped from the underwater soil.

It was the events at Tully which inspired Doug Bower and Dave Chorley's mischievous efforts a decade later.

A Ball of Sparks   Tom Gwinnett, a farmer from Woolaston, Gloucestershire, England, was driving past a wheat field one July evening in 1988, when his car's electrics suddenly failed. He was trying to rectify the problem, without success, when he became aware of a strange whirring noise. He looked into the adjacent field, where he saw a dull red ball about the size of a football. It was not a solid sphere; rather, it appeared to consist of a cluster of red sparks, and the sparks seemed to be coming from the tops of the wheat.

Spellbound, Gwinnett watched the mysterious ball for a minute or two, the mechanical sound continuing throughout. The object then suddenly disappeared and all was quiet. At that precise moment, the electrical fault on his car righted itself, his headlights came back on and he was able to continue his journey. He didn't inspect the field that evening, but the following morning he discovered a six-metre crop circle in the spot where he'd seen the mysterious ball of red sparks.

Pair of crop circles and (inset) a series of crop circles which seem to form a pictogram

Earth Energies

Above: The Double Stones, Yorkshire

In 1921, a 65-year-old Englishman named Alfred Watkins made a discovery which changed the way we view the British landscape. Travelling through his native Herefordshire one day in the summer of that year, Watkins was struck by the fact that ancient sites throughout the land were linked by a network of straight lines or 'leys'. Ancient burial mounds, standing stones, wells, even churches that were known to have been built on pre-Christian sites - all were laid out along perfectly straight lines.

While Watkins was content to think of leys simply as direct routes linking places of importance, other researchers came to a startlingly different conclusion. It was suggested that they were actually lines of the Earth's energies, and that not only were our ancestors aware of this, but their rituals and ceremonies were designed to activate and harness these flows of power. Just as an acupuncturist manipulates the energy in the human body, so the flows of energy across and through the body of the Earth itself were used by our forebears.

This theory has led to a re-evaluation of other sites associated with ancient civilizations. For example, the huge stones that are a feature of such sites throughout the world may have done more than simply mark out sacred areas. Configurations of these stones, particularly circles, have long been associated with powerful energy flows, and many people have reported being physically and emotionally affected by the potent forces at work in the vicinity of these sites. Dowsers have gone even further, claiming that their ancient skills enable them to measure and describe the patterns of energy that exist at these places.

The search for harmony between man and the Earth has inspired the creation of religious buildings of many faiths. Examples of Geomancy, as this is known, can be found in cathedrals, mosques and temples around the world. Circles, spirals, pentagons and other geometric shapes are an integral part of the design of such buildings, and the power derived from them is a matter of deeply-held belief. In the Chinese tradition this art - or science - is known as Feng Shui and is still practised very seriously today. An expert in Feng Shui will invariably be consulted regarding the most harmonious siting, orientation and shape of a new building, and this even extends to ordinary homes, offices and factories.

Sceptics will point out that these phenomena owe more to conviction than to objective science, but many people remain convinced that the Earth generates its own energy flows and that it is important to seek to harmonise with the powerful forces at work.

Above: Alfred Watkins discovered ancient sites throughout Britain were linked by ley lines

Ley Lines

Here, Alfred Watkins describes in his own words the discovery he made on June 30, 1921:

'I had no theory when, out of what appeared to be a tangle, I got hold of the one right end of this string of facts, and found to my amazement that it unwound in an orderly fashion and complete logical sequence....

A visit to Blackwardine led me to note on the map a straight line starting from Croft Ambury...over hill points, through Blackwardine, over Risbury Camp and through the high ground of Stretton Grandison where I surmise a Roman station.

I followed up the clue of sighting from the hilltop....the straight lines to my amazement passing over and over again through the same class of objects.'

The Old Sarum Ley

Perhaps one of the clearest examples of Alfred Watkins' 'leys' is the dead straight 18-mile 'Old Sarum' line. It starts at a prehistoric burial mound, passes through Stonehenge, then a prehistoric man-made hill called Old Sarum, Salisbury Cathedral, and finally through an ancient earthwork called Frankenbury Camp.

Above: The medicine wheels of the American Indians use stones as markers of sacred sites

Below: The Old Sarum ley line

Many hundreds of leys have now been identified and there are many more waiting to be discovered by 'ley hunters'. These detectives usually begin their search with a map and a transparent ruler. If four or five ancient sites are found to be in alignment over a short distance, they often undertake field work to establish whether or not it is a true ley.

Watkins himself devised a scoring system whereby 'genuine' leys could be differentiated from chance alignments. In the British landscape there are many different kinds of ancient sites which qualify as potential ley indicators, including standing stones, stone circles, encampments, tumuli, barrows and mounds. Even wells and churches dating from a later period could often have older roots. Watkins allocated points to these different kinds of sites as a way of ascertaining which were the genuine article.

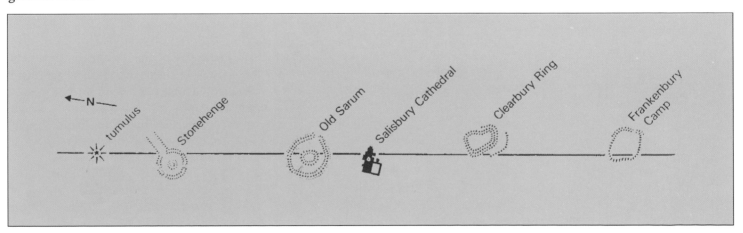

Ley Markers

At first sight it may seem strange that sites of such widely differing ages could form the basis of ley lines. Watkins' theory - which has been supported by many experts since - is that many modern churches were built over previously pagan sites. This is not just a matter of speculation - the process is described, for example, in a letter (dated 604 AD) from Pope Gregory to Abbot Melitus, who had been given the job of converting England to Christianity:

'I have come to the conclusion that the temples of the idols in England should not on any account be destroyed. Augustine must smash the idols, but the temples themselves should be sprinkled with holy water and altars set up in them in which relics are to be enclosed....I hope the people (seeing their temples are not destroyed) will leave their idolatry and yet continue to frequent the places as formerly, so coming to know and revere the true God.'

Above right: Medicine wheel, near Sedona, Arizona

Below: Heptonstall church and Stoodley Pike lie on a ley line in West Yorkshire

If the Christians are known to have absorbed pagan sites, it must be a distinct possibility that the pagans themselves adapted other even earlier sites.

The St Michael Line

Exponents of the ancient art of dowsing claim that they can detect not only water and minerals, but the presence of ley lines too. Using pendulums or divining rods, dowsers say they are able to locate the changes in energies which indicate the position and width of the lines.

In the late 1980s, a dowser named Hamish Miller claimed to have followed a line of energy which snaked its way through some of the most important ancient sites in England. The 'St Michael line', as it is called, is believed to run from St Michael's Mount, off the Cornish coast, to Lowestoft, on the North Sea coast, a distance of some 200 miles. It passes through a remarkable number of churches and chapels dedicated to St Michael, including St Michael's tower on the famous Glastonbury Tor.

At Avebury's ancient temple complex Miller was amazed to discover another almost parallel line of energy, again traversing the country but this time passing through a number of ancient sites dedicated to St Mary.

While extended leys of this kind appear to be rare, there are those who suggest that many ancient sites throughout the British Isles and Europe are laid out along just such 'geomantic' lines.

Aboriginal Songlines
The mythology of the Australian aboriginal people contains many stories of their animal and human heroes undertaking sacred quests into the desert. As they journeyed, these heroic figures found and established waterholes, and these sites were linked together by songlines, very similar to ley lines. Songlines are invisible paths which are said to resonate with the aboriginal tribal songs and whose purpose was to guide future generations in their journeys across the desert.

Ayers Rock - or Uluru as it is known by the native peoples - is a giant piece of red sandstone which holds particular sacred significance for aboriginals. It features in many of their myths and it is the place where many songlines meet.

Above: Ayers Rock, Australia, is the place where many aboriginal songlines meet

Below left: The Bighorn Medicine Wheel, 10,000 feet up on Medicine Mountain, Wyoming, forms a precise astronomical observatory

The Bighorn Medicine Wheel
The Bighorn medicine wheel stands 10,000 feet up on Medicine Mountain, in the Bighorn mountains of Wyoming. It is not a perfect stone circle, nor was it intended to be; its 28 'spokes', with six prominent groups of stones, or cairns, form a precise astronomical observatory. Its alignments show the sunrise and sunset of the summer solstice, as well as the risings of at least three major stars.

It is not clear when the circle was created, or by whom. The Cheyenne people are known to have erected Medicine Lodges, and the Oglala Sioux constructed 28-spoked Sun Dance lodges from wood, but both of these were temporary structures intended for particular ceremonies. What is certain is that the Bighorn wheel stands as an impressive example of a tradition which combines spectacular form with the precise function of an astronomical calendar.

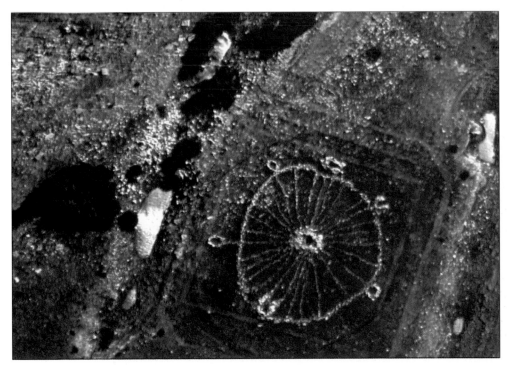

Stone Circles

The name 'Stonehenge' readily springs to mind when the subject of stone circles is raised. A lesser known fact, perhaps, is that there are up to 900 other such circles in the British Isles alone. The oldest of these structures are thought to date from Neolithic times, while the later examples could be from the Bronze Age. Their precise purpose is unknown, but more and more are found to have alignments which relate to the lunar and solar calendar.

Many people have described strange and powerful experiences in and around these configurations of stones. Some have reported a tingling sensation, while others have said a flow of energy has actually repelled them when they have tried to touch the stones. One explanation of this phenomenon focuses on the type of stones used in these structures. Many have been found to contain crystalline quartz, the properties of which are believed to include storing and transmitting energies.

Feng Shui

Feng Shui (pronounced Fung Shoi) is a practical science long established in Chinese culture, its aim being to harmonise the elements and environment in which people live and work. With a literal meaning of 'wind and water', feng shui is used during the planning stage of building construction to determine the exact site and orientation most beneficial for its intended function.

The feng shui master uses a complex compass to help him locate alignments, problem directions, conflict areas and the like. He also often employs a kind of mirror called a pak-kua, which is supposed to maintain good relations with the spirit realm and which remains in the environment when the construction process is completed.

While this may seem eccentric to Western minds, feng shui is nevertheless gaining popularity far beyond its Chinese roots. Its advocates claim that it can bring greater happiness and well-being, aid fertility and enhance the wealth-creating potential of individuals and businesses.

Above: Midsummer sunrise at Callanish stone circle, Scotland

Feng Shui In Action

When Hong Kong's new Kai-Tak airport was being built in the 1980s, workers threatened to down tools following a series of accidents in which many labourers had been killed. The feng shui master determined that the problem lay in the fact that the airport was being constructed on an old burial site. He worked with the energies of the site and the accident rate subsequently fell dramatically.

The Japanese finance company Nomura Securities was experiencing problems in its offices in London. An air of general unhappiness pervaded the building, and one of the employees had committed suicide. The feng shui master was called in to assist, and he too decided that the root of the problem was the former use of the site, in this case a Roman burial ground. In an unusual move, a Roman Catholic priest was also brought in and he performed an exorcism of the property. Once again, conditions showed marked improvement, on this occasion through the combined efforts of 'interfaith geomancy'.

The new headquarters of the Hong Kong Shanghai Bank were designed by the well known European architect Sir Norman Foster, yet even he did not enjoy total autonomy in the design process. He was required throughout to take into account the recommendations of Hong Kong's feng shui expert Koo Pak Ling. Koo determined the most favourable direction from which to enter the building, and oversaw the siting of some of the key interior features, such as the escalators. Even the fine detail, the positioning of furniture and pot plants, for example, did not escape his attention. And Koo was also responsible for the decision to purchase additionally a piece of land between the bank and the sea, which he considered vital to sustaining the harmony he had created. The bank has enjoyed continued success, which believers regard as a testament to the powers of feng shui.

Above: A feng shui master had to work with the energies of the site to reduce accidents to the construction workers during the building of Kai Tak Airport, Hong Kong

Below: The Cathedral of the Sagrada Familia, Barcelona, uses sacred geometry in its architecture

Sacred Architecture

Buildings endowed with religious or spiritual importance have always had geometric shapes incorporated into their design. Circles, squares, triangles and pentagons recur constantly in such buildings, and each shape is imbued with its own significance and power. The great cathedrals of Europe were built by master masons who were schooled in the principles of sacred geometry. They were aware of how to harness the natural forces associated with the shapes themselves, and also how to draw on the energies of a particular site.

Perhaps less well known is the fact that number can also have sacred significance. Kings College Chapel in Cambridge is an example of the application of a sacred numbering system. Here, many of the architectural features occur 26 times, and this is no accident. Nigel Pennick, in his book The Ancient Science of Geomancy, explains the significance of this number. In the ancient symbolic system called kabbalistic gematria, letters in Hebrew and Greek were given number equivalents. 26 represents JHVH or Jehovah, the Hebrew name for God, and its incorporation in the Chapel's design is thus a way of 'storing' power in its very fabric.

As the power of religion has declined and Western society in particular has become increasingly secularised, much of this knowledge has been lost. The use of sacred geometry is no longer seen as a priority in a world which values structures in material terms, rather than for their qualities of spiritual enhancement. As a result, 20th century examples of the use of sacred geometry are rare, but a notable exception is the Cathedral of the Sagrada Familia in Barcelona, designed by the Spanish architect and mystic Antonio Gaudi.

Landscape Figures

The desire of all past civilizations to leave their mark on the landscape has provided us with a rich cultural legacy. But while the structures created by our ancestors are important sources of information, they are often sources of mystery too.

What was the purpose, for example, of the figures etched into the earth at Nazca, Peru? Why should an Indian civilization from well over a thousand years ago create images so large that they could only really be appreciated when viewed from the air? And while many of the white chalk horses which adorn the hills of southern England are comparatively recent and well documented, others are much older and with more obscure origins. One in particular, the White Horse of Uffington, has a distorted shape which, like the Nazca figures, makes it appear more realistic when viewed from above.

As so many of these figures are sculpted into the surface of the earth, perhaps it is not surprising that it was a 20th century sculptor who was responsible for perhaps the most startling theory regarding at least one set of geographical features. It was in 1929 that Katherine Maltwood published her idea that the topography surrounding Glastonbury, in the south west of England, formed a giant terrestrial zodiac and that man had played a part in shaping and adapting the terrain to that end. She believed Glastonbury to be unique in this respect, but several more landscape zodiacs have since been discovered.

At best, Katherine Maltwood has provided the key to understanding a tiny fraction of the huge number of landscape figures bequeathed to us by our forebears. But while the speculation as to their purpose goes on, we can at least marvel at their form; for in many cases they are feats of technical virtuosity and artistic accomplishment in their own right.

Above: White horse carved into the hillside at Westbury, Wiltshire

The Nazca Figures

Some of the most spectacular landscape images in the world can be seen at Nazca, in the Peruvian desert, close to the Pacific Ocean. There are more than a hundred individual designs, including representations of animals, plants and human-like figures, as well as abstract forms.

The figures were created by the removal of the surface rocks, revealing the pale yellow soil beneath, and cover an area of 200 square miles (518 square kilometres). They vary enormously in size: some of the birds are 80 feet long, while the lizard is nearer 600 feet in length. This gives an idea of the magnitude of the scale involved, and indicates that the full visual impact of these images could only be gained from an aerial perspective. And therein lies the mystery; for although the figures are believed to date from between 400BC and 900 AD, the first aerial photographs of the site were not taken until the 1940s. What, therefore, could their function have been?

Chariots of the Gods?

The countless number of lines which criss-cross the area have been a focus of much speculation over the years, and some believe it is these lines, rather than the figures, which hold the key to the puzzle. One controversial theory was suggested by Erich von Daniken in his celebrated book Chariots of the Gods? He claimed that the Nazca lines were a landing strip for alien beings, and the human-like figures were actually representations of these inter-planetary visitors.

The full visual impact of the figures created in the desert at Nazca, Peru, can only be gained from an aerial perspective

Hot Air Balloons?

In 1975, two men decided to test what was, on the face of it, a bizarre theory: that the Peruvian Indians who laid out the Nazca images had used a hot air balloon to assist them in their surveying of such a vast tract of land.

Jim Woodman, the founder of Air Florida, and Julian Nott, a British balloonist, concluded that this was at least a possibility following the discovery of an ancient pot. The pot showed a round shape supporting a people-carrying vessel, and the two set about finding out if the Indians of Nazca had the wherewithal to turn the image of a balloon on a pot into the real thing. They were helped in this by the discovery of some fabric, perhaps 1,500 years old, which was relatively intact thanks to the dry climate of the Peruvian plateau. This fabric was recreated in sufficient quantity to form a large sphere, the balloon's envelope, while a gondola for the passengers was constructed from reeds.

In November 1975, the balloon was complete and ready to be put to the test. It was filled with smoky hot air from a wood fire and, with Woodman and Nott in the decidedly rickety gondola, the whole contraption rose into the air. The flight ended twenty minutes and three miles later, but the point had been proved: the Nazcans could have turned the design on the pot into a flying reality.

Shamanistic Flying?

Another theory regarding the figures at Nazca - and similar images in other parts of the world - is that they could be evidence of shamanism. The shaman was the tribesman with responsibility for the spiritual life of the other members. It was he who initiated the others into the ways of the spirit world, or 'otherworld'. This was achieved through dance, drumming and the taking of trance-inducing plants. Once the initiates had entered this hypnotic state, their 'astral body' was able to leave the physical body and travel over the landscape. Could the figures and lines at Nazca have acted as a kind of spiritual flight path for these astral travellers, providing familiar symbols and life forms which they could identify from above?

One of the surviving tribes of shamanistic Indians are the Kogi, who live in the remote moutains of northern Colombia. The shaman priests, or Mamas, still train members of their tribe in the ways of spirit flying. Their 'Map Stone' indicates the paths taken during astral flight, and while some of these routes exist in a purely spiritual dimension, others are physical realities, stone pathways set in the landscape.

The Great Serpent Mound

Many other landscape figures found across the Americas are also associated with the rituals of death, but more discernibly so. For this continent provides a rich source of burial mounds, many of which remain intact. Typically, these contain the full skeletons of some people and the cremated remains of others, together with artefacts presumably intended to assist in the afterlife.

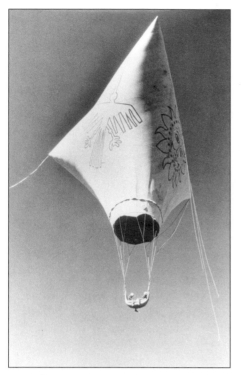

Above: Jim Woodman and Julian Nott tested their theory that the Nazca Indians had the skill to construct a hot air balloon

Below: Over 2,000 years old, the Great Serpent Mound in Ohio remains a mystery

Left: Remnants of the Serpent Temple at Avebury, destroyed in the 18th century by local villagers, with the support of the local church

Below: Cut into the chalk hillside is the Long Man of Wilmington, southern England. Some believe his two sticks are tools for sighting ley lines across the landscape

To give an idea of the scale on which such mounds were constructed, the Adena Indians alone were responsible for creating thousands over a 500-year period. Some are geometrically shaped, but the most striking are those which take the form of living creatures: bears, buffaloes, foxes, eagles - even humans.

However, the most impressive and well preserved example of these American Indian earthmounds does not appear to fit into this category. The Great Serpent Mound, which is in Adams County, Ohio, is thought to have been built by the Adena tribe between 2,000 and 2,500 years ago. Its body is three feet high and the whole structure stretches to a quarter of a mile in length. But it does not contain any remains or artefacts and is not thought to be a burial mound. In native Indian culture the serpent was often held as a symbol of the life-giving properties of water, but whether the mound was created for the purposes of fertility or spirituality is still open to question.

The Avebury Serpent Temple

The serpent theme recurs at Avebury, in Wiltshire, which is regarded by many as the site of the most significant ancient pagan temple in Britain. Indeed, some say that to compare Stonehenge to Avebury is like comparing a small church to a cathedral.

William Stukely, the 18th century British archaeologist, surveyed the site when it was being torn down by the local villagers, with the support of the local church. He produced a number of engravings to record the original layout of the complex before it was destroyed.

Stukely described the entire site as a serpent temple. The snake's body was formed by two stone avenues, which passed right through the centre of the henge. The notion of the serpent temple has been revived in the 20th century, notably by the dowser Hamish Miller, who claims to have used Stukely's plan to trace the snaking energies across the Avebury site.

White Horses

The white chalk horses that are strewn across the hills of southern England are a curious cocktail of fact and mystery. The provenance of many of them is well documented, while others present yet more puzzles regarding age and purpose.

The two best known examples of this phenomenon are at Westbury, Wiltshire, and Uffington, Berkshire. The former, which is the more abstract, is believed by some experts to have been carved by Iron Age Celts around 100 BC, although others put it much earlier still.

The white horse at Westbury stands on a steep hillside, close to the famous sites at Avebury and Stonehenge. Again, opinion is divided about its age, although there now seems to be a possibility that it is a relatively recent recutting of an older, more abstract figure. One school of thought has it that the horse was cut into the chalk in the 9th century to celebrate King Arthur's victory over the invading Danes.

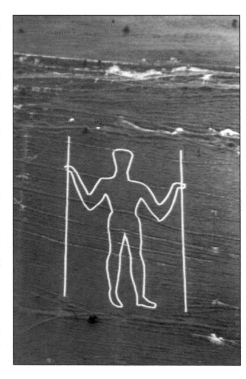

Right: The Cerne Abbas Giant has come to be revered as a fertility symbol

Below: Terrestrial zodiacs have been identified all over Britain, many corresponding to present day Christian dioceses

The Cerne Abbas Giant

The giant figure which lies on a hillside above the village of Cerne Abbas in Dorset, England is notable for the large club he wields in his right hand and his erect phallus. This is the most overtly sexual of all the figures depicted in the landscape, and, not surprisingly, the Giant has come to be revered as a fertility symbol. Childless women have been known to sleep on key parts of his anatomy. But this is a case of an image being appropriated to suit the purposes of later generations, for nothing is known about the origin of the Giant.

The 180-foot-high figure does, however, lie next to an Iron Age earthwork called The Trendle where, until recently, the local people celebrated the pagan-influenced fertility ritual of May Day. The high point of this festival was the dancing around the maypole - another phallic symbol.

If the figure is as old as some experts believe, then it has been suggested that it may depict a god. It certainly bears a resemblance to portrayals of the Roman god Hercules found on some Romano-British pottery. But if that date were to be accurate, it would simply provoke a further mystery: how could the Giant have survived intact for so long when those more puritanically minded over the intervening centuries might have been expected to erase its prominent features?

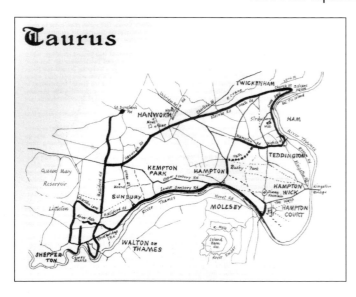

The Glastonbury Zodiac

In 1929, a sculptor named Katherine Maltwood published details of her extraordinary theory that the features in the landscape around the town of Glastonbury, in the south west of England, formed a giant terrestrial zodiac. This complete map of the twelve constellations was laid out over a circle some ten miles across, according to Maltwood. Hills, roads, rivers and other topographical features formed the various figures and animals associated with the signs of the zodiac, although not all of these representations were the ones we know today. For example, the figure of Aquarius, at the centre of the zodiac, is a phoenix, while Cancer is portrayed as a ship. However, other constellations coincide perfectly with the conventional associations: Taurus has the pronounced horns of the bull; Leo's lion has a well-shaped underbelly outlined by a river; and one of the twins of Gemini has visible ribs formed from terraced fields, with hair courtesy of a tract of flourishing woodland.

Although Katherine Maltwood's theory was revolutionary and had a startling impact, there is some evidence to suggest that others may have found the pattern before her. Queen Elizabeth 1's astrologer, John Dee, together with a medium named Edward Kelley are reputed to have discovered the Glastonbury Zodiac in the 16th century. In his biography of John Dee, writer Richard Deacon quotes Dee as saying that the area in question showed 'astrologie and astronomie carefullie and exactly married and measured in a scientific reconstruction of the heavens which shows that the ancients understode all which today the learned know to be factes.'

But it is not just 'understanding' that would have been required: the scale of the zodiac would have called for a prodigious effort on the part of some earlier civilization to shape and adapt the landscape for the purpose, not to mention an amazing grasp of surveying and mapping techniques.

Other Zodiacs

Katherine Maltwood believed the Glastonbury zodiac to be the only configuration of its kind, but since the publication of her theory, there have been claims for at least eight others in the British Isles and France. The British ones are mainly to be found in the south of England and Wales, and four of them are on the same line of latitude - 52 degrees North.

The zodiacs seem to be very precisely situated and the result of very careful surveying. Some experts believe that in pre-Christian times the whole of the British Isles was divided into 'geomantic provinces', each containing a zodiac. When Christianity prevailed, this system was replaced by dioceses overseen by bishops. The zodiacs that have been identified appear to fall neatly into these dioceses, suggesting that the Christian church may have adopted an earlier, pagan system of territorial division.

In his book Terrestrial Zodiacs in Britain, published in 1977, Professor Robert Lord writes:

'The precise purpose of the British terrestrial zodiacs we may never be able to rediscover. But with further accumulation of knowledge, it should be possible within a few years from now to build up a general theory of their significance. This will be particularly so if prejudices against their acceptance can be overcome. It will be especially significant if zodiacs are found in parts of Europe where detailed recorded histories go back further than in Britain.

'One thing we can be certain of is that the construction of these zodiacs was no passing whim of a semi-primitive people. To project sophisticated drawings onto a landscape, to arrange them in a particular order, and to incorporate natural features such as rivers and streams, would require very considerable surveying skill, a degree of skill that would make much modern surveying seem mere child's play.'

Some, then, must have taken several generations to complete; and the dedication and ingenuity put into them cannot have been surpassed, even by the cathedral builders of medieval times.

For the sceptics who remain unconvinced by such academic argument, perhaps they might find a mathematical one more persuasive. For Mary Caine, who has taken up the work of Katherine Maltwood, has said of terrestrial zodiacs:

'Preposterous? Maybe, but there on the map are the twelve signs of the zodiac in correct order in a circle all of five miles long. Can this be chance? It has been calculated that if the odds against two signs being right with each other are two to one, the odds against twelve being in the correct relationship are nearly 480 million to one.'

Below: Katherine Maltwood suggested that landscape features around Glastonbury formed a giant terrestrial zodiac

Ancient Mystery Sites

In the quest for spiritual fulfilment, mankind has always identified places of sacred significance and built structures thereon to act as a focus for ritual and ceremony. Many of these ancient structures stand as an enduring testament, not only to their creators' beliefs, but also to their technical virtuosity.

How were supposedly 'primitive' people able to create structures which measured time, which were accurately oriented to the points of the compass, and from which the movement of the planets and the stars could be plotted?

Perhaps the most celebrated of these ancient structures which also fulfil an astronomical function is Stonehenge. It is by no means unique in this respect, however. Sites at Avebury in England, Carnac in France, Callanish in the Outer Hebrides and Newgrange in Ireland also reveal astonishingly accurate surveying functions intrinsic to their design.

Clearly such precision was necessary if the dates of important rituals were to be reliably calculated; yet how that need was translated into action, with so little technology available, remains an intriguing conundrum.

Nature, too, has played its part in the creation of sites imbued with spiritual significance. There are sacred mountains on most continents, places where the line between body and spirit is blurred, where the gods are believed to make themselves known to man.

It is a paradox that while past civilizations and nature have between them bequeathed to us such a rich legacy, so much remains cloaked in mystery, answers often merely provoking further questions. There are a multitude of sites known to have religious, spiritual, mystical, ritualistic and ceremonial significance; sites which attract visitors in their hordes and are the subject of the most intensive scrutiny. But they are still a long way from divulging all of their secrets.

Stonehenge   Stonehenge, or the Giant's Dance as it was called in medieval times, is thought to be about 5,500 years old, with the construction process itself being undertaken in three separate stages over a 1,500-year period. Simply on a planning level, to execute a project of such magnitude over such a time scale is remarkable. But when one includes the surveying implications and the immense physical challenge, Stonehenge becomes an achievement of mind-boggling proportions.

The famous bluestones, 80 in number and weighing many tons each, were transported from the Prescelly mountains in Wales, a distance of almost 200 miles. The larger sandstone megaliths which dominate the site today were more local in origin, but with an average weight of 26 tons this still represents a prodigious feat.

What was the purpose of these amazing efforts? In the last 30 years, the ideas regarding the henge's function have been revolutionized by the work of 'astro-archaeologists' such as America's Professor Gerald Hawkins. He and others in this field are now convinced that the henge is a sophisticated observatory and computer. By analysing the positions of the stars, sun and moon at the time of Stonehenge's active use, Hawkins has shown a number of alignments between some of the key stones. These findings show, for example, that Stonehenge was able to accurately mark midwinter and midsummer sunrises, as well as the different phases of the moon.

Newgrange   Newgrange is the most famous of the Republic of Ireland's Neolithic 'passage graves', mound graves with associated chambers up to 70 feet long. Built around 3100 BC with great precision and impressive craftsmanship, Newgrange has been found to record the midwinter sunrise, the turning of the year, in a most extraordinary way. A special structure over its entrance - the roof box, as it came to be known - admits a beam of light which passes along the passageway within right to the centre of the grave, where it falls on a triple spiral figure cut into the stone. The sun strikes the roof box in such a way as to make this possible only on the few days of the year either side of the midwinter sunrise.

The egg-shaped and womb-like interior has led some to speculate that Newgrange was a kind of fertilisation chamber. The fact that midwinter marks the turning of the year, a symbol of rebirth and renewal, lends credence to this theory.

Avebury   Avebury can justly claim to contain the most sophisticated and impressive temple complex in the British Isles. This is in spite of the fact that religious puritans dismantled many of the stones in the 18th and 19th centuries. Indeed, had it not been for these destructive actions, the Avebury site would undoubtedly attract more attention than its megalithic cousin just 16 miles away, Stonehenge.

The Avebury complex is an extraordinary conglomeration of ancient features. The main henge area covers 28 acres and was originally circumscribed by 100 large stones; today, however, just 28 survive. Within this area there were two major stone circles, dubbed the 'solar' and 'lunar' temples by the 18th century researcher William Stukely. Outside the main henge area there is a vast double row of stones known as Kennet Avenue, and the largest artificial mound in Europe, Silbury Hill, which has been carbon dated at 2750 BC.

The thorny question then arises of the function of this 4,000 - 5,000-year-old site. Without records this naturally becomes a matter of informed guesswork. An astronomical purpose is once again, one of the theories, but an idea put forward by the archaeologist Michael Dames is more original and has caught the imagination of many. Dames' thesis is that the elements of the site were 'created as a coherent ensemble to stage a religious drama which took one year to perform, with each edifice offering in turn a special setting for the celebration of a particular event in the farming year, matched to the corresponding event in the human life cycle'.

Above: Carving on a Newgrange passage grave

Opposite page: Stonehenge, Wiltshire, England

Below: Avebury's complex of stone circles

Above: Carnac's megaliths are older than Stonehenge and the Pyramids

Below: The Temple of the Sun, Cuzco, Peru, the Incas' most holy place

But what could have justified the creation of such an elaborate theatrical setting? While we know that fertility rituals could have benefited from just such a stage, surely it is more likely that the stones and other features had a real, and not merely symbolic, function? Many scientists and dowsers accept that the stones are capable of storing and transmitting energy. Could it be that the rituals that took place at sites such as Avebury somehow allowed the participants to receive and benefit from these flows of energy?

Carnac   The 3,000 megalithic stones of Carnac, France, stand as testament to the determination and effort of the ancient people responsible for 'Europe's oldest building'. Believed to date from 4700 BC, the Brittany site is around 2,000 years older than both Stonehenge and the Great Pyramid at Giza, and ranks as one of early man's great achievements.

The most well known area of the site is near the village of Le Menec, where a collection of 1,099 stones is aligned in 11 avenues. These avenues are particularly unusual in that they diminish in height from 12 feet to 3 feet over their half-mile length. They terminate at an egg-shaped enclosure more than 300 feet across, which itself is made up of a further 70 megaliths.

One stone in particular has attracted much attention - the Fairy Stone. Although it has now broken into four pieces, it originally stood 65 feet high and weighed 350 tons. To manipulate accurately an object with such specifications would be no easy task even today; the fact that it was accomplished nearly 7,000 years ago is a staggering achievement.

Glastonbury

The town of Glastonbury, in the south west of England, is one of multi-layered significance. Some people believe it is the home of the Holy Grail, others that it is the Avalon of Arthurian legend. Then there are those who point to the fact that it is the site of England's most extraordinary terrestrial zodiac. It is a place where Christianity and paganism confront one another, a place of spirituality, myth and mysticism.

Glastonbury's two main focal points are the Christian abbey ruins and the famous Tor, with all its pagan associations. The Abbey is thought to have been founded by Joseph of Arimthea, Jesus Christ's supposed uncle. There are even stories that Jesus himself visited Glastonbury with Joseph when he was in his 20s.

Glastonbury Tor is a sculpted hill which rises steeply out of the flat plains of the Somerset Levels. Its shape suggests that it has been worked at some time, although the extent to which it is natural or man-made remains unclear. There are also claims that its terraced shape outlines a vast turf maze - a form of initiatory temple which modern pilgrims often circle to enhance the spiritual experience. As the focus of pagan power, the Tor attracts new-age thinkers in large numbers each year.

Above: It is unclear whether Glastonbury Tor is natural or man-made

Below: The Temple of Apollo at Delphi, Greece, was said to be the centre of the world and the home of the oracle

The Temple of the Sun

At the centre of the vast Inca empire was Cuzco; and at the centre of the centre, the holy of holies to the Incas, was Coricancha - the Temple of the Sun.

It is well known that the Incas laid out a road system which was focused on Cuzco - around 20,000 miles of tortuous roads running over the slopes of the Andes have been discovered. But there are also paths which run in straight lines and seem to have a different function. Researcher Paul Devereux describes the latter: 'They radiated out from the Coricancha, the so-called 'Temple of the Sun', which was a place of ancestor worship and where the Inca himself, the son of the sun, sat in state. About ten of the lines were used for 'sunwatching' - to mark the sun's position at certain times of the year to warn of planting times and also dates in the ceremonial year.....some other lines were used for conducting child sacrifices to their place of ritual death. Others were used for long, straight-line pilgrimages.'

The Temple of Apollo

Many civilizations have attempted to mark the centre of the world, or at least what they perceive to be the centre of their own world. This has often been symbolised by a stone, or 'omphalos', which represents the navel of the world. One of the best known examples of this cultural phenomenon, and the one which has had perhaps more impact than any other, is the omphalos at Delphi, in Greece.

The sacred stone at Delphi is said to mark the spot where two eagles met after being released by Apollo from the far edges of the Earth. It is a story intended to symbolise the fixing of the earth's energy to a central point, energy which becomes available to those who worship there. Since one of the forms of energy was wisdom and a knowledge of the future, Delphi became important as the site of the Oracle.

Originally, the Oracle was a priestess called Pythia, who was able to go into a trance-like state and communicate with Apollo. But perhaps Delphi's wisdom is best encapsulated in the commandment which is carved in the stone: 'Know thyself'.

Above: Sited on the top of a mountain, the Inca temple complex of Machu Picchu

Below: The Temple of the Inscriptions at the Mayan ceremonial centre in Palenque

Machu Picchu

The Inca site of Machu Picchu in Peru tells yet another tale of unaccountable desertion. This mountain top ruin - its name means 'old peak' - was found by the American explorer Hiram Bingham in 1911. Bingham had been searching for Vilcabamba, the city founded by the Incas in a remote mountain area as they retreated from the Conquistadors. It is known that in 1536 the Inca leader Manco Capac fled from his base in Cuzco to escape from the advancing Spaniards, and Bingham believed he had discovered the last known refuge of the Inca retreat. Indeed, he went to his grave thinking he had found Vilcabamba, although it now seems very likely that Machu Picchu is a completely different site. Recent research indicates that it was not a town, but a temple complex peopled by the Inca ruling elite. What made these Incas desert their mountain hideaway has proved much more difficult to establish.

The architecture at Machu Picchu presents a puzzle in its own right. It is of a staggering quality, and the craftsmanship of the stonemasons would be hard to reproduce even today. The joints between the stone blocks used in the buildings are not only impossibly thin, but the blocks themselves have many surfaces - each, in effect, being a complex polygon. Some have been found to possess as many as 33 faces, each tessellating with the surfaces of its neighbours. When one adds the fact that no cement or bonding agent has been used, one begins to appreciate the magnitude of this achievement. It is not known what tools and techniques were used which enabled the granite to be cut so accurately; and on top of everything else there was the small matter of transporting the stones - some weighing as much as 200 tons - to the top of a remote mountain, before the wheel had even been discovered.

The most enigmatic of all the blocks is the Intihuatana, a sacred stone dedicated to the Sun God, Inti. Its many complex shapes and alignments, together with the shadow configurations that it generates, reveal an astronomical function; it was an instrument capable of predicting equinoxes, solstices and the movements of the moon.

Palenque

Before it was rediscovered in 1773, the Mayan ceremonial centre of Palenque had lain undisturbed in the Mexican jungle for about 1,000 years. Investigators were baffled to find that the Mayas had deserted the site for no apparent reason.

It was not until 1949 that the Temple of the Inscriptions started to give up some of its secrets. It was in that year that the Mexican archaeologist Alberto Ruz Lhuiller discovered a hidden staircase leading to a tomb which had been unopened for 1,000 years. The tomb contained the sarcophagus of the Mayan ruler Lord Pacal, his remains covered in green jade. But it was the lid of the sarcophagus which generated the most interest - possibly more than any other ancient artefact. It appears to depict an object in flight, although researchers have interpreted it in different ways. Conservative theories say that it is a symbolic representation, portraying the journey of the spirit. Others, however, have placed a more literal interpretation on it, suggesting that the lid shows a man operating a flying machine, or even an alien craft. This strange image continues to divide opinion to this day.

Chartres Cathedral

Chartres Cathedral, in northern France, has been a place of Christian worship for well over a thousand years, but its site may hold secrets that are far older and much closer to nature.

Several Christian churches and cathedrals have stood on the site since around 740 AD, but before then it had been the home of a pagan dolmen - a large stone supported by two or three others - over a spring within an earth mound. These sites were important markers for potent earth energies, and visitors believed that they had the power to heal and to bless.

Above: The gothic cathedral at Chartres, northern France, is built on the site of a pagan dolmen

Below: For both Buddhists and Hindus Mount Kailas has been a place of pilgrimage for hundreds of years

The same is true today, although the stone structure is very different. Chartres has been described as the most perfect Gothic cathedral in the world. Indeed, there are stories that the design and execution of the building draw on a perfect understanding of sacred geometry. Some have gone further and claimed that it was built with the secrets of Divine Law from the Ark of the Covenant; that the Knights Templar returned from the East in the Middle Ages with secret knowledge that was used by the Cistercian Order to build the magnificent edifice we see today.

Chichen Itza

The great civilizations of Central America - the Aztec, Mayan, Toltec and Inca peoples - continue to fascinate archaeologists, historians and amateur enthusiasts alike. Millions are drawn each year to what remains of these civilizations, intrigued by their high culture, ceremonies and rituals - which included human sacrifice. Not least among the questions raised by an investigation of these sites is why many of them were apparently so hastily deserted.

Chichen Itza, on the Yucatan Peninsula in Mexico, was an important Mayan ceremonial centre. It is a massive site consisting of a number of temples, and from the foremost of these, the Temple of the Sun, a causeway led to one of the two 'cenotes' or open wells. The cenote's grisly purpose was to receive sacrifices, which were often human. This was attested to by Bishop Landa, who arrived along with the European conquistadors:

'Into this well they have had the custom of throwing men alive as a sacrifice to the gods in times of drought, and they believed that they did not die, though they never saw them again. They also threw into it a great many things, like precious stones and things which they prized.'

Mount Kailas

Mount Kailas, in Chinese-occupied Tibet, has been the most important pilgrimage site for both Buddhists and Hindus for hundreds of years. To walk around its crystal-shaped dome, performing many thousands of ritual prostrations, represents the fulfilment of a lifetime's spiritual journey to adherents of those faiths.

Lama Anagrika Govinda described the pilgrimage thus: 'To see the greatness of the mountain one must keep one's distance; to understand its form one must move around it; to experience its moods one must see it at sunrise and sunset, at noon and at midnight, in sun and in rain, in snow and in storm, in summer and in winter, and in all other seasons. He who can see the mountain like this comes near to the life of the mountain, a life that is as intense and varied as that of a human being....He who performs the Parikrama, the ritual circumambulation of the holy mountain, with a perfectly devoted and concentrated mind, goes through a full cycle of life and death!'

Pyramids

Of all the human creations which generate mystery, excite speculation and capture the imagination, there is one group which ranks above all others: the pyramids which stand on the Giza plateau near Cairo. These nine structures continue both to astonish us and fill us with awe as we consider the scale, craftsmanship and technical virtuosity involved in their construction. And when the issue of their function or purpose is raised, the pyramids seem to have a beguiling ability to absorb all theories that are proposed, to rise majestically above all attempts to unlock their secrets.

Of the nine pyramids at Giza some have been almost totally destroyed, but it has always been the Great Pyramid of King Khufu, or Cheops, which has attracted most attention. Along with the two other largest pyramids - those dedicated to the rulers Khafre and Menkaure - the Great Pyramid is believed to have been built during the Egyptian Fourth Dynasty, between 2700 and 2200 BC.

While the most straightforward and commonly accepted idea is that the pyramids were simply tombs for mummified pharaohs, the Great Pyramid seems to fly in the face of this theory, for it shows no signs of having contained Khufu's body. When the supposed tomb was opened in 820 AD by Abdullah al Mamun, he discovered that the passage leading to the king's burial chamber had been sealed by large granite blocks. When he finally broke through and gained access to the chamber, he found only an empty sarcophagus, and no means of exit. Why had the chamber been blocked off? And was it really empty when it was sealed?

Another intriguing factor which lends weight to the idea that the Great Pyramid had a purpose other than burial is that its inner chambers are above ground level. There is little evidence that the Egyptians ever buried their pharaohs above ground. But if the purpose of the pyramids was not the entombment of Egypt's rulers, what could it have been?

Above: The pyramids of Egypt have captured the imagination for generations

A Feat of Engineering

The Great Pyramid is the largest single building on the planet. It is over 482 feet high and contains approximately 22 million stone blocks. These blocks weigh over 6 million tons - 30 times the mass of the Empire State Building.

It was assembled with a precision that would be difficult to replicate even today: the joints between the blocks measure less than 1/50th of an inch; the difference between the longest and shortest sides is just 8 inches over a distance of 760 feet; and the 'pavement' around the base varies in height by just one inch over the entire perimeter - a staggering feat of surveying for a so-called 'pre-technological' civilization.

The jagged surface we see today - all 20 acres of it - was originally covered in a white limestone dressing and would have been polished to an optical precision. Many experts also believe that its capstone was covered with pure gold. These features would have given the Great Pyramid an almost unimaginable brightness in the equatorial sun, and it would have certainly earned its Egyptian name: The Light.

The construction of the inner chambers also reveals prodigious levels of achievement. Some of the blocks which form these chambers weigh 70 tons, and the dark granite from which the blocks were hewn was transported from Aswan, 500 miles further up the River Nile.

The question of exactly how the Great Pyramid was constructed remains as baffling as ever. Conventional wisdom says that it took the continuous efforts of 4,000 master masons and builders over a 30-year period, with many additional labourers drafted in at certain times. The idea that it was built by slaves or submissive cult members has largely been replaced by the theory that the skilled workmen gave their time to the project as a form of tax.

Even with this kind of manpower available, the working methods and engineering skills required are on a breathtaking scale. In fact, it was for that very reason that some refused to believe that it could have been a human achievement at all. Von Daniken and others suggested radical alternative theories, for example that alien beings had built the pyramids as giant landing pads for their spacecraft.

Strange Dimensions

Researchers have long been fascinated with the dimensions of the pyramids and the systems of measurement involved in their construction. Over the years some astonishing facts and theories have emerged from the many studies that have been undertaken.

British archaeologist William Flinders Petrie set out in 1880 to carry out the most painstaking survey of the three main pyramids at Giza. The measurements he took have formed the basis of many subsequent ideas.

The Great Pyramid is almost perfectly aligned along a north-south axis - in fact, it is less than 1/10th of a degree out of line. For a long time this inaccuracy was attributed to the surveyors, but it has since been discovered that the discrepancy could actually be due to a change in the earth's axis itself since the time that the pyramid was built; perhaps the 'error', minute though it is, is no error at all.

A Biblical Connection?

In 1859, a writer and publisher from London named John Taylor put forward the theory that the pyramids had been built with divine assistance by a non-Egyptian civilization. If this were not bizarre enough, it was followed five years later by the even more radical ideas of the Scottish Astronomer Royal Charles Piazzi Smyth.

Smyth noted that certain key numbers occurred in the dimensions of the Great Pyramid, including the length of the year, the circumference of the Earth and the distance from the Earth to the Sun. Smyth believed that God had designed the pyramid to demonstrate his divine knowledge, and that the Israelites - God's chosen people - had carried out the actual construction. He went on to analyse what he believed to be the numerological significance of the pyramid's dimensions, and expounded the view that it possessed the ability to predict God's plans for the Earth.

Above: Egyptian gods Isis and Osiris

Below: Tour guides amongst the blocks of a pyramid give some idea as to their massive scale

A Model of the Earth?

It has been known for many years that the ratio between the perimeter of the base of the Great Pyramid and its height is twice pi, the magic number identified by the Greeks for calculating the circumference of circles. This has always been dismissed as a coincidence by most Egyptologists, but Graham Hancock, in his 1995 book Fingerprints of the Gods, returned to the subject.

Hancock questioned the implications of a conscious and deliberate use of pi on the part of the Egyptians, and this led to a startling hypothesis: could the dimensions of the Great Pyramid relate to the shape of the Earth itself? For it was found that the ratio between the perimeter base of the Great Pyramid and its height is exactly reproduced in the Earth's northern hemisphere. That is, the ratio of the equator to the 'height' of the northern hemisphere is also exactly twice pi. The Great Pyramid could thus be a scale model of the northern hemisphere, the scale being 1 : 43,200.

Can any significance be attached to this number? Interestingly, it does occur in an astronomical context, being the number of years it takes the earth to pass through 20 zodiacal signs. While this may seem obscure, the Egyptians' fascination with the stars is well known, and it could have been a recognisable number to them.

If the Great Pyramid is a precise scale model of the northern hemisphere, the implications are startling. It means that the Egyptians knew that the earth was spherical, thousands of years before western civilization discovered the fact; and also that they knew its dimensions very precisely.

Right: The Sphinx may be thousands of years older than the pyramids, perhaps as old as 10500 BC

Below: At the heart of the Great Pyramid stands an empty granite sarcophagus

The Mysterious Sarcophagus

The empty granite sarcophagus which stands in the King's Chamber of the Great Pyramid presents a set of puzzles all of its own. Firstly, there is a question of access: it is too large to fit through the tunnel to the outside world. Secondly, its external volume is exactly twice that of its internal volume. Another coincidence? More mathematical games on the behalf of the designer? A deliberate act of mystical significance? Thirdly - and following on from this - there is the whole question of how a material as hard as granite could have been worked so precisely with the available technology.

The Egyptologist Flinders Petrie tried to explain how the sarcophagus might have been hollowed out using tools in existence at the time, but his experiments led him to an astonishing conclusion: 'The amount of pressure, shown by the rapidity with which the drill and saws pierced through the hard stones, is very surprising; probably a load of at least a ton or two was placed on the 4-inch drills cutting in granite....' On this evidence, Petrie was forced to admit that the Egyptians had tools 'such as we have only now reinvented'.

The Pyramids and the Stars

In the mid-1980s, researchers Robert Bauval and Adrian Gilbert began investigating the possibility of a connection between the pyramids at Giza and the stars. It was during their research that Bauval made a stunning discovery which gave rise to the most extraordinary theory of recent times:

'They (the stars in Orion's belt) are slanted along a diagonal in a south-westerly direction relative to the axis of the Milky Way, and the pyramids are slanted along a diagonal in a south-westerly direction relative to the axis of the Nile. If you look carefully on a clear night, you'll also see that the smallest of the three stars, the one at the top which the Arabs call Mintaka, is slightly offset to the east of the principal diagonal formed by the other two. This pattern is mimicked on the ground, where we see that the Pyramid of Menkaure is offset by exactly the right amount to the east of the principal diagonal formed by the Pyramid of Khafre, which represents the middle star, Al Nilam, and the Great Pyramid, which represents Al Nitak. It's really quite obvious that all these monuments were laid out according to a unified site plan that was modelled with extraordinary precision on those three stars....What they did at Giza was to build Orion's Belt on the ground.'

Cosmic Energy?

In the 1970s, Virginia Trimble, Professor of Astronomy at the University of Maryland, suggested that the ventilation shafts of the Great Pyramid may have had an altogether more important function than simply the supply of air. She calculated that at least one of these shafts would have aligned with a key star in the Egyptian sky.

Is the alignment of the pyramids at Giza a reflection of the stars in Orion's Belt? (Above and below)

The positions of the stars relative to the Earth have altered significantly since 2500 BC, due to a phenomenon known as precession - the change in the angle of the Earth's axis relative to the sky. Through computer analysis of the stars' positions, Professor Trimble was able to show that at the time of King Khufu's death the southern shaft from the King's chamber would have pointed directly at Orion's Belt.

Robert Bauval also investigated the alignment of the ventilation shafts, but he went much further than Professor Trimble. He believes that all four shafts - north and south from the King's and Queen's chambers - were aimed towards particular stars.

After death, the pharaohs underwent a ceremony known as the 'opening of the mouth', in which their eternal souls were directed along the shafts to the stars. There, the Egyptians believed, the pharaohs were reborn as their stellar counterparts. Bauval's findings concerning the four ventilation shafts led to claims that these were the pathways to the sacred stars.

The fact that the north shaft from the King's Chamber would have pointed at Draconis - the Pole Star - offers an interesting secondary theory: that the pharaoh king was offered two paths in death - the immortality of the Pole Star, or reincarnation through the return to the 'parental' stars Orion and Sirius.

Some researchers reflecting on the 'pathway' theory have suggested that it might, in fact, have operated in reverse: instead of acting as passageways from the chambers to the stars, perhaps they allowed cosmic energy to flow from the stars to the chambers.

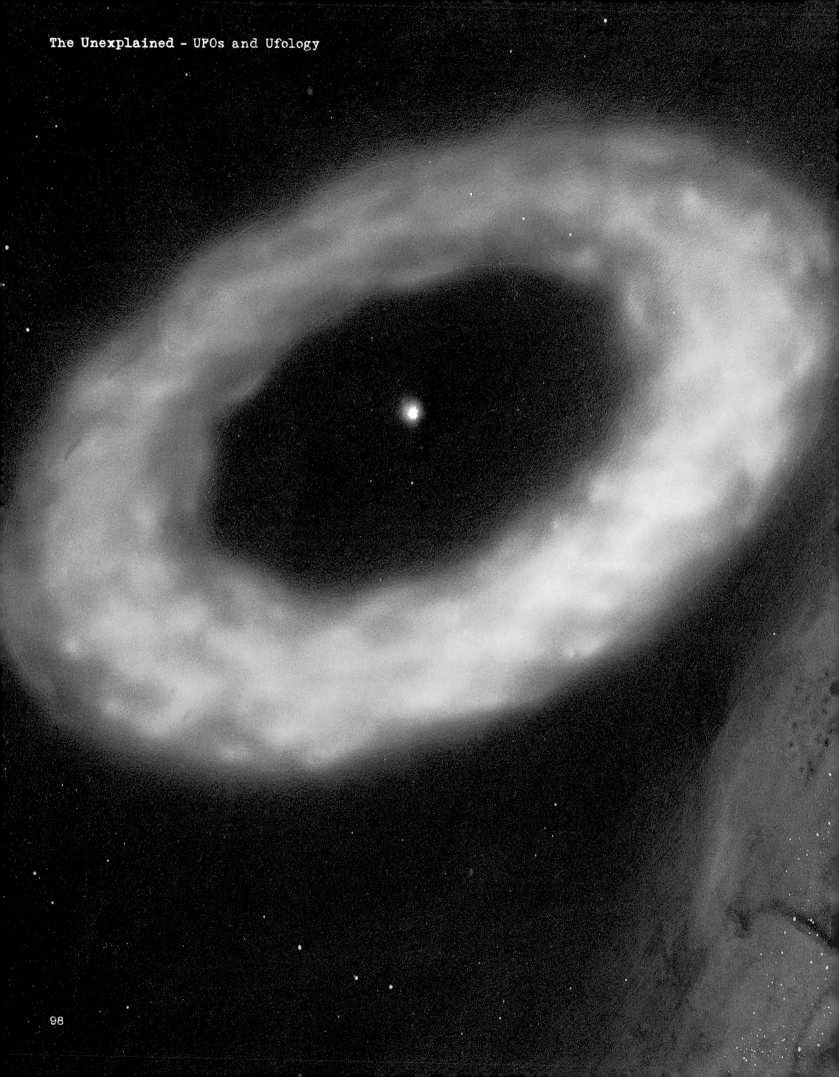

Chapter Four

UFOs and Ufology

In July 1967, three police officers watched a circular object with an orange glow around it perform extraordinary manoeuvres over the New Forest in southern England.

On December 21, 1978, Captain Verne Powell and Captain John Randall were flying from Blenheim to Christchurch in New Zealand when they saw some mysterious lights in the sky, observations which also registered on their radar equipment. Some days later, a film crew sent to investigate obtained 12 seconds of footage of the same phenomenon.

Reports of this kind are so widespread and well documented that to dismiss them all as pure invention hardly seems credible. Even the most confirmed sceptic will usually admit that the people involved saw something; it is the provenance of these unexplained sightings which provokes such divergent opinions. Are they aliens from other planets? Visitors from our own future? Manifestations from the deepest recesses of our minds? Or are they tricks of the natural world?

One of the few certainties in the field of ufology is that people are not divided into convenient camps, the doubters reflecting rational, scientific thought, with the believers given to romantic flights of fancy. Dr Maurice Biot, for example, one of the world's leading authorities on aerodynamics, readily endorses the image of UFOs so beloved by film makers and storytellers alike: 'The least improbable explanation is that these things are artificial and controlled....My opinion for some time has been that they have an extraterrestrial origin.'

It is a tantalising irony that the huge variety in reported sightings only serves to fuel the debate. Alien craft have been described as cigar-shaped or disc-like, triangular or spherical; aliens themselves as beautiful or hideous, gigantic or dwarflike; their behaviour as aggressive or benign. Sceptics have seized on this diversity. It indicates, they maintain, our susceptibility to suggestion, adding, by way of illustration, the fact that descriptions of UFOs often resemble images used in films. But others have countered that such diversity is merely indicative of our notoriously poor powers of recall.

Those who remain agnostic about UFOs can do no more than examine the evidence of others with an open mind. Mike Sacks, speaking after his experience in May 1979, delivered his contribution: 'If only I could make you believe what I saw. It was there. I know it. UFOs are real....solid, physical craft. It is just terrible knowing this and being unable to prove it.'

To arrive at a judgment, the witnesses must be heard.

History of UFOs

If UFOs exist, how long have they been visiting our planet? Ancient cave paintings, epic Indian poetry - even stories from the Bible - contain references which at the very least suggest that this is not an exclusively modern phenomenon. Some experts go even further, believing that the origins of the human race itself can be traced back to interplanetary visitors.

But if UFOs have a history on this kind of time scale, it raises an interesting secondary question: why, over a period of thousands of years, has the nature of the manifestations changed so little? Alien craft appearing before individuals, the occupants passing messages to them, and occasionally performing weird experiments on them - this has become the established pattern with regard to UFO encounters. Why, in other words, do these alien visitors appear to have learned so little over the centuries?

One theory, which neatly addresses this question, has it that UFOs do not hail from outer space at all. Rather, they are visitors from our own future. If they are able to travel back in time, the theory runs, these visitors may be sampling different eras, which may be thousands of years apart from our perspective, but which may be a matter of days to them.

If the nature of the manifestations of UFOs has changed little over time, the same cannot be said of the way in which we relate and respond to them. Before the invention of aeroplanes, UFOs were commonly described as flying boats or balls of fire. In the latter part of the 19th century, when people were becoming aware of the first man-made airships, a spate of UFO incidents in America was dubbed the 'Great Airship Flap'. Similarly, in 1930s Europe, when rocket technology was being developed, there were a number of reports involving 'ghost rockets'. Perhaps it is unsurprising that sightings of UFOs are articulated in terms of the prevailing levels of understanding.

In the middle of the 20th century, real events and fictional representations combined to create an awareness and fear of UFOs and aliens, and perhaps helped to generate the marked increase in reported sightings that occurred during this period. The Cold War, the atomic weapons programme and the space race provided a factual backdrop which fuelled the public's interest in the subject; and science fiction writers and film makers naturally found space craft and alien beings a rich and relatively untapped seam for their imaginative output. In turn, the creations found in books and on screen influenced the nature of the sightings reported by members of the public.

As a counterbalance to fevered speculation and suggestible minds, one might have expected the cool, detached authority of science - and astronomy in particular - to have provided a rational explanation of UFOs. But in 1957, Dr Frank Halstead, of Darling Observatory, Minnesota, made a dramatic statement: 'Many professional astronomers are convinced that saucers are interplanetary machines.'

The other single most powerful contributory factor in raising the profile of the UFO phenomenon is, oddly enough, probably government itself. In the USA in particular, the government has never quite managed to allay the public's concerns on the issue and there is a long history of conspiracy and cover-up theories. It is in direct reaction against the official wall of silence that a number of independent organisations have been established with the express purpose of discovering, once and for all, the truth about UFOs.

Ancient Paintings

Prehistoric cave paintings may contain evidence of the very first UFO sightings. In the Tassili area of the Sahara Desert, an ancient rock painting shows a one-eyed figure wearing what appears to be a space suit; at Val Camonica, in Italy, there are drawings which seem to show weightless beings, again wearing space suits; and at Altamira, in Spain, there is a huge chamber containing images of what we would now call 'flying saucers'.

Perhaps the most impressive of such representations can be seen at Ussat, in France. One prehistoric cave painting there shows a figure standing beneath an object which looks remarkably like the Apollo lunar module.

However, seeking to assign a particular interpretation to these images is fraught with danger. Prehistoric art might have employed stylistic conventions which yield completely different, more mundane, explanations. For example, a ring of weightless figures, looking uncannily like a formation of skydivers, could in fact represent a tribal dance; and what we see as a space helmet may have been a way of depicting something more abstract, such as imagination, inspiration, dreams or other emanations from the mind.

Ancient cave paintings may contain evidence of the very first UFO sightings

Chariots of the Gods?

In 1968, the Swiss writer Erich von Däniken published his best-selling book 'Chariots of the Gods?', which examined the evidence for 'ancient astronauts'. His astonishing theory was that the Bible, together with other ancient writings from around the world, contained descriptions of visitors from the stars who 'seeded' the human race. Our ancestors had regarded them as gods, but von Däniken decoded their stories and revealed them to be 'early UFO and alien reports'. Who else, he argued, but visitors from advanced cultures could have been responsible for the pyramids, the statues of Easter Island, the ancient electric battery now in a Baghdad museum, the Nazca lines in Peru and the maps of Admiral Piri Reis?

UFOs and Time Travel

Until a few decades ago, it was possible to speculate about the chances of the moon sustaining life. That prospect has now, quite literally, receded into the horizons as the search for extraterrestrial life-forms has gone much deeper into outer space. The fact that the net is being cast ever wider has lent support to the idea that UFOs do not come from the far reaches of space at all, but from our own future.

If aliens are the evolved human race of the future somehow stepping back in time, it would explain why people who have come into contact with them have often been able to understand their messages. The content of these communications is often connected with peace and ecology - 'Take care of the earth' is a typical example. If we have been subjected to a long-term campaign to raise our global consciousness, there would be a certain logic to it: after all, who would have a greater vested interest in the welfare of the planet than its future occupants?

Foo Fighters

During World War 2, both British and American pilots reported seeing 'balls of light' around their aircraft. The Allies thought these might be German weapons, but after the war it was discovered that German aircrews had had similar experiences. For reasons that are now obscure, these strange lights were given the name 'foo fighters'.

In August 1944, Captain Alvah Reida encountered a foo fighter while flying his B29 bomber over Sumatra. He described it as a glowing red ball, approximately 6 feet across. Captain Reida, who was flying at a height of about 14,000 feet and a speed of 200mph at the time, tried to out-manoeuvre the ball of light, but it maintained its position relative to the aircraft before disappearing at high speed.

Early in the morning of December 22, 1944, a pilot and radar operator of the American 415th fighter squadron were completing a mission, when they saw two large orange lights climbing at speed to their flying height of 10,000 feet. The pilot put the plane into a dive in an effort to put distance between it and the lights, but he was unable to shake them off. Eventually the lights peeled away and disappeared, a pattern which was typical of many accounts involving foo fighters.

Shortly after the end of World War 2, the Office of Strategic Services (the forerunner of the CIA) investigated the phenomenon and concluded that foo fighters were an unusual but natural phenomenon. There has since been speculation that foo fighters were a kind of ball lightning or plasma energy, perhaps forming because of the structural or electrical properties of the aircrafts' frames.

Ghost Rockets

It was in the early 1930s that aircraft-like lights were first reported over parts of Sweden and Norway where no aircraft should have been. Sightings of ghost rockets, as the phenomenon came to be known, continued for many years. By January 1934, over 40 reports were being received daily; and in the summer of 1946, almost 1,000 incidents were recorded.

One of the best documented cases occurred at Lake Kolmjarv in northern Sweden on 19 July, 1946. Just before noon, Knut Lindback and Beda Persson were working by the lakeside when they heard a humming sound in the sky. They saw something grey, like an aeroplane or a rocket, hurtling towards the lake. It hit the water about a mile away from them, creating a huge cascade of water. Later, Lindback said: 'I am sure it was a solid object. It was 6 feet long and had a snub nose, while the stern was pointed. I thought there were two wing-like protrusions on the side but I am not sure, everything happened so quickly.'

Following the incident, which was also witnessed by another observer from elsewhere on the lakeside, soldiers conducted a two-week search. This apparently yielded no trace of what the three individuals had seen.

Above right: 'Foo fighters' was the name given to strange balls of light witnessed by pilots during World War 2

Below: Are UFOs science fiction or science fact?

UFOs and Astronomers

There is a widespread perception that incidents involving UFOs never seem to be reported by those possibly best placed to analyse such evidence objectively - astronomers themselves. This is far from the case, however. Croste, Halley, de Rostan, Messier, Wartmann, Carrington - these are just some of the celebrated astronomers who have given accounts of UFOs.

On November 17, 1882, E W Maunder was at the Royal Observatory in Greenwich, England, when he saw 'a great circular disc of greenish light' in the sky. It moved smoothly, but faster than any of the astronomical bodies he was observing. It also seemed to grow longer, suggesting that it was perhaps a disc changing its angle. Maunder described the object as 'a definite body. Nothing could.....be more unlike the rush of a great meteor or fireball...than the steady...advance of the "torpedo"'

On June 11, 1954, one of the world's foremost astronomers, Percy Wilkins, was on a plane journey when he saw two egg-shaped objects appear out of the clouds. He described them as approximately 50 feet wide, reflecting sunlight like polished metal plates. They were later joined by a third object.

Sci-fi and Hollywood

Since the 1950s, the cinema has had an influence on the images that have later been presented in accounts of UFO sightings. The 1951 film The Day The Earth Stood Still was inspired by a spate of incidents involving flying saucers in the late 1940s, but it also contained images not yet reported. It shows a circular room inside a flying saucer, lit from no obvious source, with a platform bed used for medical examinations. The saucer itself is indestructible - a feature reported in later crash retrieval research. And the outfit worn by the character Klaatu is almost identical to that worn by the alien George Adamski claimed to have met in California some two years later.

The 1956 film Earth Versus The Flying Saucers was loosely based on UFO research carried out by Major Donald Keyhoe. Fascinatingly, it contains many images which Betty and Barney Hill were to describe following their encounter with a UFO in 1961: the encounter on a lonely road; the saucer first becoming visible in the form of distant lights; witness denial as the first reaction; subliminal messages blocked from conscious recall; the sleepy state of the witnesses; and interference with watches as a clue to what had happened.

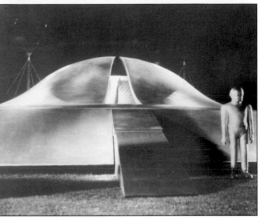

Hollywood has produced numerous films based on the idea of visitors from outer space. Top: 'Alien' Bottom: 'The Day the Earth Stood Still'

Cover-ups and Incompetence

A feature of the modern era of UFOs is that it has been media driven. Kenneth Arnold's sighting in 1947 led newspapers to speculate that the objects were alien in origin, and this in turn fired the public interest.

The contribution of the US government only served to increase speculation on the subject. Throughout the 1950s and 1960s, many investigations were conducted, but they were blatantly ineffectual. Some investigators, including Major Donald Keyhoe, were so disillusioned that they left. Others, like J Allen Hynek, were dismissed. Whether these investigations were undermined by the incompetence of individuals or by conspiracy, the net result was that the findings inspired little confidence. They also gave rise to a proliferation of independent organisations committed to the thorough investigative procedures that were deemed to be lacking at government level. The first major group of this kind was APRO (the Aerial Phenomena Research Organisation), formed by Jim and Coral Lorenzen in 1952.

Keyhoe and Hynek also went on to do important investigative work at civilian level. Keyhoe encouraged the research carried out by NICAP (the National Investigation Committee on Aerial Phenomena), which sought to exert pressure on the US Congress on the subject of UFOs. Hynek went on to create the Centre for UFO Studies in 1974, along with his 'Invisible College' - a group of scientists who were afraid to go public because they might lose their funding or credibility. The raison d'etre of CUFOS was the belief that the US Air Force had acted neither openly nor truthfully in their own UFO investigations.

Lights and Discs

Thousands of people worldwide have given vivid accounts of mysterious objects in the skies. There are similarities and recurring images in many of these stories, the most obvious, perhaps, relating to the shape of objects observed. Disc or cigar-shaped UFOs have become something of a cliché - one which film makers over the years have played a part in perpetuating - yet there have indeed been numerous descriptions of just such objects. A sceptic might suggest that the witnesses - consciously or unconsciously - take cues from other reported incidents or from Hollywood, and the stories feed off each other in an imaginative spiral.

But there is a huge diversity in the reports too. There have been spherical and triangular UFOs; they have ranged in size from quite small to, in one case, an object six miles across; some have travelled at extraordinary speeds, while others have hovered in the air; they have appeared singly and in clusters, and in the latter case, they have been known to fly in strict formation; some UFOs have appeared to play games with aircraft, while other pilots have described more hostile intent; flashing lights have been seen, lights which some investigators believe to be interactive responses.

The evidence of some sightings goes beyond the anecdotal and subjective. UFOs have registered on tracking equipment, and objects have been photographed, even filmed. Unfortunately, even objective evidence of this kind is often inconclusive. The authenticity of photographs is frequently challenged, and the camera is capable of playing tricks, just as our own eyes are. Mistakes, misinterpretation, flights of fancy, deception, tricks played by equipment or nature - these might explain some of the strange objects that have appeared in the sky. They might even explain many of them. But can all UFOs be accounted for in this way?

The First Flying Saucer
In 1878, a farmer from Texas witnessed a dark object in the sky which he described as 'a large saucer'. It was the first time that the word had been used in connection with UFOs, but it was to be almost another 70 years before it would enter general usage.

On June 24, 1947, pilot Kenneth Arnold was flying near Mount Rainier in the Cascade Mountains of Washington State, USA, when he saw nine objects travelling in formation. He estimated their speed at between 1,300 and 1,700mph - faster than any plane of the day. Each object was approximately two thirds the length of a DC-4 airliner, and the formation was stretched out over a distance of about five miles. Arnold was some 23 miles away when he observed this phenomenon, which lasted only a few seconds. It was not corroborated by radar or other sightings.

Arnold described the objects as moving 'like a saucer would if you skipped it across water'. A reporter translated this description into the term 'flying saucer', a catchy expression which caught the public imagination. Ironically, Arnold had meant to describe the movement of the objects, not their shape. Subsequently, however, the word 'saucer' became widely used in connection with the physical appearance of mysterious flying craft. The modern era of ufology was born.

UFOs on Radar
If Kenneth Arnold's story was somewhat weakened by the fact that there was no other witness and no corroboration from any tracking equipment, the same cannot be said for an incident which occurred on August 13, 1956. On that day, a cluster of UFOs that appeared in the skies over RAF Bentwaters, in Suffolk, England, was confirmed by several independent sources. The objects registered on both ground-based radar equipment and the aerial system of a Venom night fighter. There was also visual confirmation from the ground and the aircraft. Radar contact indicated that the objects were moving at 4,000mph, well beyond the capabilities of the aircraft of the day. The incident was filmed by a gun camera, but this was never released.

In June 1974, Lieutenant Colonel Toshio Nakamura and Major Shiro Kubuta were flying an F-4EJ Phantom jet on what they thought was a mission to intercept a Soviet bomber. Once airborne, however, they were informed that they were in fact being sent to investigate a brightly-coloured UFO that had been sighted and also tracked by radar. At 30,000 feet they encountered a red disc-like object which Major Kubuta said appeared to be 'made and flown by intelligent beings'. The object manoeuvred around the plane, forcing Nakamura to make violent dives and turns. Eventually, the UFO hit the aircraft. Kubuta and Nakamura managed to eject, but the latter's parachute caught fire and he plummeted to his death.

Shadowed Over Tenerife
On January 16, 1993, Captain Adolfo Morales was flying a Boeing 727 over Tenerife, when he and members of his crew watched as a UFO shadowed them for 22 minutes. This is his account of what happened: 'It followed our flight path, going up when we went up and down when we went down. Then, without any warning, it suddenly moved at incredible speed to the right and stopped dead over the town of Santa Cruz on the island of Tenerife. It covered the distance, approximately 100 miles, in less than one and a half seconds. It hovered there, shining with a brilliant red and violet light as it started to descend. Finally it disappeared beyond the island. The UFO was seen by all members of my crew. Even the stewardesses came into the cabin to see it. It was amazing.'

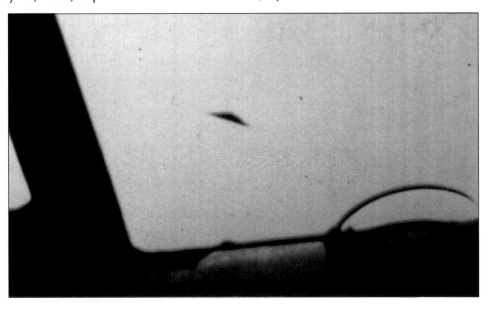

A UFO sighting from the cockpit of a plane

Giant UFOs

In November 1979, Captain Francisco Lerdo de Tejada was flying from Austria to Tenerife when he saw a UFO as large as a jumbo jet. It hurtled towards his Super Caravelle at astonishing speed and then took up a position nearby, apparently playing games with him. Tejada reported that the object was making movements 'quite impossible for any conventional machine to execute'. The UFO was later confirmed visually by the airport director, Señor Morlan, and some of his ground personnel.

Captain Kenju Terauchi of Japan Air Lines was making a cargo flight over Alaska in November 1986, when he and his crew became aware that their Boeing 747 was being accompanied by some lights emanating from a strange object. Terauchi described the object as 'walnut-shaped' and at least twice the size of an aircraft carrier. It kept pace with the 747 for over half an hour before vanishing.

Large as the UFOs in these two accounts are, they are dwarfed by the object reported over Gansu Province, China, on June 11, 1985. The captain of a Boeing 747 flying from Beijing to Paris saw a UFO which sped across his flight path, causing him to consider making an emergency landing. The object was estimated to be six miles wide.

Above right: There have been many accounts in which UFOs have appeared in clusters rather than singly

Below: Frederick Valentich (in photo held by his father) disappeared after he reported a strange object flying around his plane

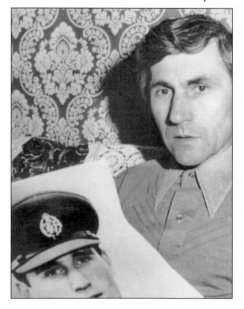

Death by UFO

Frederick Valentich was flying a single-seater plane across the Bass Strait in November 1978, when he radioed the Melbourne Flight Service Unit to report a strange observation. Although the Unit had no knowledge of any other aircraft in the vicinity, Valentich described a large bright object with a green light which flew all around his aircraft for several minutes 'playing some sort of game'. During one period in which the object came very close to his plane, Valentich indicated that his engines were being affected. Towards the end of the transmission, the flight controller sensed that Valentich was 'definitely concerned for his safety'. There was then an unidentifiable sound and communication from the plane ceased. Valentich has never been seen since.

Formations of UFOs

Just ten days before Kenneth Arnold's famous sighting in 1947, pilot Richard Rankin was flying over Bakersfield, California, when he saw 10 objects travelling at a speed calculated to be 560mph. These objects, which were about 30 feet wide, were flying in a triangular formation. There have been many accounts in which UFOs have appeared in clusters rather than singly, and in such instances they have often been observed to fly in strict formation.

In the Solomon Islands, in August 1942, Sergeant Stephen Brickner reported one of the most extraordinary groups of UFOs ever seen. He described how he had witnessed 150 UFOs flying in an enormous rectangular formation, 15 objects long and 10 deep.

Formations of UFOs were seen over several US states on July 31, 1965. The US Air Force claimed that these objects were the planet Jupiter and the stars Betelgeuse, Aldebaran, Rigel and Capella. Later, however, this explanation was roundly refuted by the director of the Oklahoma Science Foundation Planetarium, Robert Risser, who commented: 'This is about as far from the truth as you can get'. Apparently, none of the stars mentioned were visible in the USA at the time of the sightings. It is incidents such as this which, particularly in the USA, have made many people sceptical about official pronouncements on the subject of UFOS and have given rise to a host of conspiracy theories.

The Flap of 1973

On March 1, 1973, 40 brightly-lit circular objects were observed over Saylor's Lake, Pennsylvania. A group of a dozen people watched the objects for two hours. This marked the beginning of a sensational period in UFO history, during which a host of dramatic sightings were documented.

In the autumn of that year, seven major UFO incidents occurred in the USA over a 19-day period. On October 7, Mississippi policeman Charles Delk chased a UFO in his car; on October 11, Larry Booth reported seeing a UFO in Pascagoula, Mississippi; and the following day, two fishermen at the local shipyard claimed to have been abducted by aliens.

In Falkville, Alabama, on October 17, Police Chief Jeff Greenhaw investigated a UFO report and managed to photograph an entity on the road. The entity subsequently ran away, outpacing Greenhaw's car.

On October 18, Captain Laurence Coyne was flying a helicopter from Columbus, Ohio to Cleveland Hopkins Air Force Base, when a grey, cigar-shaped object appeared. It proceeded to hover in front of the helicopter, the story being substantiated by three crew members and five observers on the ground.

In Blackford County, Indiana, two men reported similar experiences on October 22. DeWayne Donathan and Gary Flatter both encountered figures dancing by the roadside, and Flatter said he watched them levitate into the sky.

In Greensburg, Pennsylvania, on October 25, Stephen Polaski was one of 15 witnesses who saw a UFO landing in a field. Polaski and two boys rushed to investigate and found a 'bigfoot-like' creature, seven feet tall and smelling of burning rubber.

UFOs Over the White House

In July 1952, there was a wave of sightings around the American capital, Washington DC. Many UFOs were seen or detected on radar at Andrews Air Force Base; some even entered the restricted air corridor near the White House.

In one dramatic incident, Paul R Hill, an aeronautical research engineer, witnessed an apparent rendezvous of UFOs over Chesapeake Bay. Two of the mysterious craft revolved around each other at 500mph before being met by a third 'falling in' several hundred feet below, thus creating a V-shaped pattern. A fourth UFO joined the group, which then flew south at high speed. The US Air Force stated that they had no aircraft in the area at the time.

Captain Ruppelt, a former co-ordinator of UFO investigation for the Air Force, later wrote a book alleging a government cover-up over the spate of incidents that year. Ruppelt said: 'The summer of 1952 was just one big swirl of UFO reports, hurried trips, midnight phone calls, reports to the Pentagon, press interviews and very little sleep.'

Hovering Triangles

On November 29, 1989, two Belgian police officers were driving from Eupen to Eynatten when they were almost blinded by three lights passing low above their car. The lights seemed to be attached to an enormous dark triangle. They followed the object and found it hovering above the dam of the Gileppe. Several other witnesses confirmed what the policemen had seen.

In 1989, two Belgian police officers were among a number of witnesses to the sighting of a triangular shaped UFO

Mufon UFO Journal

Official Publication of the Mutual UFO Network Since 1967

Number 286
February 1992
$3.00

MUFON

TRIANGULAR OBJECT OVER BRUSSELS, BELGUIM
December 1, 1989

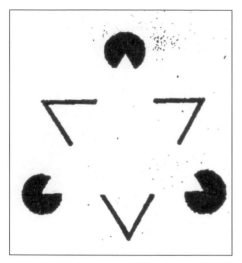

Above: How many triangles are there? There are in fact none, but the brain seeks to make patterns - a crucial factor to consider when examining UFO reports

Below: Could the mysterious lights at Hessdalen be the result of geophysical activity?

Reports of mysterious triangles continued in Belgium for over a month. The sizes varied, and some witnesses described features such as domes or cupolas. Even the Air Force issued reports of triangular-shaped UFOs, and the number of sightings from Belgium and the surrounding countries soon rose to over 700.

On March 30, 1990, these eye-witness accounts received corroboration when the phenomenon was captured both on radar and on film. Since then, there have been many other reports of triangular UFOs, including several in England and in the area north of Goteburg in Sweden.

Photographic and Televisual Evidence

Investigators of UFOs use a range of devices to record their observations, chief among which are still and movie cameras. Some of the most remarkable photographs in the field were taken by Ed Walters at Gulf Breeze, Florida, between November 1987 and May 1988. Walters took over 50 Polaroid and stereoscopic photographs of objects he claimed to have sighted on many occasions. One object kept appearing again and again, while at other times several objects appeared simultaneously. Walters also captured these incidents on video, and there were other witnesses who backed up his claims.

Captains Verne Powell and John Randle were flying from Blenheim to Christchurch in New Zealand on December 21, 1978, when they encountered a UFO. The object also showed up on their radar equipment, and this incident, together with a series of other sightings, led the government to initiate an investigation. This resulted in a mysterious glowing ball being captured on film, generating huge media interest, as the following news report indicates: 'Worldwide attention was focused on the sky above Kaikoura after a film of the sightings was broadcast on American, British and Australian television. An international debate has erupted over possible explanations for the large white glowing ball captured on film. Captain Verne Powell, one of the first to see the UFO, says he watched in astonishment as the object sped across 24 kilometres of sky in five seconds. He was annoyed by suggestions that he may have mistaken Venus for a UFO. A pilot since 1944, Powell said: "I know Venus when I see it".'

Study Projects

In the 1970s, a scientific study was carried out after a wave of sightings of strange lights was reported over Missouri, USA. The study, named Project Identification, was headed by Dr Harley Rutledge, who not only observed the phenomenon, but came to believe that the lights were making interactive responses to stimuli transmitted by his research team.

Between 1981 and 1985, the Hessdalen valley in Scandinavia was the centre of a prolonged study of UFOs. Many witnesses had reported seeing illuminations of various shapes, and over a four-year period investigators took many photographs of these

mysterious lights. Apart from cameras, a range of sophisticated monitoring equipment was used, including seismographs, magnetometers, spectrum analysers, infrared viewers, Geiger counters and an Atlas 2000 radar system. As in Project Identification, there were reports of interactive lights responding to the investigators.

Earthlights and Hallucinations

In 1982, researchers Paul Devereux and Paul McCartney published the book 'Earthlights', in which they proposed a radical new way of studying many UFO reports. The suggestion was that there could be a link between unusual sightings of lights and geophysical activity. This theory was developed after it was found that many UFO incidents involving LITS (lights in the sky) occurred over geophysical fault lines. The implication was that these lights were the product of natural energy released prior to earthquakes. Experiments

suggested that certain rocks under pressure produce patterns of light emission - possibly an electrical plasma discharge.

Earthlights could be a plausible explanation for the mysterious lights in Hessdalen. There are many fault lines in the area surrounding the Norwegian fjords; indeed, the whole of Scandinavia is undergoing geographical readjustment, still rising after the melting following the last Ice Age.

Devereux has speculated that the plasma might respond to personal disposition - in other words, creating what the witnesses wanted to see. Meanwhile, Canadian researcher Michael Persinger has suggested that these energies could affect the electrical activity in the brain, resulting in hallucinations. This might explain the seemingly bizarre accounts of contact with alien beings, and even abduction.

Main picture: Experiments have suggested that certain rocks subjected to pressures like those in the San Andreas fault produce patterns of light emissions which could be mistaken for UFOs

Easy Explanations?

Countless explanations of UFOs have been given, the commonest being that they are nothing more than aircraft lights or astronomical bodies. It is also widely believed that lenticular clouds are often mistaken for UFOs. Lenticulars are natural cloud formations which are disc-shaped and often metallic grey in appearance, and can look stunningly like hovering UFOs. There are also mock suns and noctilucent clouds, while light reflecting on ice crystals in the air is known to cause a red or orange glow and have a solid-looking appearance. These are just some of the naturally-occurring phenomena which can all too easily be misinterpreted as something more sinister.

Satellites re-entering the earth's atmosphere have also been known to stimulate UFO reports. In 1977, the launch of Kosmos-955 generated stories of a jellyfish-shaped UFO over Petrozavodsk, Russia. Even laser shows and searchlight displays at rock concerts can have the appearance of something far more outlandish. The UK Ministry of Defence anticipated exactly this problem before a concert by French musician Jean-Michel Jarre and alerted the British UFO Research Association to expect a spate of false alarms.

It is clear that a large number of UFOs can be explained rationally, but equally, not all sightings fit conveniently into categories such as those above; a significant number remain in the realm of the unexplained.

Traces and Evidence

UFOs arrive without warning, but they don't always leave without trace. Scottish forester Robert Taylor is one who would attest to that statement from first-hand experience. On November 9, 1979, he was confronted by a dome-shaped object hovering silently just above the ground. Two spiky protrusions then grabbed his legs and he lost consciousness. When he came to, the object had vanished, leaving two parallel tracks about nine feet long and studded with holes.

This is an example of 'close encounters of the second kind' - cases where UFOs have left visible marks on the landscape. Physical evidence supporting anecdotal claims of UFO activity can take many forms: interference with car and aircraft controls; power failures, sometimes on a huge scale; animal carcasses stripped to the bone with surgical precision; a child healed of cancer; metals which baffle scientists when they are subjected to examination. The most crucial and dramatic evidence, however, must be actual wreckages of UFOs that have crashed. The most celebrated incident of this kind was said to have occurred at Roswell, New Mexico, in 1947.

With the power that UFOs appear to have, benign or otherwise, it is unsurprising that governments around the world have shown concern. In the USA in particular, this has been characterised by evasion and cover-ups. Other countries, such as France, Spain and Brazil, have pursued policies of greater openness and released previously classified information on UFOs into the public domain.

A large percentage of alleged UFO sightings undoubtedly have mundane explanations; but the global figure for such reports is so huge that even a small percentage of unexplained incidents represents many thousands of cases. And it is in everyone's interest that these cases are rigorously investigated, for, in the words of Air Commodore J Salutun, of Indonesia: 'The study of UFOs is a necessity for the sake of world security...In the event...we have to prepare for the worst in the space age, irrespective of whether we become the Columbus or the Indians.'

Above: UFO pictured above Sao Paulo, Brazil in 1984

Ground Traces   There is a commemorative plaque in the forest near Livingstone, Scotland, indicating the spot where Robert Taylor had his bizarre experience in 1979. This was the first time that a UFO encounter had been marked in such a way, but it was not the first incident in which ground traces had been left.

In November 1972, a remarkable example of this phenomenon occurred at Rosmead Junior School in South Africa. There had been a number of UFO reports in the area before Rosmead's principal, Harold Truter, witnessed a mysterious light in the sky while on his way to school. He arrived to find the surface of the tennis court seriously damaged, with tar and ash scattered over a distance of 600 feet. There was a pattern of symmetrical holes around the damaged surface, and blue gum trees which stood just outside the tennis court had been burned.

The crop circle phenomenon has long been connected with speculation over UFO landings. Even if the admissions of the self-confessed hoaxers are taken at face value, this still leaves a significant number of crop circles unexplained, and these are believed by some to be indicative of UFO activity.

Residual Traces   At Delphos, in Kansas, USA, 16-year-old Ronnie Johnson reported seeing a mushroom-shaped UFO hovering above trees near a shed on his family's farm. The object flew off, but Ronnie was left temporarily blinded and paralysed. On recovering, he rushed to tell his parents, who also saw the UFO before it vanished into the distance. They examined the ground over which Ronnie had seen the object hovering, where they found a 9-foot circle of grey-white powder which glowed in the dark. When Mrs Johnson touched the material in the ring, her fingertips became numb. Rubbing her fingers on her legs, they too became numb, and remained so for a fortnight.

Analysis of the ground trace revealed that it contained some kind of fungus, but 18 separate laboratory examinations failed to reach a consensus. On May 27, 1973, the National Enquirer magazine awarded the Johnsons their $5,000 prize for the UFO story that 'supplied the most scientifically valuable evidence' of the year. They described it as 'a major scientific mystery - the most baffling case the panel encountered in a full year of investigation.....The panel carefully investigated the possibility of a hoax, but are completely satisfied that the sighting was real.'

Residues that have been found following other incidents include tin, silicon and ferrochromium. But some substances attributed to UFOs have baffled analysts, such as the stinking yellow oil which fell over Ireland during the 19th century, and the cotton-like fibres known as 'angel hair', which some believe to be held together by the electrostatic field surrounding UFOs.

Above: Robert Taylor came face to face with a dome shaped object hovering silently just above the ground

Below left: UFO landing traces near Richmond, Virginia, USA in 1967

Crash Retrievals

In July 1978, UFO researcher Leonard Springfield addressed the annual conference of the Mutual UFO Network and made a dramatic assertion: that the US government had retrieved numerous UFO wreckages and stored them on military bases. He referred to specific incidents, including that at Roswell in 1947, and talked of secret film footage, studies by metallurgists and eye-witness accounts of dead aliens.

There may be a mundane explanation. The retrievals cited are generally in militarily sensitive areas, such as the White Sands proving ground, and Trinity and Los Alamos, where both the atomic bomb and the space programme were developed. Some of these projects included experimentation using monkeys, and this might account for some of the stories of small humanoids.

More recently, there have been claims suggesting that alien technology is under examination at a location called Area 51 (also referred to as Groom Lake and Dreamland), some 80 miles from Las Vegas. The book 'Alien Liaison', by Timothy Good, refers to the existence of the Alien Technology Centre in this geographical area, and there have also been theories that aliens and humans are collaborating on top-secret projects.

The Roswell Incident

In July 1947, a rancher named William Brazel informed the local sheriff that he had seen the wreckage of an explosion scattered across his ranch in New Mexico. The sheriff reported the incident to the Roswell Army Base, whereupon Brazel was apparently held by the military while an investigation was carried out. A team headed by Major Jessie A Marcel collected the debris, which was loaded onto a B-29 aircraft and flown to the Wright-Patterson Air Base on the orders of the commanding officer, Colonel William H Blanchard.

Major Marcel confirmed that chunks of material had been recovered, but no pieces of any flying craft. Later, however, witnesses did report finding a flying disc, largely intact, buried in the side of a mountain. Years later, some people claimed to have seen the bodies of aliens, either at the crash site, at autopsy, or in storage.

The official line from the Roswell Army Air Base was that a weather balloon had been recovered, and wreckage consistent with that story was duly paraded before the media. But Major Marcel insisted that this was not the wreckage he had recovered - the material he had seen was thin and foil-like, but would not dent; it also had strange hieroglyphics printed on it.

In 1995, the General Accounting Office admitted that the weather balloon story was indeed bogus, an attempt to cover up details of a secret listening device that had crashed. Also casting doubt on the UFO theory is the president of the USA himself. Speaking in Belfast, Northern Ireland, on November 30, 1995, Bill Clinton stated: 'As far as I know, an alien spacecraft did not crash in Roswell, New Mexico, in 1947. And if the US Air Force did recover alien bodies, they didn't tell me about it either.'

Above right: Examining marks thought to have been caused by a UFO landing

Below: In 1995, Ray Santilli claimed he had a film showing the autopsy of an alien body recovered from the Roswell site

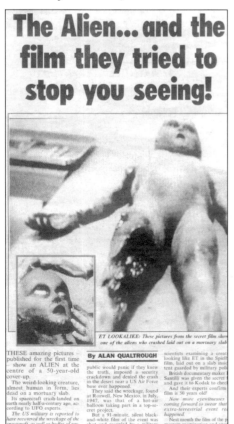

The Alien... and the film they tried to stop you seeing!

By ALAN QUALTROUGH

THESE amazing pictures – published for the first time – show an ALIEN at the centre of a 50-year-old cover-up.

The weird-looking creature, almost human in form, lies dead on a mortuary slab.

Its spacecraft crash-landed on earth nearly half-a-century ago, according to UFO experts.

The US military is reported to have recovered the wreckage of the spacecraft, as well as bodies of several aliens – one of which may have

ET LOOKALIKE: These pictures from the secret film show one of the aliens who crashed laid out on a mortuary slab

public would panic if they knew the truth, imposed a security crackdown and denied the crash in the desert near a US Air Force base ever happened.

They said the wreckage, found at Roswell, New Mexico, in July, 1947, was that of a hot-air balloon taking part in a top-secret project.

But a 91-minute, silent black-and-white film of the event was shot and recorded by a military cameraman who hid it away for

scientists examining a creature looking like ET in the Spielberg film, laid out on a slab inside a tent guarded by military police.

British documentary maker Santilli was given the secret and gave it to Kodak to check and their experts confirm film is 50 years old!

Now more eyewitnesses coming forward to swear that extra-terrestrial event really happened

Next month the film of the post mortem examination and another showing close-ups of the

But in March 1995, Ray Santilli claimed he had a film showing the autopsy of an alien allegedly recovered by the US Army at Roswell. Santilli agreed to speak at an international symposium of the British UFO Research Association in August of that year, and his revelations attracted huge media interest worldwide.

Santilli claimed to have been in contact with the original photographer, Jack Barnett, who had made the film at the request of the US government. Barnett had shot over 60 reels of film, but had retained 20 of them because of processing problems.

John Spencer, chairman of BUFORA, immediately set up a team of specialists to examine the film, including film archivists and special effects experts. Santilli was asked to co-operate, but so far he has allowed very little of the film to be scrutinised by BUFORA's team. That which has been examined has yielded suggestive but inconclusive results.

Unknown Metals

On September 14, 1957, Brazilian journalist Ibrahim Sued received an anonymous letter describing how several witnesses had seen a flying disc. The disc had seemed to be about to crash into the sea near Ubatuba, then recovered height, only to explode in mid-air. 'It disintegrated into thousands of fiery fragments,' the letter ran, 'which fell sparkling with magnificent brightness. They looked like fireworks.'

Some of these pieces had been recovered and were enclosed with the letter. The fragments were passed to the chief chemist at the Mineral Production Laboratory. Analysis revealed that they were made of magnesium of an extraordinarily high quality and with no trace elements.

Writer Timothy Good recently interviewed an employee of the Weapons Research Establishment in Australia about an object found near the Woomera Test Range in the late 1950s. It was a perfect sphere, some 30 inches in diameter, grey and very light. It resisted all forms of penetrative examination. The witness thought it more likely to be a UFO than debris from the space programme, citing as his reason: 'Quite simply, there was not then the technology to produce what we had in our hands.'

Vehicle Interference

In 1979, the British UFO Research Association produced their Vehicle Interference Project report. It listed 420 known cases of the phenomenon, with the number growing all the time.

On the night of November 2, 1957, on Route 116 near Levelland in Texas, Jim Wheeler almost drove into a huge bright object. It was about 200 feet wide and egg-shaped, and was sitting in the middle of the road. As Wheeler's car drew near, his engine and headlights went dead. He got out of the vehicle to investigate, but the object drifted up into the sky and vanished. As it did so, his car engine and headlights came back to life.

Mr W Collett was driving a Ford Transit towards Reading, England, on October 26, 1967, when the electrics suddenly cut out. He noticed a dark shape hovering above the road. The interference occurred two more times, and on each occasion he could see the object hovering close by. He was able to complete his journey only after the object had moved on.

Perhaps the strangest case involving vehicle interference happened to the Knowles family, who sighted a UFO while driving through the Nullabor Plains in Australia. Their car was lifted into the air, then dropped so hard that it burst a tyre.

Above: Military personnel with wreckage from the Roswell site

Below: UFO over the Empire State Building, 1963

Above: In 1965 Boston was caught in a blackout covering 80,000 square miles, said to have been caused by a UFO

Below: Luminous object photographed at Hessdalen in 1982

Blackouts

In the Great Northeast Blackout of November 9, 1965, power was lost over a vast part of the USA and Canada. An area of 80,000 square miles was blacked out, affecting 26 million people. Just before the loss of power, three people in different locations - including the deputy aviation commissioner of Syracuse - had seen a huge light or fireball over Clay substation.

In his report to the House Committee on Sciences and Astronautics in July 1968, atmospheric physicist Dr James McDonald stated: 'Just how a UFO could trigger an outage on a large power network is...not clear. This is a disturbing series of coincidences that I think warrants more attention than they have so far received.'

Two weeks after the Great Northeast Blackout, two areas of St Paul, Minnesota, also had power failures which coincided with UFO sightings. The same thing also happened at Cuernavaca, in Mexico, on September 23, 1965, where the witnesses included such prominent figures as the governor, mayor and military chief. And in the Great Chinese Blackout of September 1979, UFOs were reported over the cities of Xuginglong and Huaihua.

Mutilated Creatures

On September 8, 1967, a colt went missing from a ranch in Alamosa, Colorado. When the horse's body was found the next day, a quarter of a mile from the ranch-house, its condition triggered a wave of speculation. The carcass had been mutilated, but in the most mysterious way: the head was completely denuded of flesh, with the body intact from the neck down. There was no blood around the animal. The line along which the flesh had been removed was described as surgically precise. There had already been many reports of UFOs in the area, and rumours soon began linking UFOs with the mutilation of the horse.

In his book 'Alien Liaison', Timothy Good says that there have been thousands of similar incidents since 1967, with cattle being the chief victims. Often, specific areas of the body have been targeted, such as the reproductive and sensory organs.

Could these animals have been preyed upon by terrestrial predators, creatures able to eat their way through soft tissue with apparently surgical precision? Or could aliens be using the animals for experimental purposes or for food? In January 1996, Timothy Good, together with researcher Linda Howe, made their position clear. They declared on British television that the best evidence for UFOs would come from examining mutilated carcasses.

Healing Light

Not all encounters with UFOs have such harmful or destructive outcomes, as this report of an incident in 1957 shows: 'In Petropolis, Brazil, a young girl's miraculous recovery from cancer has been linked with UFO activity. The girl's family claim that on the night of October 25, they were comforting her, when a flying saucer landed outside the house. A beam of light came from the saucer, and two four-foot-tall aliens with yellow-red hair and green slanting eyes emerged. The beings, apparently, went to the girl's side and laid out medical instruments. The father states that they telepathically obtained details of her illness from him. Then, using another light, they revealed the girl's internal organs and removed the cancer. According to reports, they gave the father a box of pills for the girl to take, before they flew off into the sky.'

Official Openness

Fifteen days after Captain Thomas Mantell was killed chasing what he thought was a UFO, the US government set up Project Sign. Seven months later, on August 8, 1948, Project Sign reported to General Vandenberg, the head of the US Air Force. The astonishing conclusion contained in the report was that UFOs did exist and were interplanetary. The project was shut down and its findings rejected.

Other governments around the world have encouraged greater openness on the subject of UFOs. The Brazilian Navy declared that photographs of a UFO taken from their ship Almirante Saldanha in 1958 were genuine, and these were released into the public domain on the orders of the country's president.

In 1976, the Air Ministry in Spain handed over a file containing case histories of UFO encounters to a reporter, Juan Benitez. In an article for 'Flying Saucer Review', Benitez stated: 'When you read these files....it becomes definitely and categorically clear that UFOs exist and, quite evidently, are a matter of the deepest concern to the governments of the whole planet.'

On April 14, 1992, the joint chiefs of staff of the Spanish Army, Navy and Air Force decided to declassify their UFO files, which contained details of 71 sightings. The reports revealed 16 radar detections, 14 orders for military aircraft to intercept, 22 sightings by civilian air crews, 10 photographed incidents, 9 close encounters and 5 cases involving humanoid entities. Researcher Ballester Olmos studied the material and found 'no trace of smokescreens or any deliberate deceptions'; he expects another 50 case histories to be declassified soon.

Above: UFO over Trindade Island in the South Atlantic, photographed from the ship Almirante Saldanha

Below: A Soviet rocket launch in 1973 mistaken for a UFO

Sewage and Other Solutions

If UFOs are not extraterrestrial craft piloted by aliens, then what are they? The alternatives put forward over the years are numerous, ranging from the mundane to the fantastic. One suggestion is that UFOs are themselves life forms that live in the upper atmosphere. Another early idea was that UFOs were the surface scum from sewage works, lifted skywards by storms and high winds.

Modern theories address themselves to the perceiver as well as the perceived. Brief sightings of distant objects can easily be misinterpreted by witnesses; objects as familiar and ordinary as stars and aircraft are prime candidates for misidentification, and a large percentage of UFO incidents may be explained in this way.

Yet that still leaves an impressive number of reports unaccounted for. According to figures published by Jacques Vallee in his book 'Confrontations', even if the proportion of unexplained UFO reports is only 5 per cent, that is still numerically significant - between 5,000 and 50,000 sightings. And this figure could be much higher if some of the 95 per cent of 'solved' cases are classified thus on dubious grounds. One who believes they are is Robert Bull, of the British UFO Research Association. He maintains that the criteria by which cases are judged to be solved are neither universally agreed nor strictly adhered to, and the figure put on unexplained UFO incidents is therefore a gross underestimate.

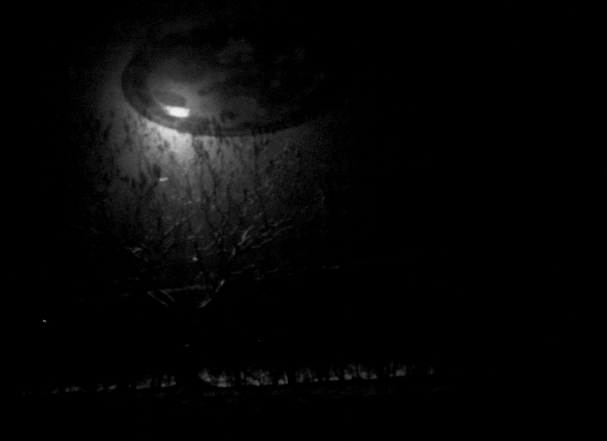

Close Encounters of the Third Kind

'Close encounters of the third kind': this is the term ufologists use to describe actual contact with alien beings. George Adamski became the first person to claim such an encounter, in 1952, although others may have had similar experiences before, but not publicised them for fear of being ridiculed. What is certain is that since Adamski made his story known, thousands of people have come forward to relate their own close encounters.

The alien with which George Adamski came into contact was benign, convivial even, but others have spoken of beings with more malevolent intent and suffered physical injury. The appearance of alien forms has been equally diverse, although most are described as humanoid. This in itself has created a conundrum, as scientists regard the chances of humanoid life developing on other planets and visiting Earth during our brief period of tenure as extremely remote.

When science tells us that alien beings in humanoid form are an illogicality, we may be swayed strongly against an individual, however adamant, who claims to have had contact with just such a being. But what of the occasions where large numbers of people have witnessed the same incident and given remarkably consistent versions of what they have seen?

One way or the other, case histories involving close encounters of the third kind will continue to be crucial to UFO research.

Adamski and the Aliens
According to George Adamski, his first contact with an alien occurred in the California Desert at 12.30pm on November 20, 1952. It was ten miles from the town of Desert Center that the encounter took place, and Adamski gave a vivid description of the being which confronted him: approximately 5ft 6in tall, well built, youthful-looking, with green eyes, long blond hair and a tanned complexion. The alien was wearing a brown ski-type suit and sandals.

Adamski claimed he used telepathy and sign language to communicate with the alien, who came from Venus. He related how the alien had taken him on a tour of the solar system in his flying saucer, and how he had met inhabitants of Mars, Saturn and Jupiter.

This account sparked off thousands of similar stories in the years that followed, and indeed, Adamski himself was to have further contact with aliens. In February 1965, he and Madeleine Rodeffer filmed a flying saucer performing manoeuvres outside the latter's Maryland home. Rodeffer claimed she had been able to make out figures looking through the craft's portholes.

Analysis of the film has been controversial and inconclusive. Among those who doubted its authenticity was Dr Paul of NASA, who said: 'My own strong impression is that these frames show a small object, perhaps two or three feet across, a short distance from the camera.'

Above and below: George Adamski who claimed to have first had contact with an alien in 1952, communicating with it through telepathy and sign language

Under Siege
Eight adults and three children had an extraordinary encounter on the night of August 21, 1955 at Kelly, in Kentucky. At 7pm Billy Ray Taylor saw a huge shining UFO landing in a dried-up riverbed near his farm. An hour later, the farmhouse was besieged by a number of weird creatures with long arms and claw-like hands. The creatures were about three feet tall, with large crack-like mouths, round bald heads and huge elephant-like ears. They had eyes which glowed yellow at the side of their heads, while their bodies had a silver glow.

Over the next few hours, there were many attempts to shoot the creatures, but they seemed impervious to gunfire; indeed, their response was to float gently in the air.

At 11pm the occupants of the house managed to escape and ran for the local police chief, who returned with them. Although he saw no alien creatures himself, he was amazed by the amount of damage done by the guns. 'Something frightened these people,' he said, 'something beyond their comprehension.'

Man with a Mission
In 1959, there was a UFO incident in Papua New Guinea in which 38 witnesses reported being able to make out individual entities inside the craft. It took place near the Boianai Mission where, at around 6pm one evening, medical assistant Annie Borewa saw something extraordinary in the sky overhead and summoned Father William Gill to come and see. Together they watched as two small UFOs and a larger circular object hovered nearby. It had a wide base and a narrower upper deck, with four legs protruding from it. A beam of light was seen pointing up into the sky at a 45-degree angle.

As Father Gill and his congregation looked on, four figures were seen operating equipment on the upper deck. When Father Gill waved to them, they all started waving back. Gill then flashed his torch at the UFO, which apparently responded by swinging to and fro.

According to some, Father Gill and the other witnesses saw not a UFO but a 'ghost ship' in the sky - a phenomenon more common in the days of sailing vessels than rockets. This demonstrates the fact that the classification of UFO incidents is often no straightforward matter.

Above: Cults have been a part of the UFO phenomenon for many years. Here the Aetherius Society, which communicates between the cosmic masters and the Earth, mounts 'Operation Prayer Power'

Below: Joe Simonton with a pancake he received from alien visitors

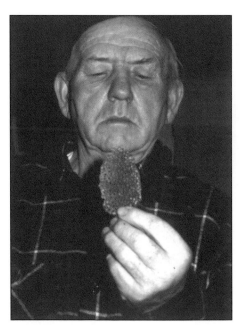

Footprints and Fertiliser

When police officer Lonnie Zamora saw a flame descending over a hill in Socorro, New Mexico, on April 24, 1964, he immediately went to investigate. At the scene he saw a shiny, egg-shaped object and two figures. Reacting with apparent surprise at seeing Zamora, they got back into their craft and flew away across the desert. Subsequent investigation revealed landing marks in the sand, burnt vegetation and footprints. A metal-like substance was also discovered on some of the rocks.

There is some possible corroboration of this sighting. On the previous day, farmer Gary Wilcox reported seeing an object very like that described by Zamora; and the civilian investigator Ray Sandford also saw something very similar just a few days. In Wilcox's case, he too saw two humanoids, who asked him for a bag of fertiliser. When he went to fetch one, the craft sped off. Wilcox left the bag of fertiliser anyway, and the next day it had vanished.

Ufologist Dr J Allen Hynek investigated this case officially on behalf of the US government. He later declared: 'Of all the close encounters of the third kind, this is the one that most clearly suggests a "nuts and bolts" physical craft.'

Grays, Nordics and Troglodytes

In recent years, descriptions of aliens have become somewhat standardised. Many reports refer to aliens known as 'grays' - small thin beings, with tiny mouths and noses and huge almost pupilless eyes. Grays have figured in both crash retrieval incidents and cases of abduction.

Earlier in the 'modern era' of UFOs, however, the standard type of alien was known as 'Nordic'. The being encountered by George Adamski in 1952 possessed all the Nordic characteristics: very human-like, tall, handsome and graceful, with long blond hair. Nordics differ from grays in disposition as well as physical appearance, tending to be respectful and co-operative, whereas grays are said to treat humans as fodder for experiments.

While grays and Nordics are predominant types, there is a huge variety in the descriptions of aliens which have been reported. Elephant-skinned, floating, one-footed aliens were encountered in Mississippi in October 1973; red-skinned, one-eyed creatures have been seen in South America; aliens wearing space-suits, helmets and flexi-tubes featured in many accounts in Europe in the 1950s and 1960s. The aliens who abducted Jose Antonio da Silva in Belo Horizonte were described as 'troglodytes'.

Why Humanoids?

The fact that the vast majority of aliens have been described as humanoid in form is puzzling. On the planet Earth, which may be considered as just one biosphere where life has developed, only a tiny fraction of the millions of species in existence are humanoid. In a completely different biosphere, random forces would presumably produce different results. That even one other humanoid race should have evolved and reached a level of technology allowing it to visit Earth during the brief time-span that humans happen to be in the ascendancy would be coincidence enough. Yet we seem to have had not one but countless different humanoid visitors.

Some have attempted to explain the preponderance of humanoid aliens by distinguishing between intelligence and technological development. Even on Earth, the argument runs, some creatures might have a higher intelligence that we cannot comprehend. Dolphins, ants and bees might fall into such a category. However, perhaps it is only the humanoid forms who are also capable of developing the technology allowing them to cross the gulfs of space.

At present levels of understanding, this explanation would not appear tenable, and the arguments against humanoid aliens currently hold sway.

Non-humanoid Forms

Although reports of most aliens have described them as humanoid, there have been a few cases involving contact with non-humanoid forms. Early one morning in 1971, John Hodges and a friend were on Dapple Grey Lane in Los Angeles, when they saw two objects resembling human brains on the road. They were approximately three feet high and seemed to be alive. After driving his friend home, Hodges realised that he had lost two hours.

Regression hypnosis revealed that Hodges had been telepathically contacted by the brain-like entities, which told him that they would meet again. Seven years later, there was further contact, in which Hodges was warned of the dangers of nuclear war.

At 1am on January 27, 1977, Lee Parrish was driving home through the town of Prospect, Kentucky, when he was buzzed by a bright rectangular UFO. On arriving home, he too discovered that he had lost time, half an hour in this case.

Under hypnosis he recalled being transported into the UFO, where he was surrounded by three machine-like but living entities. One of them, a huge black slab 15 feet tall, has been compared to the monolith in the film '2001 - A Space Odyssey'.

Above: A typical depiction of a 'gray'

Below: A depiction of a humanoid-looking entity

Men in Black

Some UFO witnesses have been scared into keeping quiet about their experiences by oppressive figures known as the 'Men in Black'. Those who have encountered these sinister individuals report that they generally travel in groups of two or three, wear dark suits and hats, and drive old but pristine black cars.

The founder of the International Flying Saucer Bureau, Albert Bender, claimed he was visited by three Men in Black after he announced a theory to explain UFOs. They told him to keep silent or face 'dire consequences'.

In 1976, Dr Herbert Hopkins was visited by a Man in Black - or MIB - enquiring about an abduction case that he was investigating. The MIB had a bald head, no facial hair, had skin like plastic and wore lipstick. Throughout the meeting he was described as behaving like a robot. At one point, the MIB asked Hopkins to hold a coin, which then slowly dematerialised from his hand. The MIB finally ordered him to destroy his tapes of the case in question, and Hopkins was so shaken that he later complied.

If the whole meeting was extraordinary, its end was particularly bizarre. The Man in Black began talking very slowly - almost as if he had a power supply that was running low - and then he left.

Some people believe these sinister Men in Black are government agents; others that they are themselves aliens.

Repeater Witnesses

Most people who witness a UFO incident do so only once, but there are also repeater witnesses who report a number of sightings. These generally take the form of close contact, and often a 'kinship' emerges: the witnesses come to believe that the encounters have a special significance.

There are two schools of thought relating to the phenomenon of repeater witnesses. One theory is that UFOs can best be perceived by a certain state of mind, and this can be developed over a period of time. The counter argument has it that some people become so fascinated by a first sighting that a desire is created, and subsequent events are then misinterpreted to fulfil this inner need.

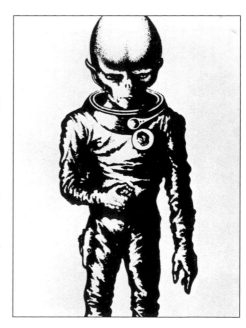

Above: Contactees are equal participants in the experience, whereas the role of abductees is that of unwilling victim

Below: Drawing by a schoolboy witness from Broadhaven Primary School, Wales

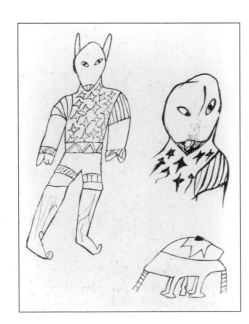

The distinction between contactee and abductee is particularly relevant to the subject of repeater witnesses. Contactees are equal partners in the experience, whereas the role of abductees is that of unwilling victim. But movement between the two is possible, at least, according to Betty Hill and Charles Hickson. Betty Hill's well documented first experience with UFOs, in New Hampshire in 1961, was clearly an unwelcome abduction; but in recent years she has spoken more as a contactee, claiming to use secret codes to communicate with aliens.

Charles Hickson was badly shaken by his encounter, which occurred at Pascagoula, Mississippi, during the 'great flap of 1973', but he later found meaning in the experience. He maintains that the encounters have continued, and he now refers to them as 'contacts'.

Child Witnesses
Some people might feel that children would not make the most reliable witnesses to UFOs, but there have been instances where large groups of youngsters have given convincing and consistent accounts of what they have seen.

In April 1967, over 200 children and staff at Crestview Elementary School, near Carol City, Florida, saw mysterious objects in the sky in broad daylight on several occasions. Many children described them as solid and aluminium-like in appearance.

At Broadhaven Primary School in Wales, on February 4, 1977, 14 children and their teacher saw a circular silver object in a marshy field. Later, the headmaster asked the children to draw what they had seen, and the resulting pictures - done in separate rooms - were remarkably consistent.

Researcher Cynthia Hind has taken a long-term interest in this case, and in 1995 she reported that the witnesses - now grown up - were unchanged in their memories of that day.

Hind has also investigated a strikingly similar incident which took place in Zimbabwe. On September 16, 1994, 62 children at Ariel Primary School in Ruwa, near Harare, told their teachers that they had seen a mysterious object and figures from the playground. The children spoke of 'little men' with 'eyes like rugby balls', and, once again, the pictures that were drawn contained a high level of consistency.

'Star Children'

'Star Children' are human beings who believe they have been seeded on Earth by a higher, extra-terrestrial civilisation. Many are convinced that the nature of their extra-terrestrial intelligence is kept dormant until a particular event or trigger releases it for some greater purpose. Star Children often identify their own origins through dreams, and may have contactee-type encounters with UFOs. They typically work as teachers, doctors, nurses, lawyers, or in other positions from where they can play key roles at the appointed time.

-Author Brad Steiger lists 'the essential pattern profile of the star people' as:

-Having been born unexpectedly to parents

-Having had unseen childhood companions

-Having personal charisma and compelling eyes

-Being attractive to children and animals

-Having lower than normal body temperature

-Being hypersensitive to electromagnets

-Having low blood pressure

-Requiring little sleep

-Showing a sense of urgency, as if a special mission has to be completed

-Expressing alien environments in dreams, fantasies and artwork

-Yearning for their real home beyond the stars

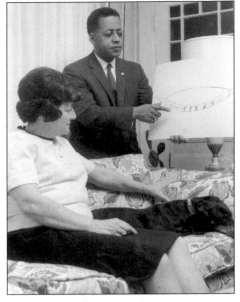

Above: Betty and Barney Hill with a drawing of a UFO they witnessed in 1961

Below: Still from the film 'Close Encounters of the Third Kind' in which contact between aliens and humans was depicted as benign

Ray Guns and Unfriendly Fire

In September 1954, Marius Dewilde saw two entities near his house at Quaroble in France. They were short and dressed in what looked like diving costumes. Dewilde attempted to grab them but was repulsed by a powerful light from a nearby object. The beam paralysed him and the object flew off.

On March 14, 1965, rancher James Flynn was rendered unconscious by a beam of light from a UFO, which also left charred ground traces. Flynn's doctor found impairment of muscle and tendon reflexes which he believed were not faked.

On St Valentine's Day, 1975, Antoine Severin saw a small domed object landing in a field on Reunion Island in the Indian Ocean. Several short entities emerged and fired a white beam at him, knocking him out. For several days, Severin's vision and speech were badly impaired.

9-year-old Gregory Wells was returning to his home in Beallsville, Ohio, on March 14, 1968, when his mother and grandmother heard him screaming. They found Gregory on the ground, his jacket on fire. He later said that he had seen a huge bright object hovering above the road, and that he had been struck by a beam of flame. Other witnesses also reported seeing the object.

Strange Compulsions

Encounters with UFOs can cause witnesses to display some strange forms of compulsive behaviour. Sometimes these compulsions can reflect fears or aspects of the experience that the witness does not want to face; in other cases they are part of what is perceived as a special purpose or mission.

Kristina Florence described how as a young girl she had had a fear of ants which compelled her to seek out and destroy anthills. Hypnosis sessions revealed that she was making a subconscious connection between the shiny skins of the ants' eggs and the skins of the entities that had once abducted her.

Researchers John Spencer and Steve Gamble, of the British UFO Association, investigated the case of a man who had dedicated most of his life to UFOs in the belief that he had been specially chosen by higher beings. He was a maintenance worker on a factory production line, but was convinced that the factory was in fact a disguised flying saucer, which at the appointed time would take selected people away from Earth. He believed, therefore, that he had a crucial role in keeping the machinery in good repair.

Abductions

Of all the manifestations of UFO activity, the one which strikes most terror into people's hearts is abduction. Reports of such encounters awaken our innermost fears, and yet we are endlessly fascinated by them.

The first attested case of abduction took place in 1961 in New Hampshire, local couple Barney and Betty Hill being the protagonists in the drama. The Hills maintained that they were abducted on September 19, although it was to be more than two years before events of that night were pieced together. More than 30 years later, this case continues to provoke intense argument among investigators and psychologists. Did the hypnosis the couple underwent elicit real memories? Or did deep-seated fears give rise to a fictitious account of what happened.

Publicity surrounding the Hills' case sparked off hundreds of similar reports, many of which have been subjected to the closest scientific scrutiny. One such story concerned Charles Hickson and Calvin Parker, who claimed they were abducted on October 12, 1973 after three alien beings appeared from a large oval craft. The men were subsequently examined by Dr Bernard Best of Harper Hospital, Detroit. Dr Best could find nothing in their version of events that suggested falsehood, fantasy or delusion, and concluded that they were telling the truth.

Did the well-publicised details of Barney and Betty Hill's case inspire a wave of copycat accounts? Or did the Hills act as a catalyst, paving the way for others who might have been afraid to tell their stories? Naturally, there is huge scepticism over such extraordinary incidents, but some cases contain evidence which is more difficult to refute. Abductees have been left with inexplicable wounds on their body, or have suddenly acquired amazing new talents and powers.

But the crucial question relates to purpose: what do the aliens want? The main theory is that abductions are part of a systematic programme of the study of human genetics, a biological experiment which is being continually monitored and updated. Alternatively, the aliens may require something which is missing from their own genetic make-up.

The case histories are all we have to go on in determining whether abductees are victims of self-delusion, or guinea pigs in some bizarre interplanetary experiment.

Betty and Barney Hill   Late in the evening of September 19, 1961, Betty and Barney Hill were returning to their New Hampshire home, when they noticed a bright light in the sky which seemed to be following their car. The object finally got so close that Mr Hill stopped the car, got out and walked towards it. He saw humanoid entities looking down at him through a row of windows and, fearing that he was about to be captured, returned to his car in a panic-stricken state and drove off. The couple arrived home two hours later than planned.

Over the next two years, the Hills were haunted by dreams and fears about that night. They finally agreed to undergo regression hypnosis with Boston psychiatrist Dr Benjamin Simon. An extraordinary story emerged as a result: the couple had somehow driven to a lonely side road that September night, where they had been stopped by humanoids from a flying saucer. They had been removed from their car, taken aboard the craft and subjected to a medical examination.

Betty Hill later became a repeater witness, often driving to remote locations, where she would communicate with UFOs by flashing her car headlights.

'What Have They Done?'   On October 12, 1973, Charles Hickson and Calvin Parker were fishing at the Shaupeter shipyard in Pascagoula, Mississippi, when they suddenly became aware of an oval-shaped object with a blue light nearby. A hatchway opened, and out floated three entities with wrinkled skin, conical projections instead of ears and noses, and crab-like pincers for hands.

The aliens 'floated' the terrified fishermen into their craft, at which point Parker apparently fainted. After being removed from the vessel, Hickson's main concern was for his friend. 'My God, what have they done to him?' he exclaimed when he saw the agonised expression on Parker's face.

Once freed, the pair drove around, unsure of what action to take. Eventually they went to the sheriff's department and told him their story. They were interviewed separately about what had taken place, and their accounts tallied so closely that the sheriff was convinced that they were telling the truth. Dr Bernard A Best, of Harper Hospital, Detroit, came to the same conclusion when he later conducted his own examination.

Above: Betty and Barney Hill who only discovered their alien abduction after undergoing regression hypnosis

Below: An artist's impression of a UFO

Travis Walton   On November 5, 1975, a gang of seven woodcutters were working in the Sitgraves National Park, near Snowflake, Arizona, when they saw a large golden UFO above the treetops. One of the men, Travis Walton, ran towards the object and was hit by a blue ray. The others immediately fled to report what had happened to the police.

The police initially refused to believe the men, in spite of the fact that lie-detector tests corroborated their story. They were accused of having murdered Walton and hidden his body.

Five days later, Walton reappeared. He said he had been abducted by humanoids and 'grays', and had been taken on a space flight. He was amazed to discover that he had been away for five days, even though he had a growth of beard commensurate with that passage of time. He, too, took a lie-detector test, following which examiner Dr Gene Rosenbaum stated: 'This young man is not lying....he really believes these things.'

The witnesses received $5,000 from the 'National Enquirer' magazine for the most valuable UFO report of the year, and the incident was the inspiration for the film 'Fire in the Sky'.

Above: Out working in a gang of wood cutters, Travis Walton (inset) was hit by a ray from a UFO and disappeared for five days

Below: Fishermen Charles Hickson and Calvin Parker were abducted from their fishing boat

'My Greatest Experience'

Like Charles Hickson and Calvin Parker, Alfred Burtoo was engaged in the peaceful activity of fishing, when he was an abduction victim. It happened in the early hours of an August morning in 1983, at the Basingstoke Canal, in Aldershot, England. Burtoo, who was in his late 70s, was approached by two entities wearing one-piece green suits and visors. They indicated that they wanted him to go with them, and, apparently unafraid, he followed them onto an object 45 feet wide and resting on runners.

On board, he was subjected to an examination and then told: 'You are too old and infirm for our purpose.' Burtoo claimed that they spoke in English but with a foreign accent, and thought they originated from somewhere on Earth. He was allowed to return to his fishing spot, where his dog was waiting for him. He then watched as the object took off at high speed and disappeared.

Unusually, Burtoo suffered no obvious after-effects. He believed that at his age there was nothing to fear, although he was irritated by the fact that he had been rejected. Nevertheless, he described the encounter as 'the greatest experience of my life'.

Following Burtoo's death three years later, researcher Timothy Good asked his wife if he had ever admitted his story to be a hoax. Mrs Burtoo said that to the very end her husband had maintained that he had been telling the truth.

Out-of-body Abductions

One radical view of abductions is that they take place not in the physical world but on the astral plane, and that it is the astral body, not the physical one, which undergoes the abduction experience.

Finnish medical expert Rauni-Leena Luukanen-Kilde has experienced several out-of-body visions during surgery. She also recalls an abduction in which a medical examination was involved, a recurring characteristic of this phenomenon. She believes that her physical body remained in bed throughout, while her astral body was on a spacecraft.

Other witnesses have reported seeing their own bodies during abductions, suggesting that an out-of-body experience was taking place. This is precisely what happened to Betty Andreasson Luca on several occasions. She has referred to a 'world of light' which was 'indescribably beautiful', much in the same way that people who have had out-of-body or near-death experiences have spoken of entering another world on a spiritual level.

Screen Memories

It is perhaps understandable that the victims of abduction should seek to block out the memory of such a terrifying experience. That seems to be what happened in the case of Whitley Streiber, who claimed he was abducted by alien beings on December 26, 1985.

Streiber replaced his actual memories of the incident with false or 'screen' memories, involving an owl and the light of a snowmobile. It was some time before he realised that these images were masking a more sinister truth.

Memories of cars, houses in fields and shops with 'strange shopkeepers' have featured in many reports by abductees, and these have been interpreted as displaced images of flying saucers. Similarly, recollections of animals with large eyes - owls, deer and cats, for example - are thought to conceal memories of aliens themselves.

Some researchers have suggested that the screen memory is imposed by the aliens to prevent the witness from recalling the real experience; others that it is a natural self-defence mechanism, the mind protecting itself from facing a horrific reality, as commonly happens after other traumatic experiences.

Lost Time

In August 1975, Alan Fellows was driving towards the village of Mossley, in Yorkshire, England, when he was surrounded by a thick mist and saw a bright egg-shaped light. It appears that he then passed out, and there was later evidence that he had been afflicted by some kind of temporary paralysis. When he came round, he found he was clutching a screwdriver as if holding a weapon. He had no recollection of picking it up.

Helene Giuliana was returning home late one night in June 1976, when her car engine cut out as she was crossing the bridge at Romans, France. She saw a huge orange glow in the sky, but it quickly disappeared, power was restored to her car and she was able to continue her journey. On arriving home, however, she discovered she had lost a considerable period of time. Regression hypnosis subsequently revealed that she had been abducted by small figures, who had tied her to a table and conducted an examination.

Luli Oswald and a friend had a similar experience while driving from Rio de Janeiro to Saquarema on October 15, 1979 . The pair saw three UFOs and also suffered vehicle interference. The next thing they could remember was finding themselves on a side road some distance away, where they realised that they had lost two hours. Regression hypnosis was again employed and this revealed all the classic elements of an abduction by aliens.

Artistic Powers

An unexpected but not uncommon by-product of the abduction phenomenon is the development of creative and artistic powers in the victims. Peter Holding's encounters with UFOs turned him from a gardener who had never displayed any artistic talent into an artist whose work commands high prices. Many of his photographs and paintings have religious themes, reflecting the spiritual nature of his experiences.

Above: Betty Andreasson Luca has reported that during her several abductions she also experiences an out-of-body experience

Below: Peter Holding developed an artistic talent after his encounters with UFOs

Above: In the 'bedroom visitation' scenario aliens appear and take the victim to their flying saucer

Below: Burn marks on the skin of an abductee

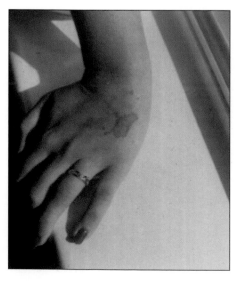

Mark James had encounters with UFOs which he found frightening and disturbing, but he acknowledges that they were also the springboard which led him to seek personal development. He now expresses his creative drive through music.

Researcher John Spencer has investigated this phenomenon, which he discovered to be relatively common. It seems doubtful that aliens abduct people primarily to develop their creative talents. It is more likely that the enlightenment they experience is a side-effect of their struggle to come to terms with their abduction. Perhaps, as the mental horizons and perspectives are changed by the abduction experience, the artistic, creative and intuitive side of the brain is simultaneously activated. But it is one thing for abductees to develop the will to create; it is quite another for them to suddenly acquire the ability to give expression to these newfound desires.

Mrs Elsie Oakensen, from Northamptonshire in England, also discovered new talents following an abduction experience. The incident, which occurred in November 1978, involved what she described as a 'scanning': 'There was some kind of examination, and by that I don't mean necessarily a medical examination. It could have been a spiritual examination.' Since then, she has developed psychic abilities and is now a healer and a dowser.

Types of Abductions

Abductions freqently seem to occur in particular circumstances, prominent among which are the 'lonely road at night' scenario and the 'bedroom visitation' scenario. In the former, the encounters tend to happen at times of potential sensory deprivation - on long, straight, dark roads, when the driver is alone or, if accompanied, when others in the vehicle are asleep or dozing. The abductee often experiences an 'isolation factor', described as an incredible quiet and stillness.

In the 'bedroom visitation' scenario, aliens appear and take the victim to their flying saucer. The abductee may be physically carried by the aliens, or levitated out of the window and 'sucked up' into a UFO above. Characteristics of the experience include witness paralysis and the fact that other persons in the room - such as a husband or wife in bed beside the victim - are immobilized or cannot be woken. Bedroom visitations do not always involve an actual UFO, but only the implication of one in the form of bright lights, often from unseen sources.

There are factors which are common to both 'lonely road at night' and 'bedroom visitation' scenarios. Chief among these is what is known as 'doorway amnesia', where abductees have no recollection of the transition from the 'real world' to the environment of the aliens' craft.

The Build-up Phase

Many abductees have spoken of strange feelings or unusual behaviour patterns as prior indicators of their experiences - what French researcher Jean-Francois Boedec called the 'build-up phase' to UFO abductions.

On October 21, 1954, Mrs Jessie Rostenberg and her two young sons saw both a UFO and alien entities. This had been preceded by a feeling of uneasiness throughout the day.

In July 1954, an 11-year-old girl on holiday at Wegierska Gorka in Poland was gathering mushrooms with her friends in the woods, when she uncharacteristically decided to go off on her own. She saw a glowing oval light and walked towards it, whereupon she encountered a being who took her aboard a craft. Her next memory was of being found by her friends seven hours later. Her mushroom basket was empty and all she had was a vague memory of flying. The girl's urge to leave her friends, as if summoned or controlled by unseen forces, is typical of many cases investigated by Boedec.

The 'Gray' Abductors

Aliens known as 'grays' are particularly associated with abductions. Descriptions of grays tend to be similar, although not totally consistent:

'His face was long and thin with a flat chin, and extremely pale - almost ghost-like. The most prominent features were the eyes, large and round, with just a tiny dot pupil, pink and no larger than a match-head. There was almost no mouth - just a thin line......'

'I saw two strange grey-faced creatures....with dingy white skin, almost grey, and eyes that were pitch black in colour, liquid-like, shimmering in the dim light.....'

'Their presence was unimaginably powerful, and so strange. There was a sort of jollity about these beings....They seemed happy....'

The Human Experiment

Are aliens engaged in a systematic programme of genetic examination and manipulation of human beings? When Betty and Barney Hill were abducted, they described how they were subjected to separate examinations. There have been many similar reports, sometimes involving several abductees being examined together. Some victims have been left with physical evidence of their experience - wounds or strange 'scoop' marks. This phenomenon seems to be associated with how passionately the abductee believes in the experience, in the same way that the appearance of stigmata on the hands and feet of Christians seems to be a product of devout faith.

Most of the examinations centre on the reproductive system, with samples of sperm and ova being removed. Abductees have spoken of being impregnated with alien-human hybrid offspring, which are either removed or born during a later abduction. They are sometimes bonded with these offspring during subsequent abductions.

British abductee Maria Ward was the victim of a bedroom visitation abduction, after which she remembered 'having something done to me in my womb. I could feel something moving around inside me.' Ed Duvall, another abduction victim, was told that the aliens needed his sperm 'to create special babies' and 'for work we are doing to help the people on your planet.'

Above: Artist's impression of the aliens that abducted Betty and Barney Hill

Below: Whitley Streiber who 'screened' his abduction memories to block out the terrifying truth

Fake Reports and Suggestibility

In 1977, Professor Alvin Lawson made a study of the nature of the abduction experience. He conducted a series of 'imaginary abductee experiments', in which he studied the differences in testimony between those who genuinely believed they had been abducted and those who deliberately fabricated stories for the purposes of the test.

Subjects were given the outline of an abduction story, then hypnotically regressed to recall the experience. It was found that imaginary abductees could match the detail of the 'genuine' reports, indicating that people can create fake reports, albeit subconsciously.

In 1992-3, John Spencer of the British UFO Association conducted an experiment using no genuine abductees. Researchers acting as volunteers were asked to learn an imaginary abduction scenario, which they would then recall under hypnosis. In one case, examiners used suggestive words, eye contact and body language to change a female subject's terrified 'recall' of being raped by aliens into a pleasant spiritual recollection. This implies that witnesses' stories can be influenced in a major way by suggestion.

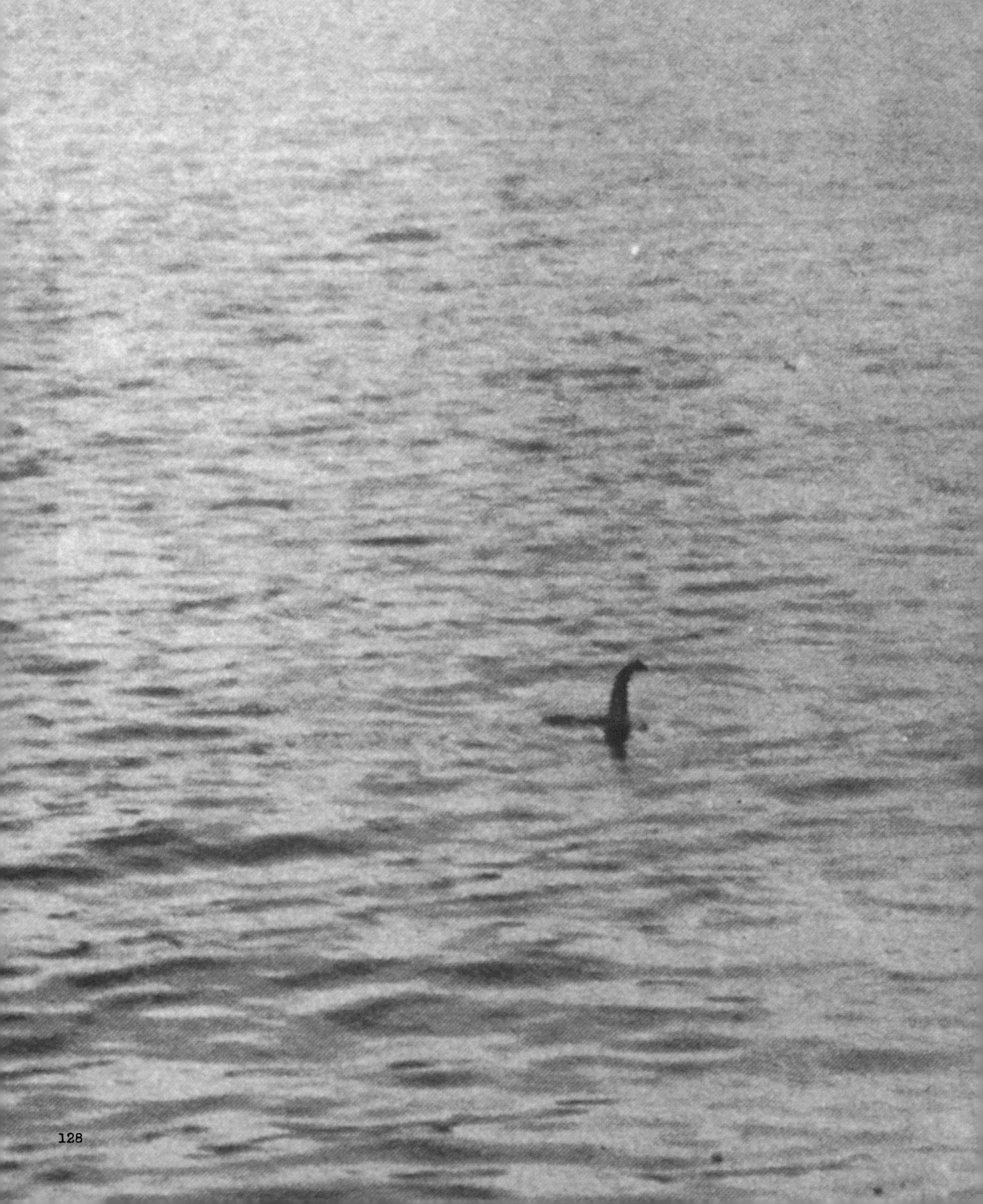

Chapter Five

Mysterious Beings

The notion that we live on a shrinking planet is well established. Communications systems are becoming ever more sophisticated, developing technologies in the field of transport allow us to move around the globe with increasing ease. One might think that everywhere on Earth is now accessible, and, by implication, that little or nothing remains to be discovered about the creatures that inhabit it. But the idea that the great unknown lies in outer space is certainly misguided. Scientists might not agree about the number of unknown species with which we share our planet, but that number is unquestionably large. Relatively small areas of remote jungle can reveal hosts of insect species previously unknown to science. And there are people who believe we have much larger unknown neighbours in our global village.

When the early explorers told of strange creatures that lived in the oceans and faraway lands, exaggeration and hearsay turned these into terrifying beasts. Orang-utans and giant squid became hairy giants and sea monsters. Today we might think nothing so large could exist without our knowing about it. But comparatively recent discoveries, such as coelacanth and megamouth, show that this is not the case. And if the mythical creatures of past ages are the textbook entries of today, who knows what other legendary beasts may follow? The Loch Ness monster, the yeti, werewolves, vampires: there is evidence for all of them, albeit inconclusive. Who can say which creatures will continue to exist only in the imagination, for the boundaries between myth and reality are being constantly redrawn.

The Loch Ness Monster is probably the most famous of all the mysterious creatures of the deep

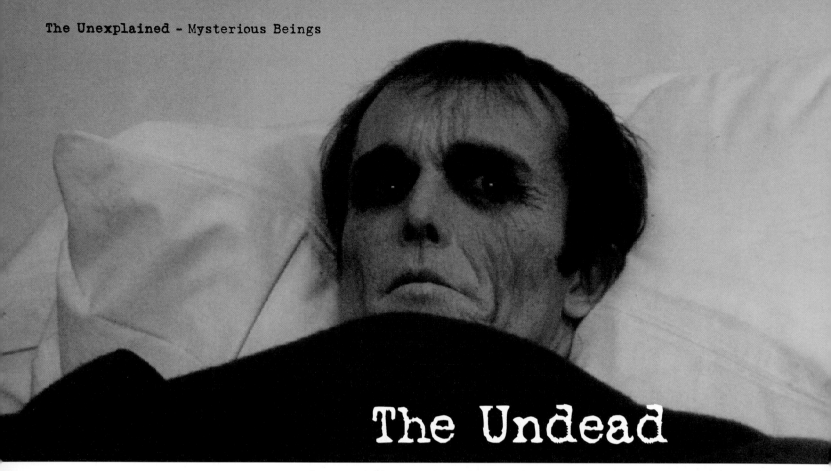

The Undead

Vampires, werewolves, zombies: these are the inhabitants of the twilight world of the undead. Horrific acts have been laid at the door of these creatures over many centuries, and in the modern era their portrayal in books and particularly films has rendered them the stuff of nightmares. But the pattern which emerges from ancient legends and documented case histories is rather different; indeed, far from being the perpetrators of unremitting evil, there is evidence to suggest that these creatures of the night are often unfortunate victims of circumstance.

The word 'vampire' immediately conjures up images of Bram Stoker's famous creation. Stoker was certainly fascinated by vampire legends, but for the character of Count Dracula he also drew on factual accounts of historical figures infamous for their callousness and blood-lust. Most people are aware of Dracula's need for human blood to quench his thirst and reinvigorate himself. Traditionally, however, vampires were created when people died under certain circumstances - stillborn, suicides and murder victims, for example - and whose souls as a result were trapped in their bodies, unable to pass into the spirit world.

The transformation of man into wolf has a history that extends back to ancient Greece and beyond. Once again, popular mythology has presented us with a defined image-a human who takes a bestial form when exposed to the light of the full moon. In two celebrated cases of the werewolf phenomenon, those involving Peter Stubbe and Jean Grenier, neither conformed to this stereotype. Although both were guilty of unspeakable acts of savagery, the way in which they were initiated was markedly different: Stubbe confessed to being the architect of his own misfortune, making a pact with the devil, while Grenier was a mere child, an innocent lured to a terrible fate.

It seems that the undead, if not exactly alive and well, are at least still with us. In the Caribbean island of Haiti, belief in the power of sorcery and voodoo remains intense. People continue to live in fear that the bodies of the departed may be stolen from their graves by voodoo priests and returned to a semiconscious life as one of the living dead - a zombie. It has been suggested that voodoo priests in fact administer a poison which induces in the victims a death-like coma from which they can later be revived; but when French anthropologist Alfred Metraux, a sceptic by inclination, studied the zombie phenomenon, he found cases which challenged his preconceptions.

Above: Zombies are the bodies of the dead reawakened into semi-conscious life

From Vlad the Impaler to Dracula

Bram Stoker's Dracula was published in 1897 to immediate popular acclaim, a play based on the novel being performed in the same year under the sponsorship of the famous actor-manager, Henry Irving. But it was not until the many film versions of the 20th century that the story of Count Dracula gained widespread international recognition. While most people are familiar with the Dracula story, perhaps less well known is the 15th century tale which provided Stoker with his inspiration.

Abraham Stoker, who was born in 1847 near Dublin, was himself an avid reader of fantasy novels, and was fascinated by vampire legends. He also had a strong interest in the occult, and was a member of the esoteric Order of the Golden Dawn. The catalyst for channelling these interests into a creative form was a meeting with Arminius Vamberry, a professor of Eastern Languages at the University of Budapest. It was Vamberry who told Stoker the horrific tale of Vlad the Impaler, the character who would form the model for Count Dracula.

Vlad the Impaler was the historical figure most closely associated with the legend of the vampire. Born in 1431, he was prince of an ancient kingdom now part of Romania. Vlad actually bore two surnames: Tepes (the Impaler) and Dracul (his father's name, meaning 'dragon'). He was cruel and tyrannical, infamous not only for the way he mercilessly impaled and dismembered enemy prisoners, but for murdering many of his own people too. The German chronicles which record his terrible deeds rank him 'among the most bloodthirsty tyrants of history, such as Herod, Nero and Diocletian'. These shared a gluttonous self-satisfaction at the death of their many victims. It was Vlad's seemingly insatiable blood-lust which, some 400 years later, inspired Stoker's tale of the Count with the more literal thirst for human blood.

Above: Countess Erzebet Bathory is believed to have murdered 300 young girls whose blood she drank in the belief that it would preserve her youth

Below: The seemingly insatiable bloodlust of Vlad the Impaler inspired Bram Stoker's 'Dracula'

Erzebet Bathory

Another historical figure whose terrible atrocities helped to shape the vampire legend as we know it today was Erzebet Bathory. When she was brought to trial, in Hungary in 1611, the barbaric cruelty of this aristocratic woman was exposed. Bathory was believed to have murdered as many as 300 young girls, who were tortured horrifically, then bled to death after being stabbed with sharp needles. All the accounts of Bathory's heinous crimes indicate that she drank her victims' blood, and even bathed in it in the belief that this would preserve her youth.

Bathory's activities were only halted when a small army, led by one of her cousins, broke into her castle during one of her bloody orgies. She was subsequently tried and convicted, but ironically, she was saved from death by her own aristocratic blood. Instead, she was imprisoned for life in a room where the doors and windows were sealed.

The castle of Csejthe, where Bathory lived and in whose dungeons the gruesome deeds were carried out, became the model for Bram Stoker's castle in Dracula.

Detecting Vampires

Legends dating back over many centuries have helped to identify those said to be at risk of becoming vampires after death. These include suicides, witches, the excommunicated, the stillborn, victims of murder and violent death and those not buried in hallowed ground.

When people in these high-risk categories died, special precautions were frequently taken. In Romania, for example, the head of the deceased had a nail driven through it. Sometimes, objects perceived to be imbued with special powers were buried with the dead: a piece of holy bread, a lemon or the famous clove of garlic - these were supposed to prevent the vampire from re-entering the body after its nightly wandering.

More stubborn cases called for more drastic measures: piercing the heart. This was sometimes done with a stake made of aspen, the wood of Christ's cross; otherwise a sanctified dagger might be used. If the corpse did not turn immediately to dust, the head was cut off, and the rest of the body burned, the ashes being scattered to the four winds.

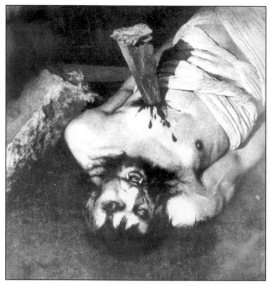

Above: Piercing the heart with a stake was believed to prevent those corpses most at risk from turning into vampires

Below: A voodoo ceremony on All Saints Day

Lycanthropy

Belief in lycanthropy - the existence of 'wolf people' - may stem from a genetic disorder which causes excessive facial hair. A classic case of this condition, which can affect both men and women, was that of Petrus Gonsalvus. Gonsalvus's hirsute appearance led to him being nicknamed 'the wolf-man of Bavaria', although he never displayed any wolf-like behaviour. His daughter also developed the condition, and a portrait of her, showing her fur-covered face, was presented to the King of Bohemia by William, Duke of Bavaria.

There have also been cases of delusions of lycanthropy, with patients insisting that they turn into wolves under certain conditions. A US soldier became convinced he was a werewolf after taking LSD and strychnine in a German forest. His drug-induced delusion included the belief that his hands and face were covered with hair. This case might provide a clue to some historical incidents of lycanthropy, where the same effect may have been created by plants and fungi with narcotic properties.

Werewolves in History

The werewolf featured in Roman legends, and accounts of people being transformed into wolves appear in Virgil, Petronius and Ovid. Herodotus wrote of the Neuri people: '(They) are sorcerers, if one is to believe the Scythians....for each Neurian changes himself, once in the year, into the form of a wolf, and he continues in that form for several days, after which he resumes his former shape.'

In Norwegian and Icelandic culture, it was once believed that certain people were 'not of one skin'. Originally a pagan idea, this was a belief that people could take on the form and nature of any chosen creature: '...if he has taken the form of a wolf, or if he goes on a wolf's ride, he is full of the rage and malignity of the creatures whose powers and passions he has assumed.'

The Case of Peter Stubbe

One of the most shocking cases of the werewolf phenomenon occurred in 16th century Germany. Peter Stubbe was convicted of a series of gruesome murders and acts of cruelty and immorality. It was said that he had made a pact with the devil in which he was given a wolfskin belt that would transform him into a bloodthirsty wolf. He roamed the area around Cologne for 25 years, killing and eating cattle and sheep, but his name was to go down in history for far worse crimes. Women and girls were raped, killed and eaten. Even his own family did not escape his cruelty: he is said to have abused his daughter and sister, and violated and killed his son before eating his brain.

Stubbe was apparently captured as he was turning himself back into human form. He discarded his wolf-pelt, which was never found, but he was tortured and confessed to 16 murders and his pact with the devil. He was decapitated, his body being burnt with those of his wife and mistress, while his head was put on public display to serve as a warning to others.

The Case of Jean Grenier

Jean Grenier's story featured in The Book of Werewolves, written by Sabine Baring-Gould in 1865:

'Jean Grenier was the son of a poor labourer in the village of S. Antoine de Pizon, France. The story he related of himself before the court was as follows: "When I was 10 or 11 years old, my neighbour, Duthillaire, introduced me, in the depths of the forest, to a M. de la Forest, a black man, who signed me with his nail and then gave to me and Duthillaire a wolfskin. From that time I have run about as a wolf."

'In the parish of S. Antoine he had attacked a little girl who was keeping sheep. She was dressed in a black frock; he did not know her name. He tore her with his nails and teeth, and ate her. Jean said that he had the wolfskin in his possession, and that he went out hunting for children at the command of his master, the Lord of the Forest.

'He usually ran from one to two hours a day, when the moon was at its wane, but very often he made his expeditions at night.'

Vrykolakas

Belief in the 'undead' - souls whose bodies did not decompose and which could leave their tombs - can be traced back as far as ancient Greece. Throughout the Europe of the Middle Ages, these wandering souls were often called 'vrykolakas', which means 'werewolf' in the Slavonic language. Vrykolaka usually referred to someone who had not been buried in consecrated ground, perhaps because the person had been excommunicated or had committed suicide.

By the 16th century, Vrykolaka was used throughout Eastern Europe to refer to the living dead as well as the bloodthirsty werewolf; it was also sometimes used in connection with vampires. Such was the level of concern regarding this phenomenon within the Roman Catholic church that an investigation was carried out over a 200-year period. During this time, around 30,000 cases of humans adopting the form of a wolf emerged.

The Narcisse Case

In Haiti, on April 30, 1962, Clairvius Narcisse was admitted into an American-run hospital in Deschapelles, suffering from a terrible fever. His condition deteriorated and, on May 2, with his sister Angelina at his bedside, he was declared dead. His body was buried the following day near the village of l'Estere, where the family lived.

In 1980, 18 years after Angelina believed she had witnessed the death of her brother, a man approached her in the village market. He claimed he was Clairvius, and that their brother had arranged his zombification following a land dispute. He explained that he had been resurrected from his grave and taken by a group of men to north Haiti, where he worked as a slave along with other zombies. This lasted for two years, ending only with the death of the zombie master. The man claimed he then lived a nomadic existence for 16 years, daring to return home only after learning that his brother had died.

The Narcisse case generated great interest. With the help of the family, a series of tests was devised aimed at confirming the man's story or exposing him as a fraud. He was questioned about Clairvius's childhood in such detail that not even the closest family friend could have known the answers. He passed these tests unerringly, and over 200 of l'Estere's residents were convinced that Clairvius had really been brought back from the dead.

Voodoo and Slavery

With its emphasis on communion with the spirit world, voodoo has often been viewed by Christian churches as a form of satanism. Its roots lie in the ancient religions of Africa. When the slave trade began in the 17th century, and Africans of many tribes were transported to the Americas, one of the justifications for their appalling treatment was that they were savages, virtually sub-human. The churches of the time conspired in this attitude, believing that these primitives needed to be converted from the corrupting influence of their satanic forms of worship.

Under threat of violence, even death, many slaves naturally agreed to convert to Roman Catholicism, but they also continued to practise their native religions. The two forms of worship were even sometimes amalgamated, a practice that persists in voodoo ceremonies to this day.

Raised from the Dead?

The creation of zombies represents the 'dark' aspect of a tradition that employs both black and white magic. French anthropologist Alfred Metraux made a study of the zombie phenomenon and was sceptical at first. One case in particular did impress him, however. It concerned a woman who, after death, had had her head twisted in order to fit her coffin; she had also received burns to the foot during burial. Prior to her death, she had rejected the advances of a suitor, and some years after her burial her zombie was seen working for the same man. She was positively identified by her brother, who was particularly struck by the fact that her neck was twisted and her foot burned.

Above: Voodoo developed from an amalgam of Roman Catholic ceremony and the native beliefs and rituals of slaves forced to convert to Christianity

Below: Felicia Mentor who died and was buried in 1907, was photographed in 1937. Is she a zombie?

Monsters

It is axiomatic that we fear the unknown, but we do not have to look as far afield as alien beings from outer space as a source of such fears. With all the technological strides that man has taken, with all the references to the shrinking world, the unknown lies much closer to home. For we share the planet with all manner of weird and wonderful unseen creatures. Some inhabit the remotest, most inhospitable areas of the earth's surface; others are much nearer neighbours.

The ocean depths continue to be huge repositories of mystery, a world where no light penetrates and where innumerable secrets await discovery. Even with the modern equipment which enables us to dive ever deeper, these mysteries are being uncovered but slowly. Only recently, for example, have we learned of the coelacanth, a fish which has inhabited the oceans for millions of years. Other awesome creatures of the deep include the megamouth shark and gulper eel.

One might have expected the inhabitants of inland waterways to be known quantities in comparison with their counterparts of the open seas. But there have been reports of strange creatures in over 300 lakes worldwide, none more famous than the monster that is said to lurk in the depths of Scotland's Loch Ness.

On land, it seems to be the larger members of the cat family which terrify yet fascinate us. Stories involving big cats abound, even in places where no such animals are supposed to exist in the wild. In 1983, for example, in the English town of South Molton, Devon, more than 200 animals were attacked over a five-month period by a creature dubbed 'the beast of Exmoor'. It was described as an enormous black cat, with a tail as long as its body, capable of running at speeds of 35mph and jumping hedges and gates with ease.

Some of the monsters of the planet remain for the time being in the realm of the unknown, the stuff of myth and legend, such as Loch Ness's celebrated occupant. Others, like megamouth and coelacanth, have taken their place in marine biology textbooks. As we learn about them, so their power to frighten diminishes. But, paradoxically, this knowledge provokes new fears; for the discovery of such large creatures previously unknown to science prompts an unnerving question: what else is out there?

Sea Serpents

For his book In the Wake of the Sea Serpents, Bernard Heuvelmans collected 587 separate reports concerning these mysterious creatures of the deep. Instead of trying to bracket all these sightings together, Heuvelmans created a number of categories to fit the great diversity in the descriptions. These included the many-finned, the super-otter, the many-humped, the super-eel and the merhorse. For the entry relating to the merhorse, he refers to a 1947 sighting by a Vancouver Island fisherman named George Saggers. Saggers described the creature as having 'two jet black eyes about three inches across and protruding from the head....It appeared to have some sort of mane, dark brown in colour.'

In 1966, British yachtsmen Chay Blyth and John Ridgeway rowed across the Atlantic. One night, unbeknown to Blyth, who was asleep, the pair had a perilously close encounter with a sea monster. Ridgeway describes what happened:

'I was shocked to full wakefulness by a swishing noise to starboard. I looked out over the water and suddenly saw the writhing, twisting shape of a great creature. It was outlined by the phosphorescence in the sea, as if a string of neon lights was hanging from it. It was an enormous size, some 35 feet or more, and it came towards me quite fast. I must have watched it for some 10 seconds; it headed straight at me and disappeared right beneath me. I stopped rowing. I was frozen with terror at this apparition. I forced myself to turn my head to look over to port side. I saw nothing. But after a brief pause I heard a most tremendous splash.

'I am not an imaginative man and I searched for a rational explanation. Chay and I had seen whales and sharks, dolphins and porpoises, flying fish, all kinds of sea creatures, but this monster of the night was none of these. I reluctantly had to believe there was only one thing it could have been - a sea serpent.'

The key objection to the whole sea serpent phenomenon is the lack of physical evidence: a carcass has never been found on shore. Heuvelmans has a simple explanation for this: 'All belong by nature to the category of animals least likely to be stranded, and quite capable of getting off the shore again if by misfortune they are.'

Lindorms

19th century Swedish scientist Gunnar Hylten-Cavallius also investigated the sea serpent phenomenon, but he concentrated his research on one creature in particular, the lindorm. In 1885, he published details of 48 accounts involving lindorms, of which the following is a summary:

'Usually the lindorm is about 10 feet long, but specimens of 18 or 20 feet have been observed. Its body is as thick as a man's thigh; its colour is black with a yellow-flamed belly. Old specimens wear on their necks an integument of long hair or scales, frequently likened to a horse's mane. It has a flat, round or square head, a divided tongue, and a mouth full of white, shining teeth. Its eyes are large and saucer-shaped, with a frightfully wild and sparkling stare. Its tail is short and stubby and the general shape of the creature is heavy and unwieldy.'

The Kraken

In 1861, the French gunboat Alecton struck a huge sea monster in the Atlantic Ocean. The crew managed to rope the creature but it escaped, leaving just a small piece of its tail. Scientists who heard the sailors' story and examined the physical evidence concluded that they had either been hallucinating or were mad.

What the crew saw was probably Architeuthis - the giant squid or octopus. The animal was described as about 24ft long, well within the compass of the Architeuthis. Specimens 60ft in length with a 90ft reach have been recorded, and its awesome appearance is thought to be behind the legend of the kraken.

Tales related by 19th and 20th century whalers have provided much of the evidence for these massive beasts. Whales in their death-throes have been known to vomit pieces of squid of huge proportions: tentacles the thickness of a man's chest, with suckers the size of saucers.

Above: Giant squid, which can be as long as 90ft are thought to be behind the legend of the kraken

Below: Sightings of sea serpents have been recorded for hundreds of years. When John Ridgeway rowed the Atlantic in 1966 with Chay Blyth he believed he saw a sea serpent

Above: The kraken came to symbolise the awesome potential of the sea to swallow man up

Below right: The creature which most fits the reported sightings of the Loch Ness Monster is a dinosaur - the zeugladon

More recently, divers and scientists have begun to discover that the giant squid has an intelligence and learning capacity, making it a fascinating creature to study as well as one to instil fear.

The Coelacanth

The coelacanth is a genuinely prehistoric fish which was discovered as recently as 1938. It lives in waters up to 1,300ft deep around the Comoro Islands, which lie off the coast of East Africa. Only a few coelacanths have ever been caught, and their rarity is giving cause for concern as they have been targeted by hunters. Although coelacanths can hardly be described as monsters of the deep - adults grow only to about 6ft in length - they can justly claim to be the ocean's dinosaurs. It is a sad irony that this rare creature seems in danger of becoming extinct little more than half a century after being discovered by man.

The Loch Ness Monster

Probably the most famous of all the mysterious creatures of the deep resides not in the open seas but in a Scottish lake. The search for the monster said to inhabit the waters of Loch Ness has gone on for a hundred years, although the phenomenon really caught the imagination in the 1930s, when many local people reported seeing a large elephant-grey animal with a long thin neck and a small head. The creature was even seen out of the water near the edge of the loch, but these land sightings stopped in the 1930s.

Those convinced of 'Nessie's' existence received a setback in 1994, when the most famous photograph of the monster - the 'surgeon's photo' of 1934 – was exposed as an elaborate hoax. That revelation does not mean, of course, that the monster does not exist; but if it does, it has certainly been sticking to the deep, dark waters of the Scottish loch. Conclusive proof of 'Nessie's' existence remains as elusive as ever.

Left: Operation Deepscan, in which Loch Ness was systematically scanned using sonar equipment

Below: Could the Loch Ness Monster be something as simple as a large sea cow?

Loch Ness Theories

With the abundance of eye-witness accounts, photographic and film evidence of the Loch Ness monster, not to mention a bank of scientific data, perhaps the question that ought to be asked is not 'Does it exist?' but 'What is it?' If the sceptics are to be believed, it is merely a piece of driftwood, a seabird, a large fish, an hallucination or a hoax.

If it is animate, but not a known species, such as a sea cow, large eel or elephant seal, then some theorists have suggested that the answer might lie in prehistory. The creature which fits the reported sightings most closely is a dinosaur thought to have been extinct for millions of years - the zeugladon, the appearance of which is something between a snake and a whale.

The search for the monster has become an increasingly hi-tech operation in recent years. In 1972, a team from the Academy of Applied Sciences, Massachusetts, took a series of photographs which were enhanced by computer. These seemed to show a flipper of about 4-6ft in length. Three years later, the same team published two more photographs, apparently showing the creature's torso and face. In 1987, 20 vessels took part in Operation Deepscan, in which the southern half of the loch was systematically scanned using sonar equipment. During the three-day operation, 10 'contacts' were recorded, signifying movements of large, unexplained objects. The source of these is still unknown, another chapter in the ongoing mystery surrounding Loch Ness's celebrated occupant.

Lake Okanagan's Ogopogo

The North American continent's most famous lake monster is probably Ogopogo, which reputedly inhabits the waters of British Columbia's Lake Okanagan. In 1974, a woman identified only as 'Mrs B Clark' described her brush with Ogopogo: 'It was travelling north, away from me. It did not seem to be in much of a rush and it swam very slowly....Five to ten feet behind the hump, about five to eight feet below the surface, I could see its tail. The tail was forked and horizontal, like a whale's, and it was four to six feet wide. As the hump submerged, the tail came to the surface until its tip poked above the water about a foot.'

A composite description based on 200 sightings provides more detail of Ogopogo's appearance: the creatures look most like a log, elongated, serpentine, no thickened body centrally; about 12 metres long, although a range of smaller sizes has been reported and a few larger, up to 20 metres.

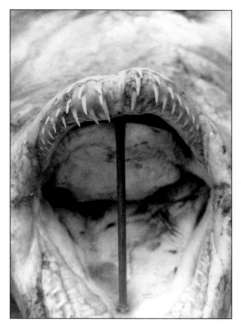

Above: Even the shark has the power to terrify us

Below right: Beast of Exmoor photographed in 1987

Lake Champlain's Champ

Stories of the monster of Lake Champlain, Vermont, go back over a hundred years. In those early days, an age when there was less interest in the natural world and conservation, this serpent-like creature became the target of many hunts. In the 1880s, one such party claimed to have found their prey and killed it: 'Only about 25 feet was between us and the infuriated serpent. (We) discharged each a shot at it, when the head was seen to turn, the immense body begin to curve....Streams of blood spurted from its head...At last, the excited party observed the serpent give one spasmodic twist of its immense length....never to rise more by its own exertions.'

Many believe the creature known as 'Champ' to be a plesiosaur - a prehistoric throwback thought to have become extinct about 65 million years ago. Perhaps the most convincing piece of evidence for the existence of 'Champ' is a photograph taken by Sandra Mansi when she was holidaying in the area in 1977. This clearly shows a huge animal with a humped body, long neck and small head. The photograph has been subjected to close scientific scrutiny, but no doubt so far has been cast on its authenticity.

Big Cats

The terrestrial equivalent of these monsters of the deep - creatures on land which terrify yet fascinate us - would appear to be the larger members of the cat family. Not surprisingly, many reports involving big cats occur in countries where they still roam free. In the United States, for example, Northern California is home to the puma, while panthers are known to live in Florida. On the other hand, sightings of big cats also occur in countries less readily associated with such animals. In the United Kingdom, where the wild cat is believed to have been extinct for more than 70 years, reports of creatures resembling pumas, leopards and panthers are increasing.

These animals are an even stranger notion in Australia, for they are not native to the continent at all. And yet even here reports are rife. A big cat was blamed for 340 livestock killings in 1957, although no conclusive proof was ever found. And rumours still circulate regularly of a Queensland tiger, described as having a striped body, lance-like claws and protruding fangs. But the beast which most commonly seems to fill this gap in the popular imagination is the Tasmanian tiger. This animal, which is in fact a marsupial cousin of the kangaroo, is thought by many to be extinct, yet sightings of this strange striped creature are still occasionally reported.

The Surrey Puma

In the mid-1960s, in Surrey, England, there were repeated sightings of a puma-like animal. Between September 1964 and August 1966, official records show 362 separate incidents, with many more sightings claimed but not

reported. In other words, this animal, belonging to a species that is secretive by nature, was seen, on average, once every other day for a period of two years.

Reports stretched as far afield as Cornwall and East Anglia, over an area of southern England of approximately 10,000 square miles. Many of the sightings were obviously mistaken - there were cases of the animal being seen simultaneously in places many miles apart. The police estimate that of the 362 sightings, 47 were 'solid', but that still means that this secretive creature was showing itself about once every fortnight over a two-year period.

Above: Big cats are the terrestrial equivalent to the monsters of the deep

Below: Many sightings of big cats are supported by evidence of attacked farm animals, mysterious claw marks and footprints

The 'Beast of Bodmin'

The beast which is said to roam Bodmin Moor in the south-west of England became the subject of a government report following numerous complaints by farmers that they were losing livestock to the animal. There were 77 reported incidents in an 18-month period up to June 1995. The Cornish Guardian described one woman's encounter with the 'Beast':

'The hunt goes on following the latest mysterious sighting of the "Beast of Bodmin Moor". Fresh enquiries have been launched following last week's incident in which a woman was reported to have been knocked unconscious by a large cat. Inspector Richard Kneebone, at Bodmin Police Station, said that wildlife experts were looking into the case of the 37-year-old woman who was reported to have been knocked to the ground and left unconscious by a large cat with a three-foot tail. Police are not revealing the identity of the woman or the exact location of the incident, but say the woman was attacked while out walking her dog. The report has rekindled speculation that there is at least one large cat on the moor.'

The Government published its findings on July 19, 1995, concluding that there was no verifiable evidence that a big cat existed, and that there was 'no significant threat' to farmers' livestock.

Five days later, three teenagers found a skull of what appeared to be a large cat in the River Fowey. It became a media sensation as an expert from London Zoo declared that the skull came from the panther family. But a second report by the Natural History Museum two weeks later told a different story. The skull was that of a young male leopard, possibly from India. Since its death, the animal had been kept 'either in a warm country or stored in a building where it was exposed to the attentions of tropical cockroaches.' The fact that the back of the cranium had been cut off was also seen as significant, for this technique is used when a leopard's head is mounted on a leopardskin rug. How the skull got into the river remains a mystery.

Big Cat Theories

Theories which seek to account for reports of big cats in areas where no such animals ought to exist fall into three distinct groups. The first is that they may be escaped zoo or circus animals which have managed to establish a population, perhaps by cross-breeding with other feline species. In the UK, where many sightings have occurred, the Dangerous Animals Act of 1976 led to some big cats, which had been kept as pets, being released into the wild by irresponsible owners. Evidence for populations of these beasts is scant, however.

The second, and less likely, possibility is that they are survivors of an ancient species thought to be extinct. The weakness of this case is that no forensic evidence of such animals - skulls, skeletons etc. - has ever been found. Moreover, both of these theories suffer from a general weakness that any large cat would need to eat large quantities of meat in order to survive. Up to now, however, none of the cases investigated has revealed evidence of an animal taking deer, sheep or cattle in the amounts that would be expected.

The third theory focuses on the simple notion of misidentification - that the animals featuring in 'big cat' reports are nothing more than large examples of the domestic variety. Where cases involve attacks on livestock, the perpetrator could be a different animal altogether, a dog, for instance.

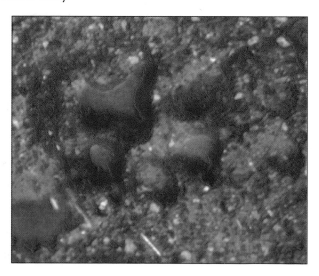

Wild Things

The Yeti In 1960, Sir Edmund Hillary returned from a trip to the foothills of Mount Everest with what was reported to be the scalp of a yeti. The scalp, which had been borrowed from a monastery, was later shown to be that of a goat, which meant that there remained - and still remains - scant physical evidence of this, the most famous of the BHMs - Big Hairy Monsters.

Lack of tangible proof there may be, but there is the evidence of numerous first-hand experiences, which have certainly convinced the individuals concerned of the existence of the yeti, or 'abominable snowman'. For this creature has inspired more expeditions than any other, and descriptions of its physical appearance and the footprints it leaves have filtered back from the Himalayan Mountains since 1832.

To many in the West, the combination of inhospitable mountainous terrain and a wild, unidentified creature might sound both geographically and conceptually remote; but those who live on the doorstep certainly take a different view. The Sherpa people not only believe that the yeti exists, but they even differentiate between three types of creature: the 'DzuTeh', standing about 7 or 8ft tall; the 'Meh-Teh, which is somewhat smaller, between 5 and 6ft; and the 'Yeh-Teh' (from which the word 'yeti' is derived), which is smaller still.

Edward Cronin, a member of the 1972 Arun Valley Wildlife Expedition, has put together a generalised description of the man-beast: 'Its body is stocky, apelike in shape, with a distinctly human quality to it, in contrast to that of a bear. It stands 5-6ft tall and is covered with short, coarse hair, reddish-brown to black in colour, sometimes with white patches on the chest. The hair is longest on the shoulders. The face is robust, the teeth are quite large - though fangs are not present - and the mouth is wide. The shape of the head is conical with a pointed crown. The arms are long, reaching almost to the knees. The shoulders are heavy and hunched. There is no tail.'

Above: A Bigfoot footprint measured against a man's

'Like a Human Being'

The British photographer N A Tombazi encountered a mysterious creature during an expedition to the Himalayas in 1925. Tombazi, who was also a member of the Royal Geographical Society, describes what he saw: 'The intense glare and brightness of the snow prevented me from seeing anything for the first few seconds; but I soon spotted the "object" referred to, about two or three hundred yards away down the valley to the east of our camp. Unquestionably, the figure in outline was exactly like a human being, walking upright and stopping occasionally to uproot or pull at some dwarf rhododendron bushes. It showed up dark against the snow and, as far as I could make out, wore no clothes. Within the next minute or so it had moved into some thick scrub and was lost to view.'

'A Black Apelike Shape'

In 1970, the world-renowned climber Don Whillans gave an eyewitness account of a yeti he had seen on Annapurna: '...this creature, which looked to me in its movements apelike, sort of bounded along in a funny gait towards what obviously, in a few weeks' time when the snow had gone, would be a clump of trees....I got the binoculars out and all I could make out was a black apelike shape. Then, quite suddenly, it was almost as if it realised it was being watched, it shot across the whole slope of the mountain. It must have travelled half a mile before it disappeared into the shadow by some rocks....And the actual tracks that I saw had very peculiar indentations between the actual footprint (which didn't strike me until about 12 months later, when I was looking at a picture of a gorilla in a normal animal book) that could well be the knuckle marks of this creature, between the actual footprints...'

Above: Artist's impression of the Abominable Snowman or Yeti

The Wooldridge Photographs

Briton Anthony Wooldridge was on a charity run through the Himalayas when he observed a yeti-like creature. He managed to capture this shape on film but it was not to prove the decisive breakthrough that was first thought. Wooldridge himself takes up the story: 'Standing behind a shrub was a large, erect shape, perhaps two metres tall. Convinced that whatever it was would disappear quickly, I took several photographs rapidly and then moved up about 50 metres nearer to a rocky outcrop....It was difficult to restrain my excitement as I came to the realisation that the only animal I could think of which remotely resembled this one in front of me was the yeti....its head was large and squarish, and the whole body appeared to be covered in dark hair, although the upper arm was a slightly lighter colour. The creature was amazingly good at remaining motionless.'

Below: Paul Freeman with cast of what is now believed to be a hoax Bigfoot footprint

Wooldridge's photographs attracted worldwide media and scientific attention, but it was a bubble that was quickly burst. Investigation of the site revealed an outcrop of rock which was very yeti-like in shape, and Wooldridge accepted his error, saying: 'I appear to have jumped to a false conclusion. This is obviously very disappointing.'

Tracks in the Snow

If the yeti itself is still proving to be camera-shy, at least, some believe, we have photographs of the tracks it leaves behind. Footprints would appear to remain the most tangible evidence of the creature's existence, although even these do not go unchallenged.

Many pictures have been taken which are claimed to show the yeti's footprints, notably those from F S Smythe's 1937 expedition, and the now world-famous photograph taken by Eric Shipton on the Menlung glacier in 1951. Another member of that expedition, Michael Ward, described the prints thus: 'They were really well defined....we could see the toes of all the feet....there was absolutely no blurring round the edges.' Measurements taken showed the prints to be 13 inches long and 8 inches wide.

Sceptics have offered more prosaic explanations of these markings in the snow. They are the tracks of other animals, such as snow leopards or bears, it is claimed; or even the impressions left by Buddhist lamas who walk barefoot in the snow. The prodigious size of many of the prints could be due to the melting of the snow since the tracks were first made.

Above: The Himalayas is the home of the legend of the Yeti but (inset) many countries and cultures have their own 'big hairy monster' legends

Below: Photograph of footprints on Annapurna, taken by climber Don Whillans who believes they may be those of a Yeti

Despite this note of scepticism, such evidence that there is would seem powerful enough to render the yeti more than a creature of myth; but the search for irrefutable proof will doubtless go on.

Bigfoot

The American continent boasts its own version of the yeti. When the first European settlers arrived in California, they were told by native Indians about a strange man-beast which lived in the mountains. The legend lives on to this day, the creature being known as Bigfoot in the United States and Sasquatch in Canada.

The evidence for Bigfoot, like the yeti, is mixed. There have been thousands of sightings, and innumerable casts of footprints have been taken. Bigfoot has also been photographed and, even more impressively, captured on film. It was in 1967 that Roger Patterson and Bob Gimlin shot the only known footage of one of these mysterious creatures. But once again, the sceptics have ammunition for their argument too. For all the sightings and photographic material, there is a distinct lack of hard physical evidence. It is difficult to believe that in a country as highly populated as America Bigfoot should have evaded capture for so long, or at the very least that a skeleton should not have been found.

The Patterson Footage

Roger Patterson was an ex-rodeo rider who had been scouring the Pacific Northwest woods in search of Bigfoot for some time before the famous encounter of 1967. He had even written a book on the subject, published in 1966, but it was the unique film shot on October 20, 1967, at Bluff Creek, Northern California, for which he is remembered.

The first 'independent' investigator to arrive on the scene was Bob Titmus, who found tracks which were consistent with the movement of the beast in the film. He made plaster casts of ten of them. The way in which the creature moved was carefully scrutinised to try and determine whether it was consistent with a human or non-human physique. But in order to ascertain this it was necessary to know whether the film was shot at 16 or 24 frames per second; Patterson was unable to remember.

The sensational film quickly became engulfed in controversy. The fact that Patterson was struggling financially at the time led many to accuse him of an elaborate hoax. Having spent a long time searching for Bigfoot, and written a book on the subject, he would certainly have been aware of the potential gains to be had by being the first person to capture it on film. But if the Patterson film was a hoax, it was one which its perpetrator took to his grave. Patterson never wavered from his story, right up until his death in 1972; and Bob Gimlin also continued to maintain that the film was genuine.

The Case of Paul Freeman

The biggest case since the mystery surrounding the Patterson film occurred in 1982 and centred on an alleged sighting by Paul Freeman. Freeman, a part-time employee in the US Forest Service, was driving through the mountains of the Umatilla National Forest in June of that year, when he saw some elk and decided to follow them on foot. It was at that point that Freeman claims he was confronted by an 8-foot-tall creature. There was a stand-off, the two staring at each other for some moments, after which both fled. Later, Freeman returned with colleagues to where the incident was supposed to have taken place, and 21 footprints were found, each measuring 14 inches long and 7 inches wide. Photographs of the prints were taken and casts were made.

Over a period of weeks, further prints were discovered in the surrounding area. Freeman came under the media spotlight, and the footprints themselves were subjected to even greater scrutiny. Expert opinion on them was divided. Some researchers were impressed, while others felt the markings were too regular, too perfect.

Doubts also surfaced about Freeman's credibility. He resigned from his post, citing the stress of the experience, then subsequently claimed further sightings and produced a photograph of an alleged Bigfoot. But he also later admitted that he had faked the footprints, and most experts now believe Freeman's story to have been an impressive hoax.

Above: Artist's impression of the Chinese Wildman

Below: The Australian big hairy monster is known as the Yowie

The Chinese Wildman

Stories of BHMs exist in virtually all parts of the world, but are particularly prevalent in Eastern countries which have large areas of jungle. There is the Malaysian 'wildman', or kaki besar as it is known to the local people; the Sumatran apeman, first spotted in 1916 by a Dutch scientist; and in Borneo and Pakistan, too, reports of large hirsute bipeds are legion. But perhaps the best-known creature of this ilk, and the one for which the most documentary evidence exists, is the wildman of China.

The people of southern China have spoken of the wildman, or 'yeren', for centuries. Anthropologist Zhou Guoxing of the Beijing Natural History Museum has spent 10 years studying the creature also known as the 'man-bear', the 'hill-ghost' and the 'monster of the mountains'. His researches have led him to compile the following picture of the wildman: 'There appear to be two types of yeren: a larger one of about two metres in height, and a smaller one, about one metre in height. Also, there are two types of footprint: one is large, 30-40cm, remarkably similar to that of man, with the four small toes held together and the largest one pointing slightly outwards; the other type is smaller, about 20cm, and more similar to the footprint of an ape or monkey, with the largest toe evidently pointing outwards.'

Fairies

Sprites, elves, gnomes, trolls: just some of the inhabitants of the fairy realm which most people simply associate with childhood tales. Small, cheeky, helpful, occasionally threatening, these are the weird and wonderful characters occupying a fantasy landscape sustained, it is commonly thought, only by the innocence of those early years. For most people the maturing process itself slowly but comprehensively dispels all belief in the fairy world; but for some adulthood merely reinforces these beliefs and turns them into conviction.

If anything, this is a trend which is becoming more widespread. This is because fairy lore is rooted in the Gaelic and Celtic traditions, and has strong links with nature spirits. As interest in New Age ideas and environmental issues has burgeoned in recent years, so these traditions have been experiencing something of a revival.

Certain seers and psychics claim to have special knowledge of the fairy realm and the different classes of beings which inhabit it. These beings are often associated with particular elements, leading to the identification of the so-called 'elemental' spirits: gnomes, sylphs, salamanders and undines, the spirits of earth, air, fire and water respectively. In the modern era, reports involving fairies tend to centre on nature spirits, the forces behind the creation of trees, flowers and even animals. These ideas are reminiscent of what Plato called 'ideal forms'.

Historical records show how belief in fairies has been an accepted part of many cultures, and this has manifested itself in many ways. In the Middle Ages, for example, it was widely thought that fairies were responsible for replacing pretty babies with uglier offspring, or 'changelings'. Ugly or unfit babies believed to be changelings would be left to die.

Above: 13 year-old Frances Griffiths faked fairy photographs in 1917 in order to convince her father that she had not been lying when she said she had got wet when playing with fairies at a nearby pond. Even as an old woman she maintained she was telling the truth

Left: The Findhorn community in Scotland put its success in growing crops down to their 'connection' with the spirits responsible for the growth of plants - the 'devas'

Below: The brothers Jacob and William Grimm collected many folk or fairy tales

Even today, fairy lore is widely respected in some countries, particularly those where the Celtic tradition is strong. In Iceland, for example, the fairy-faith has survived relatively intact. A recent survey suggested that 55 per cent of people regarded the existence of elves as certain, probable or possible; only 10 per cent thought the notion preposterous. Icelanders certainly feel there is a need to accommodate their nature spirits, and this manifests itself when new buildings or roads are constructed. With echoes of the Chinese practice of Feng Shui, psychics are called in to negotiate with the fairy realm and ensure that these projects take a harmonious course.

The suggestion that a fairy realm exists outside children's storybooks will no doubt provoke scorn and derision in many; but more surprising, perhaps, is the large and growing number of people who subscribe precisely to that view.

Celtic Fairies

One of the most famous works on the subject of fairy lore, including many detailed first-hand experiences, was compiled in the early 20th century by the American scholar W Y Evans Wentz. Here, he quotes an incident which occurred in Ireland:

'I have never seen a man fairy nor a woman fairy, but my mother saw a troop of them. She herself and the other maidens of the townland were once out....They were milking cows in the evening gloaming, when they observed a flock of fairies reeling and setting upon the green plain in front of the knoll. And, oh King! but it was they the fairies themselves that had the right to the dancing, and not the children of men! Bell helmets of blue silk covered their heads, and garments of green satin covered their bodies, and sandals of yellow membrane covered their feet. Their heavy brown hair was streaming down their waist, and its lustre was of the fair golden sun of summer. Their skin was as white as the swan of the wave, and their voice was as melodious as the mavis of the wood, and they themselves were as beauteous of feature and as lithe of form as a picture, while their step was as light and stately and their minds as sportive as the little red hind of the hill.'

The Secret Commonwealth

Robert Kirk was a rare individual: an Episcopalian minister from the highlands of Scotland who was convinced that fairy folk were real. In his famous work of 1691, The Secret Commonwealth, Kirk set down the fairy lore of his region. He described fairies as a 'middle nature between man and angel', and whose physical appearance was 'somewhat of the nature of a condensed cloud, and best seen in twilight. These bodies are so pliable through the subtlety of the spirits that agitate them, that they can appear or disappear at pleasure.'

Legend has it that Robert Kirk did not die, but passed into the fairy realm himself at a hill in Aberfoyle which still bears his name. It is said that this extraordinary minister remains to this day available to any who seek him out.

An 18th Century Journal

Author and teacher Ted Andrews claims that we all have the ability to make contact with the fairy realm. He maintains that he has always been aware of the fairy people and that there has never been a time when they were not with him.

A journal dating from the 18th century elaborates on the theme of establishing contact with the 'People of Light':

'There are many classes or orders of the People of Light....Some are well known to mortal men and women, others are invisible and hidden away....It is mainly of these hidden orders that I shall treat here....there is a more secret art by which the hidden orders are found and this shall be the core....of my account. This art I learned....from an aged woman in Devonshire, and some Irish-Scottish seers in Virginia in the Colonies. Thereafter it is given to converse and learn direct with the People in their own manner, according to their realm. By this deep art one may reach

Above: Do we all have the ability to make contact with the fairy realm?

Below: Fairies dancing around a fairy stone. For the psychic Edgar Cayce fairies were his playmates

through pools, enter hills and trees, meld with stones, and come at last to the halls of the People of Light, who are within the body of the Land. And they may also come to you, for the threshold once opened may be crossed in either direction. You may also see with their eyes and they likewise shall see with yours for mutual learning.'

Cayce's Playmates

Edgar Cayce was one of the 20th century's most famous psychics. He was known as 'the Sleeping Prophet', for in a career spanning 45 years the 14,000 psychic 'readings' he gave were dictated while he was in a hypnotised state. Many of these readings were for people experiencing health problems, and Cayce's record in providing diagnoses was extremely impressive. At the time of his death, in 1945, he had a waiting list of over two years.

Edgar Cayce's psychic talents first revealed themselves in early childhood, when he would play in his garden with a host of 'imaginary' friends. These 'nature playmates', as his mother called them, came to be a secret between the two of them after Cayce was ridiculed by his school friends. It was many years later that Cayce read about the fairy realm, and thereafter he was convinced that this was the true source of his childhood experiences.

Nature Spirits

While Edgar Cayce was seeking to reinterpret his early experiences in the light of knowledge gained much later, others have recognised particular natural forces at work more immediately and from an adult perspective. The cases of Dorothy Maclean and Machaelle Small Wright also differ in the respect that they feature nature spirits rather than playmates; an overarching power rather than a physical embodiment.

Dorothy Maclean, who was also a trained psychic, was a member of a small community on the northeast coast of Scotland which became famous for growing vegetables of a prodigious size, despite the poor quality of the soil. The group who tended the garden at Findhorn Caravan Park put their extraordinary success down to their 'connection' to the nature spirits responsible for the growth of plants - the 'devas'.

Dorothy Maclean claimed she was able to receive messages from the devas of different plants, and these were intended not just for the practicalities of work in the garden, but for general enlightenment too. One of the early messages came from the deva of the golden lily:

'The theory of evolution that puts man at the apex of life on earth is only correct when viewed from certain angles. It leaves out the fact that God, universal consciousness, is working out the forms of life. For example, according to generally accepted regulations, I am a lowly lily, unable to be aware of most things and certainly not able to talk with you. But somehow, somewhere is the intelligence that made us fair and continues to do so, just as somehow, somewhere is the intelligence that produced your intricate physical body.'

Machaelle Small Wright has not described such direct contact in tending her garden in Virginia, but she is an equally strong advocate of the effects nature spirits can produce:

'....most people think of nature spirits in terms of elves, gnomes, fairies...the "little people" of the woods. I experience nature spirits as swirling spheres of light energy. I have walked through the woods with one of these "balls of energy" moving beside me and, when necessary, I've moved around a tree while the ball of energy continued to move straight through the tree, coming out the other side....I was not familiar with or comfortable with the concept of fairies, elves and gnomes. Having read horse books during my childhood, I simply didn't have a background steeped in fairy tales and folklore. So....when the nature spirits chose to be visible, they chose a context with which I was comfortable - energy. Had I seen an elf or a gnome come toward me, I definitely would have checked into a rubber room.'

Psychologists such as Bruno Bettelheim have stressed the value of fairy tales as a rich source of meaningful myth, an important vehicle for the healthy development of the human psyche. Instinctively, parents have recognised this too, and there is a long tradition of these tales forming part of the child-rearing process. But is there any more to it than that? Science would consider those who take the concept of the fairy realm any further to be victims of hallucination or self-delusion; but there have been many examples of individuals, rational to all appearances, whose belief has indeed gone further. The fairy realm might present a rich seam to the sceptic, but those who are advocates of its existence and its powers are more numerous than might have been imagined.

Above: Fairies are often closely associated with nature spirits

Below: The Nereids of classical Greek mythology are akin to nature spirits or fairies

Angels

'What idea is more beguiling than the notion of lightsome spirits, free of time and space and human weakness, hovering between us and all harm? (It) is to allow the universe to be at once mysterious and benign. Even people who refuse to believe in them may long to be proved wrong.'

This comment, by Time magazine correspondent Nancy Gibbs, followed a 1993 report which found that 69 per cent of American adults believe in angels. This figure might seem astonishingly high, but that is at least in part due to the breadth with which angels were defined and the range of experience which people directly associated with this phenomenon. If a narrower, more stereotyped definition had been taken - fluttering wings, bright lights and a heavenly voice - the survey's findings would doubtless have been rather different.

Many of the interviewees were not speaking of angels as an abstract, ethereal concept, nor in terms of how they were portrayed in early religious writings; rather, concrete experiences were described, incidents in which the people concerned were convinced that angels had interceded. One such person, Joan Wester Anderson, started compiling a collection of modern accounts of angels after she was convinced that one was responsible for saving her son's life. The son's car had broken down in freezing conditions, when a mysterious being in a truck appeared and towed the car to his mother's house. When the truck drove away, no tracks were left in the snow.

This incident has many of the characteristics found in latter-day reports of angels. The appearance usually occurs at a time of great stress or need, perhaps in response to a prayer; the interventions seem to be based on a benevolent concern for individuals in difficulty, as opposed to crises of national or global magnitude; and for those who believe they have witnessed the benign power of an angel at first hand, it is invariably a life-changing experience.

Above: A 1993 report found that 69 per cent of American adults believe in angels

Guardian Car Mechanics?

From early times, the Roman Catholic church taught that every human is possessed of an angel who guides and guards the individual soul. The great medieval mystic Bernard of Clairvaux gave this advice to his monks on the subject: 'In whatever place you may be, in whatever secret recess you may hide, think of your Guardian Angel....If we truly love our Guardian Angel, we cannot fail to have boundless confidence in his powerful intercession with God and firm faith in his willingness to help us...'

Marie Utterman had reason to give thanks for a most unlikely form of assistance, at a time when it proved to be most desperately needed. Marie had been feeling particularly anxious one morning about her daughter, who was due to give birth in a few weeks' time. There was no reply when she tried to telephone her daughter, but she decided to pay a visit anyway.

On the journey, her car engine cut out and she was forced to pull over to the side of the road. With that same feeling of apprehension, she prayed for help that the car would restart. Just then, a white van pulled up and three young men jumped out. They were dressed all in white and resembled ambulance personnel. Without asking what was wrong they simply said that they would try to get the car going. After five minutes of careful, almost surgeon-like work on the engine, one of them tried the ignition and it started perfectly. Marie was profuse in her thanks and offered the men payment, but they refused, saying it was their job. Only then did Marie notice that their pristine white clothes bore no marks of having been in contact with a car engine - they were still spotlessly clean. One of the men then suggested that Marie ought to get on her way to see her daughter. They got into their van and it sped out of sight - quite literally; for Marie stated that the vehicle disappeared from view long before it reached the horizon.

Marie completed her journey without incident, but when she arrived, it was to find her daughter sitting in a pool of blood. She had haemorrhaged and her blood pressure was dangerously low. Neither mother nor child suffered any ill effects from the experience, a happy outcome which Marie Utterman believed was entirely down to her guardian angel mechanics.

Saved from the Blast

In 1941, the German blitzkrieg on British cities was at its height, with London on the receiving end of some of the most intensive night-time bombardments. In one two-month period that year, the capital was bombed on 60 consecutive nights.

Donovan and Doris Cox, who lived in London at the time, had already sent their son away to school, but realised that they themselves were in constant danger. One night, Donovan told his wife that they were going to be disturbed, but that there was

Above: 14th and 15th century paintings first portrayed angels with musical instruments, establishing a link between the angelic realm and music

Below left: Many people who report seeing angels say that the angel appeared in response to a prayer

Below right: The Roman Catholic church taught that every human is possessed of an angel who guides and guards the individual soul

Right and far right: There are many reports of guardian angels protecting people from harm

Opposite page: The Angel of the Lord destroys the wicked (Frank C Papé)

Below: Angels appear in Christian, Jewish and Islamic faiths, but winged deities like this Egyptian figure exist in many beliefs and cultures

nothing to fear. Asked how he could be so sure, Donovan replied: 'I can see an angel over our house protecting us.' He described how he had seen a huge angelic figure floating over their property in a horizontal position.

The Coxes were indeed awoken that night, by a terrific explosion above their house. Doors were blown open and a pressure wave threatened to shatter the windows, but nothing was damaged. When the warden arrived on the scene the following morning, he told them that the explosion had been caused by a parachute bomb. These bombs normally exploded on impact with the ground, with devastating effects. But on this occasion, the bomb had detonated in mid-air, the warden himself having witnessed the explosion directly above the Coxes' house. Donovan Cox did not put this extremely unusual occurrence down to good fortune: he was certain in his own mind the vision he had seen had afforded them protection that night.

Artists and Angels Manifestations of angels are not solely associated with times of crisis, however. Several famous artists have cited angels as a source of inspiration for their creative output. Michelangelo - whose name means 'the angel Michael' - said he was able to see angels trapped in the stone he was working from. William Blake, who had visions of spiritual beings throughout his life, went even further, attributing his artistic talent itself to an angel - he claimed that one had taught him to paint when he was a young child. And when he portrayed angels in his celebrated engravings, he said that the visions had been given to him by the angels themselves.

A more recent example of this phenomenon has been described by the musician Carlos Santana. He has spoken of how his work has been influenced and inspired by angels, and of one experience in particular which had an enduring effect on him. It concerned the singer Julio Iglesias, and the time when he wanted permission to record a version of one of Santana's songs, Europa. Iglesias also wanted Santana to play on the record, but the latter, feeling that there would be a vast difference in their musical approaches, declined the invitation. That same evening Santana was playing tennis, when an extraordinary occurrence caused him to change his mind. As he threw the ball into the air to serve, it disappeared. A voice then asked him: 'Who gave you this song?' Santana had already recognised that the true provenance of the song rested with the angels, and asked what he was to do. 'I want you to record the song with Julio,' the voice replied, 'and all the money that you get from it, I want you to pledge it to the children of Tijuana. You don't need it.'

Santana recorded the song with Iglesias, and he later described the whole experience as having changed his life: 'To me, it is all a lesson in humility. I have to be wise and follow the voice. It has got me this far.'

Above left: Joan of Arc heard the voice of Archangel Michael

Above right: Still from the film 'It's a Wonderful Life' which features a guardian angel

Opposite page: Gustave Dové's view of paradise

Below: The Angels of Mons inspired Allied troops to victory

Joan of Arc

Of all the reported occasions when angels have intervened with dramatic effect, two famously stand out: the story of how an illiterate young peasant girl was inspired to lead her country against an invading force in the 15th century; and events that occurred during the Battle of Mons in the First World War.

Joan of Arc began hearing voices and seeing bright lights at the age of 13. She soon realised that the voice was that of Archangel Michael, and that the guidance and instruction she was being given was for a special purpose. At the time, France and England were at war, and the invading forces were threatening to take the French throne. The messages that Joan received inspired her to encourage her compatriots in their struggle. She led the French army to victory in many battles while still just 17 years old herself, and, with victory assured, took her soldiers to Rheims to see the new king, Charles, crowned. At the coronation ceremony she and 300 others present witnessed an angel carry a crown to the king.

When she was later captured by the English-supporting Duke of Burgundy, King Charles abandoned her to her fate. The voices which had so inspired her were used against her at her trial, and she was declared a witch. She was condemned to burn at the stake, and died aged 19.

The Angels of Mons

Reports of how angels influenced the Battle of Mons, in 1914, were even more sensational. For instead of merely acting as a source of inspiration, galvanising beleaguered soldiers to victory, an army of angels was actually seen on the Belgian battlefield. The phenomenon occurred when the French and British forces were in danger of being overwhelmed by the German army. A host of white-clad figures was seen, after which events turned in the Allies' favour.

Accounts of these 'war angels' circulated among troops on all sides. One German soldier described how his army had been forced to retreat when a host of figures appeared dressed all in white. They had been armed with bows and arrows and led by an officer on a white horse. German soldiers had fired on the officer without effect. Others spoke of seeing the figures of Joan of Arc, St George - the patron saint of England - and St Michael the Archangel. A number of British soldiers described how they had watched for half an hour as the three huge celestial figures hovered in the sky, St Michael apparently protecting them with outstretched wings.

Chapter Six

Ghosts and Spirits

Avaunt! and quit my sight! let the earth hide thee!
Thy bones are marrowless, thy blood is cold;
Thou hast no speculation in those eyes
Which thou dost glare with!

Thus speaks Macbeth when he is confronted by what is probably the commonest of paranormal experiences. In Macbeth's case, of course, the terror he feels when confronted by the ghost of Banquo is self-inflicted: it is he who has arranged Banquo's murder and his past is returning to haunt him.

But the commission of such heinous acts is not a prerequisite for spectral appearances. Nor does one have to seek out the archetypal haunted house. In fact, the very diversity to be found in ghostly encounters is in itself amazing. Ghosts have been seen by day and by night, within buildings and on the open road; they have manifested themselves in a host of different ways, from shadowy, floating figures to solid human form; witnesses have perceived them through a range of senses: sight, hearing, touch - even smell; some have been described as benign, others malicious; some interact with the living, others do not.

With shades of Dickens's A Christmas Carol, ghosts of past and future have even been seen. In February 1907, a police officer on duty at the royal palace of Hampton Court, near London, reported seeing an extraordinary procession. A dozen men and women, dressed in a style of a bygone age, walked past him, then disappeared. This bizarre occurrence, which is by no means an isolated example, is still registered in the incident book at the local police station.

Of course, ghosts can inflate bank balances as well as induce terror, and there have been many instances where an apparition has been found to have a more corporeal origin. But the number of reported incidents is so vast that even a small percentage would represent a significant body of evidence.

Sceptics might put the whole phenomenon down to susceptible minds and fertile imaginations; surely, ghosts can have no place in a world ruled by science and logic? But in Norway, hardly a primitive backwater, the commonest ghostly encounter of modern times - the phantom hitchhiker - has been accommodated in the highway code. In that country there is one notorious phantom which, it is believed, will cause any driver who gives her a lift to have a terrible accident. This problem is taken so seriously that warning signs have been put up: a red triangle containing a picture of a ghost!

Haunts

Ghostly manifestations can occur anywhere and at any time, but they do seem to be more frequent at certain locations. Haunted buildings themselves can be divided into two categories: those where the spectral presence is incidental, and those where the ghost has a specific association with its past history. In the latter case, there is often a tale to be told involving all manner of dark deeds.

Of course, to hotels, pubs, stately homes and the like, a resident ghost and a chilling tale are a marketing dream, and the spectral pudding is doubtless over-egged by those with an interest in perpetuating the idea that a place is haunted. On the other hand, the owner of the inn which is said to contain the most haunted room in England might have reason to feel that his ghostly incumbent is doing too good a job. For in a field notorious for its lack of hard evidence, John Humphries, of the Ancient Ram Inn in Gloucestershire, can point to something quite tangible - a file of letters all saying the same thing: 'I booked for two weeks, but after what I saw, I had to leave after two days.'

Above: At Newby church in England a ghost with a sinister skull-like face appears

England's Most Haunted House

In the 1930s, Borley Rectory in the south of England gained notoriety as one of the world's most haunted houses. It was unusual in the respect that there was no association with any dark events of the past: the Rectory had only just been built when the ghostly goings-on began. Apparitions of a nun and headless men were seen; a phantom coach and horses would drive past outside; doors would lock and unlock themselves; bells would mysteriously ring and objects would fly through the air.

By the mid-1930s, not surprisingly, no one wanted to live at the Rectory, except, that is, for Harry Price. Price was a famous ghost-hunter, and he moved into the house with a team of investigators. He wrote extensively about the strange occurrences that went on at Borley Rectory, although suspicion surrounds his version of events. On one occasion, for example, he spoke of a poltergeist throwing stones, only for a reporter to discover that his pockets were full of pebbles.

Borley Rectory did not survive long enough for many other investigations to take place. It burnt down a few years later, with the ghostly nun seen at one of the windows at the height of the conflagration.

Above: The world's most haunted house, Borley Rectory, England

Below: The Ancient Ram Inn in Gloucestershire is said to have the most haunted room in England

The dubious honour of being the single most haunted room in England today is thought to go to a chamber in the Ancient Ram Inn, at Wotton-under-Edge, in Gloucestershire. It is considered to be a great challenge to spend even one night in The Bishop's Room. One guest woke up to see 'a man in an old-fashioned nightgown...just standing there. I am not a man who is scared or spooked, so what I did was to walk towards him. I got to within about five feet of him - and then I got the shock of my life. He took a step towards me. I ducked between the two beds. At this point the man disappeared.'

Researcher Mike Lewis decided to investigate, and went armed with a camcorder which had a built-in light. Every time he tried to film inside the Bishop's Room the light failed, coming back on as soon as he stepped outside.

The Ghostly Tower

The Tower of London could lay claim to being the world's most haunted building today. It is thought to contain a greater variety of ghostly manifestations than any other building, which is not surprising, perhaps, considering its long and bloody history.

King Henry VIII's second wife, Anne Boleyn, was confined in the Tower before being executed in 1536. Her ghost has been seen there on many occasions, and, it is said, was once even challenged by a sentry. The incident occurred outside the part of the Tower called the Queen's House, and the sentry in question challenged and then bayoneted a figure which appeared veiled in a mist. Two witnesses said that it was the ghost of Anne Boleyn.

Lady Jane Grey was queen of England for just nine days in the summer of 1553, before being arrested and imprisoned in the Tower of London. She and her husband were executed on February 12, 1554. On that same date in 1957, two guardsmen reported seeing a likeness of the tragic queen on the battlements.

The great English navigator Sir Walter Raleigh was another who ended up in the Tower after his star waned. He became a public attraction as he walked along the battlements while awaiting execution. That came in 1618, and since then, his ghost has often been seen on 'Raleigh's Walk' - along those same battlements where he strolled while awaiting his fate. In 1983, a Yeoman of the Guard heard the handle of a door rattling in the Byward Tower. At first he thought it was the wind, but on looking through the glass panel, he saw a solid figure staring back at him. He was convinced that the figure was Sir Walter Raleigh.

The Tower has also been used to house prisoners in more recent times. During World War II, several spies and traitors were executed by firing squad there. A ghostly reminder of that period has been seen, once again by a Yeoman of the Guard. A figure, head bowed and dressed in a drab, grey utility suit of the 1940s, appeared before one of the guardsmen near the very spot where the executions were carried out.

Dover Castle

Dover Castle stands on the famous white cliffs and looks out on the English Channel. Underneath the building there is a mysterious network of tunnels only recently opened to the public. All manner of ghosts have been reported in the precincts of the castle, but it was one in particular - an apparition of a drummer boy - which prompted ghost-hunter Robin Laurence to organise a series of vigils. Laurence has recorded many sightings of ghostly figures from the time of the English Civil War, including a Cavalier infantry officer and a pikeman. During one of the ghost-hunting sessions, in October 1991, the team managed to capture one strange incident on video: a heavy door shaking violently on its hinges. No physical explanation for the door's movement could be found.

Terrible Secrets

Glamis Castle, in Tayside, Scotland, boasts many ghosts. Two of them are heard rather than seen - the sound of men gambling with dice. Legend has it that the two men would not stop playing on the Sabbath day, and the devil ordered that they should go on for eternity. Then there is the spectral 'Grey Lady' - Lady Janet Douglas, who was burnt at the stake for witchcraft almost 500 years ago.

But Glamis Castle's most famous mystery centres on a terrible secret said to be known only to the head of the Strathmore family. It is believed that the secret is passed on from father to son when the latter comes of age. Some have speculated that it concerns the so-called 'Monster of Glamis', a son who was born deformed, having tiny limbs and no neck. According to the story, the son was kept hidden in a secret room for the whole of his life. Two pieces of evidence are put forward in support of this theory. In one of the castle's rooms there is a picture which shows a young man with a slight deformity. If he lies at the heart of the secret of Glamis, then what of the chamber where he was kept hidden all his life? Some say that more windows are visible from outside the castle than inside, and this proves the existence of the secret room where the son was locked away.

Undying Anger

Whaley House, in San Diego, California, was built in 1857 on the site where a gruesome execution took place. A man known as 'Yankee Jim' had been hanged there for some trifling offence, but the gallows had not been built properly and he suffered an agonising death, kicking and struggling on the end of the rope for an inordinate length of time.

The children of the original owners of the house, Thomas and Anna Eloise Whaley, are said to have heard ghostly footsteps around the place. After the last of the Whaley family died in 1953, the house was opened to the public. Since then, there have been numerous reports of apparitions, strange noises and poltergeist activity. One visitor gave the following description of a ghostly encounter: '....a small figure of a woman...she is wearing a long full skirt reaching to the floor....she has a kind of cap on her head, dark hair and eyes...I get the impression we are sort of invading her privacy.'

Mediums have claimed that the house contains many ghosts, but only two have been identified: Anna Eloise Whaley and 'Yankee Jim', still angry at the barbaric treatment that was meted out to him.

The White House Ghosts

If reports are to be believed, the White House is not only the abode of the current president of the USA, but that of past incumbents too. There are stories of many ghosts at that famous residence, but the name which crops up most regularly is that of Abraham Lincoln. Like many of the individuals whose ghosts are abroad, Lincoln suffered a sudden and violent death, in his case at the hands of an assassin.

When Grace Coolidge was First Lady, she saw Lincoln's figure, dressed in black, looking out from a window in the Oval Office. Queen Wilhelmina of the Netherlands was staying at the White House on one occasion, when she heard footsteps followed by a knock at her door. When she answered it, she came face to face with the assassinated president. And as recently as the 1980s, President Reagan's daughter said she had seen Lincoln's ghost.

Above: Glamis castle is home to the 'Grey Lady' - the ghost of Lady Janet Douglas, burnt at the stake for witchcraft

Opposite page: The ghost of Raynham Hall is a misty form, devoid of features

Below: The ghost of the assassinated president Abraham Lincoln is said to haunt the White House

Right: Sightings of the ghosts of animals are also reported

Below: The mummified body of Jeremy Bentham whose ghost has been seen walking the corridors of University College London

At the time of Lincoln's presidency, spiritualism was enjoying huge popularity. His wife was a devotee of spiritualist beliefs and practices, and seances were held at the White House itself. Lincoln may also have participated, perhaps in the hope of contacting the couple's dead son, William. If he didn't attend when alive, he seems to have done so after he was dead. For 25 years after he was murdered, Lincoln's spirit manifested itself at another White House seance - although on this occasion he was asked to leave, as his presence was said to be upsetting.

Murder Most Foul

Many ghostly appearances seem to feature re-enactments of violent deaths. If a witness is aware of a dark chapter associated with a particular building, then the claim could be made that - intentionally or otherwise - sounds and images are being conjured up to fit the details of the known story. But that cannot be said of the experience Detective Inspector Elvet Price had when staying at a hotel in Wales in 1969. During the night, Price heard the sound of a woman being attacked on three separate occasions. Each time, when he put on the light, the noises stopped. It was only later that he learned what had happened 50 years before: the landlord's wife, Angharad Llewellyn, had been throttled to death in one of the hotel's bedrooms.

In 1804, a woman's ghost was seen by several soldiers of the Coldstream Guards at Wellington Barracks in London. One eye-witness gave the following sworn testimony of what he saw: '....about half-past one in the morning, I perceived the figure of a woman without a head rise from the earth at a distance of about two feet before me. I was so alarmed....that I had not the power to speak to it....In about the space of two minutes, whilst my eyes were fixed on the object, it vanished from my sight.'

The ghost was believed to be the wife of a sergeant in the Guards who had been killed and decapitated by her husband 20 years before.

Ghostly Animals

There is an old superstition that the first soul buried in a new graveyard has to guard it for eternity. For many centuries, it was common practice to kill a large dog and bury it in a new graveyard, where it would protect the dead. The 'black dog', as it came to be known, is fiercely territorial, and sometimes its protective role extends to the living. In the early part of this century, a woman was walking home one night in the Midlands region of England, when she was approached by a black dog. Her apprehension turned to relief as she passed 'a group of labourers who were saying what they would have done with her if the dog weren't with her'. As soon as the men were out of sight, the dog disappeared.

In 1919, the ghost of a pit pony was seen in a Durham coalmine, rekindling thoughts of a disaster that had occurred there years before. A coalminer named Gibbon was checking the pumps when he heard the sound of hooves and the jangle of a harness and chains. He looked up to see a pony, and then an arm grabbing at it from the darkness. Gibbon found out later that a young miner had been killed at that exact spot while trying to stop a runaway pit pony.

A Ghost-hunter's Calendar

Many ghosts are reputed to manifest themselves on particular anniversaries. In The Grenadier, a small backstreet pub near Hyde Park Corner in London, locals tell the story of an officer who, one September, was flogged after being caught cheating at cards. The officer died in the cellar and is said to haunt the pub - especially during the month of September.

Other celebrated 'spectral anniversaries' in Britain include: January 19 - the thunder of Oliver Cromwell's defeated army, heard at Braddock Down in Cornwall since 1643; February 26 - the footsteps of Sir Christopher Wren in the Old Court House at Hampton Court, where the architect spent his last years; April 4 - the ghost of Lady Blanche de Warren on the battlements of Rochester Castle, where she met her accidental death during a fight between rival suitors; July 5 - the ghost of the Duke of Monmouth fleeing from defeat at Sedgemoor; August 17 - the ghost of a nun at Chicksands Priory in Bedfordshire, paying a penance for becoming pregnant; December 28 - a ghost train crossing the Tay Bridge, a re-enactment of the disaster of 1879.

Recordings and Replays

A theory has been put forward to explain the fact that some ghostly manifestations follow a recurring pattern, with the ghosts themselves seemingly unaware of any attendant witnesses. The so-called 'stone tape-recording' theory may explain bizarre sights such as that which confronted Harry Martindale in 1953. A plumber by trade, Martindale was knocking a hole through a cellar wall in the old Treasurer's House in York, England, when he heard the sound of a trumpet. This signalled the arrival of a Roman soldier, who marched right through the wall, followed by a whole infantry column. Martindale later discovered that the house was built on a Roman road, and the soldiers had been marching at exactly the height of the long-gone thoroughfare.

Various theories have been suggested as to what could cause the recording of such events to be laid down. The geographical and geological conditions are thought to be important - factors such as the minerals in the rocks, and ambient temperature and humidity. Another idea is that an intense emotion - such as mortal dread - could spark off an abnormally large discharge from the brain, which is then permanently imprinted on the environment.

But the recording is only half of the story, of course. Once the event is captured, what causes it to be replayed? Perhaps it is something in the mind of the observer, perhaps a convergence of factors which led to the event being recorded in the first place.

Above: The old Treasurer's House in York, England was the scene of a sighting of a ghostly Roman legion

Below: For many centuries it was common practice to kill a large dog and bury it in a new graveyard where it would protect the dead

Ghosts

When most people think of ghosts, images of figures draped in white sheets rattling chains spring to mind. Bizarre manifestations do occur - such as the 'Lady of the Wood', a faceless spectre seen floating high above the ground in Indiana - but more often, reports involve apparitions in human form. If the vision is that of a friend or relative known to be dead, then it is immediately obvious that the witness is being confronted by an apparition. But sometimes, it is only later that the witness learns the truth behind a visitation; indeed, ghostly manifestations have been known to occur at exactly the time of a loved one's death some distance away.

The other stereotypical image of ghosts which is not borne out by case studies is the fear factor. While most people who have gone through the experience have described initial feelings of surprise or apprehension, the nature of the experience is frequently positive, with the apparition often assuming a protective role. To this end, ghosts are regularly reported as having interacted with the physical world in some way, changing people's behaviour and affecting the outcome of situations.

Another great misapprehension is that ghostly appearances automatically imply death. The phenomena of doubles, vardogers and bilocations give the lie to this, for they are apparitions of people still very much alive. These not only make for some of the weirdest case histories, but because they concern people and their spirit doubles at large at the same time, the number of witnesses is multiplied. One of the most famous cases of this kind was that of teacher Amelie Sagee, who was observed both in her classroom and the school garden simultaneously.

A ghostly vision appearing before a subject barely awake in the middle of the night is one thing; 42 pupils all saying they saw two 'versions' of their teacher in the cold light of day is quite another.

Above: Sometimes apparitions are of people who are very much alive

Visible Ghosts   The 'Lady of the Wood' haunts a lonely stretch of woodland in Indiana, USA. Legend says that a woman and her baby died in that area, and although there are conflicting stories as to what exactly their fate was, there is common agreement that they met with a terrible death. This is supported by the ghost's observed behaviour, for it is seen scratching at car windows and screaming, 'Save my baby!'

In the winter of 1965, a rumour circulated that the ghost was appearing nightly. People drove into the woods in their hordes, hoping to catch a glimpse of her. One group of teenagers got rather more than a glimpse, for they were suddenly confronted by an awesome figure floating some 15 feet off the ground. This is how one of them described the sight which met their eyes: 'It was as white as snow. And it had no facial features, but it had a woman's form and it swung back and forth between the trees, coming right at us saying, 'Save me!....Save my baby!' And it was the awfullest sound. Oh, it scared me to death.'

Audible Ghosts   Some ghosts are heard but never seen, and the best known of these is the banshee. The cry of the banshee is regarded in many cultures as an ominous sign, often portending death. It is said that the wailing is heard only by the victim's family, not by the person who has been marked out to die.

In the 1960s, a baker from County Kerry, in Ireland, was working a night shift, when he reported hearing a banshee; 'It started low at first, then it mounted up into a crescendo...You could make out one or two Gaelic words in it.' The following morning, the baker received news which he believed the banshee had foreshadowed: the aunt of one of his employees had died during the night.

Ghostly manifestations portending death figure in other cultures too, though the form that these take can vary, and some are visible. The Welsh speak of a green hag who flies around wailing and screaming before a death; in Scotland, an old hag-like washerwoman is seen washing the bloodstained clothes of those about to die.

Tactile Ghosts   Ghostly contact in some cases can mean exactly that - a close-up, touching experience. But it needn't inspire terror, as Englishwoman Sue Henderson found when she had a very vivid tactile encounter in the early 1990s. Sue is convinced she was contacted by her late partner, George, and after the initial surprise, regarded it as an uplifting experience, literally as well as metaphorically:

'I just felt these arms come up under me and lift me up. It was a shock. I screamed, 'Oh, what is it?' And I heard my daughter say very distinctly, 'It's George, mummy.' The next thing I knew was the feeling of the warmth of a pair of hands under my legs, holding them, but I couldn't see anything...I could feel warmth, a real sensation of heat...And I was being carried down the stairs - not floating, but being carried very gently. I know that it wasn't just my imagination.'

Olfactory Ghosts   From the moment 34-year-old Eileen Courtis took a room at the Martha Washington Hotel in New York, she could smell a foul odour. Eileen had already had several psychic experiences, and she sensed straightaway that someone had died in the room. Lying awake one night, she saw two arms holding a pillow above her head, as if about to suffocate her. She fought wildly and just managed to force the pillow away from her face. Months later, she learned that two women had died in that room: one had been found in a chair, the other in the bath.

The odour which featured in an incident involving Empress Eugenie in the latter part of the 19th century was rather more pleasant, but it too was a mysterious manifestation following a tragic death. When the British Army invaded Zululand in 1879, the Prince Imperial of France - son of Napoleon III and Empress Eugenie - was killed. His body was brought back to England, with a cairn of stones left to mark the spot where he had fallen. The following year, Eugenie went to visit the battlefield where her son had been slain, but the area was overgrown and the cairn was not visible. Suddenly, Eugenie cried out: 'I smell violets; they were always his favourite flower', and with that she ran directly to the stone memorial.

When the Prince Imperial of France was killed in Zululand in 1879 his mother, Princess Eugenie, was guided to the spot where he fell by the scent of violets

Above: Most people who encounter ghosts describe the experience as a positive one

Ghostly Protector

Many people have described occasions when they have experienced a ghostly presence, through one or more of the senses. Interaction between the spirit and the physical world is rarer, but by no means unheard of. Indeed, Michelle Duggin may owe her life to the fact that a ghost was determined to act at a time of crisis.

Early on New Year's Day, 1993, a fire started in the home of Larry and Sheila Duggin. They and three of their children managed to escape, but the youngest, 8-year-old Michelle, was trapped in her room. The window in Michelle's room was high up, and, with the fire spreading ominously quickly, all the distraught parents could see from the pavement below was their daughter's hands stretching desperately up to the glass. Suddenly, an ornament smashed through the window, and Michelle followed, plunging head first onto the ground 15 feet below. Incredibly, she sustained only minor injuries.

Further astonishment followed when Michelle gave her account of events. She said that as the smoke started seeping under the door, the shining form of a man appeared. She recognised him as her great-grandfather, who had been dead for some years. According to Michelle, it was he who lifted her up and pushed her out of the window. Obviously, this is the uncorroborated story of a child; but it was certainly thought impossible for her to have propelled herself through the window unaided.

Flight 401

Perhaps the most famous protective ghosts are the air crew of a plane which crashed in the Florida Everglades in December 1972. Since this tragedy, Captain Bob Loft and Second Officer Don Repo have been seen on many occasions making safety checks and reporting faults on other Lockheed aircraft, particularly those which used parts recycled from their own crashed plane.

One engineer was carrying out the normal checks prior to take-off, when he saw Repo, who said: 'You don't need to worry about the pre-flight, I've already done it.' On another occasion, during a flight from New York to Mexico City, two stewardesses and an engineer saw Don Repo through an oven window in the galley. 'Watch out for fire on this airplane,' he warned them. On take-off during the next leg of the flight, one engine stalled and backfired, and was taken out of service. No explanation for the fault was ever found.

The protective role which Loft and Repo appear to have assigned themselves was most clearly articulated when Repo appeared before the captain of an aircraft to assure him: 'There will never be another crash of an L-1011 - we will not let it happen.'

'Sir, I Need a Ride....'

Dr Mike Barns was driving across the Arizona Desert towards Lake Tahoe, when he came across a small boy at the side of the road. The boy, who was wearing a scout uniform and a red baseball cap, was extremely agitated, waving frantically to get him to stop. Barns did so and the boy, in an obvious state of shock, pleaded: 'Sir, I need a ride. Right away, please.'

Barns naturally obliged, but after driving some distance, the boy directed him down a small dirt track and then up a mountain road. They drove for several miles, with the boy becoming increasingly anxious. Near the top of the mountain, Barns could hear distant screams. The boy told him to stop, and pointed over an unfenced section of road into the canyon below. There, Barns saw where the screams had come from: a school bus had crashed.

Left: Michelle Duggin believed she was saved from a fire by the ghost of her great-grandfather

Below left: The ghost of a child led Dr Mike Barns to the site of a school bus crash

Below right: The ghostly crew of a plane which crashed in 1972 have been seen making safety checks on similar planes

Barns had a phone with which he was able to call for medical help, and having done so, he left the boy and clambered down to the scene of the accident. He gave what first aid he could while waiting for the paramedics to arrive. When the injured children were finally removed to safety, it was discovered that there had been one fatality: a small boy wearing a scout uniform and a red baseball cap.

Promise to a Ghost

In England, in June 1887, Lucy Dodson was lying in bed, when she heard a voice call her name. It happened twice more, and by that time, Lucy identified the voice as that of her mother, who had been dead for 16 years. Her mother then appeared before her, carrying two small children. The apparition placed the children in Lucy's arms and said: 'Lucy, promise me to take care of them, for their mother is just dead.' Lucy replied that she would, at which point the ghost of her mother disappeared, leaving the two children behind. Lucy described feeling the children in her arms before falling into a deep sleep.

Two days later, Lucy was told that her sister-in-law had died, leaving two children. Lucy had not even been aware that her sister-in-law had had a second child, who was now just three weeks old. She also discovered that the apparition had come to her two hours after the time of death.

Crisis Apparitions

Ghostly appearances which occur within 12 hours of a person's death, either before or after the event, are known as 'crisis apparitions'. In 1795, in Derbyshire, England, a Mrs Howitt was lying in bed, with the curtain around it closed. She heard someone enter the room and saw her brother Francis look in at her through the curtains. Mrs Howitt noticed that he looked worried and asked him to come closer so that they could speak. Instead, she heard him leave the room. Her maid was called to search for Francis, but no trace of him could be found. Later, news reached them that at the time he was seen in the bedroom, Francis had been murdered while on his way to the house.

In the 1960s, an American woman named Bonnie Mogyorossy reported that while watching television with friends one day, she saw the picture on the screen change. It turned into 'a distinct image of a jungle...Right in the middle of it was my fiancé, shot dead on the ground'. She simultaneously heard a voice which confirmed what she had seen on screen. Her fiancé was a soldier fighting in Vietnam; a week later, she was informed that he had been killed around the time of her vision.

A famous farewell occurred on the day that World War I ended. Harold Owen was on a ship when he saw his brother Wilfred, the great English war poet. 'He did not speak, only smiled his most gentle smile...Suddenly, I felt terribly tired and I lay down; instantly I went into a deep, oblivious sleep. When I woke up, I knew with absolute certainty that Wilfred was dead.'

Doubles

The idea that everyone has a double is an intriguing thought. Most pairs of lookalikes must live in blissful ignorance of each other's existence, but sometimes, there is contact between the two. The link can be via a third party or, more dramatically, a face-to-face encounter.

One person who did become aware that he had a double was the future American president, Ronald Reagan. In 1959, he spoke about the strange experiences that this led to: 'It all started after the war. I was on a train and some man came up to me, identified himself as an ex-colonel, and said that he had served in the same army camp in Georgia that I had. I replied that I had never set foot in Georgia....I also received a letter from a man who claimed he and his wife dined with me on a train once....I just wasn't there.'

Stranger still than the thought of a mere physical lookalike is the idea of a ghostly duplicate of a living person: the Doppelganger. In 1946, Gordon Barrows was driving near Laramie, Wyoming, having just been discharged from the army. After 18 hours on the road he was tired and numb with cold, and, to break the monotony, he picked up a hitchhiker. Two things about his passenger struck Barrows: the first was that despite the cold, he was dressed only in light army denims; the second was that he bore an amazing resemblance to Barrows himself.

The hitchhiker offered to take the wheel and let Barrows get some sleep. When Barrows woke up, with the worst of the terrain now behind them, the man was sitting motionless in the driving seat. Barrows thanked the stranger, who then got out of the car and headed back towards the canyon they had just left. Barrows was convinced that no one could have survived the freezing temperatures dressed so lightly, and came to believe that he had been helped by his own double at a time of need.

One of the best known recorded examples of an individual being seen in two places at the same time was the case of Amelie Sagee. In 1846, Amelie was a 32-year-old teacher working in a school in Latvia. On one occasion, she was outside in the school garden while her double was in the classroom. All 42 pupils of the school saw one form of Amelie or the other. She later described how,

Above: The poet, Wilfred Owen, whose brother, Harold, was visited by his ghost to say farewell

Right: Graveyards seem an obvious place for ghosts but they can appear anywhere

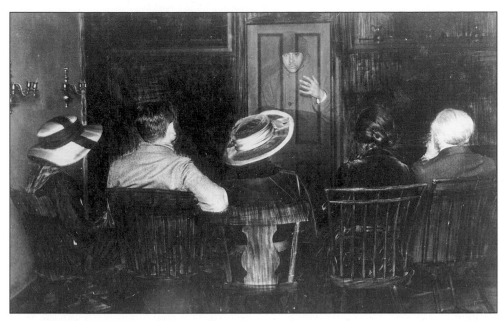

Left: Apparition at a seance

Below: Ronald Reagan discovered he had a double

although she assumed the classroom was probably unattended and that she ought to have been there, she had felt a strange unwillingness to go. One pupil spoke of actually passing through the Amelie in the classroom, suggesting a ghostly quality; in the garden, meanwhile, the 'real' Amelie was feeling drowsy and weak, as if her strength had been divided between the two forms.

This and many other similar manifestations naturally caused concern, and eventually, the school lost most of its pupils. Amelie was asked to leave, and it was then that she admitted it was the 19th job she had lost for the same reason.

Vardogers

Sometimes, the image of a person seems to be transposed to a future event. These 'forerunner doubles', known as vardogers, appear in locations and situations in advance of the 'real' person. One explanation for vardogers is that they are the result of a mental projection - a person working through a thought process so vividly and intensely that an image of the individual is projected to the location in question.

An example of this phenomenon occurred in 1955, when New Yorker Erikson Corique had to make a business trip to Norway. He was delayed several times, finally making the trip in July of that year. He had never been to Norway before, and he only made his hotel arrangements after arriving in Oslo. But when he checked in at his chosen hotel, he was greeted by a clerk who said he was pleased to see him back. The clerk assured a dumbfounded Corique that he had stayed at the hotel several months before, at which time he had made the reservation for this return trip. Further surprise awaited Corique when he visited a wholesaler who greeted him as an old friend and said he was looking forward to completing the business discussed at their previous meeting.

Bilocations

The phenomenon in which the same person is seen in two places far apart is known as bilocation. In 1917, during World War I, General Luigi Cadorna was in Slovenia, contemplating suicide after a heavy defeat in battle. But he was dissuaded from this course of action by a monk who visited him in his tent. Many years later, Cadorna visited Italy and met the psychic Padre Pio, whom he recognised as the same monk who had dissuaded him from killing himself. It emerged that at the time when Cadorna encountered him in his tent in Slovenia, Pio was known to have been in Italy.

What causes the appearance of vardogers, doubles, bilocations and crisis apparitions is unknown, but most cases seem to indicate that mental projection is a factor. In his book The Story of Ruth, Morton Schatzman describes a subject who found she could produce projections at will. On one occasion, for example, she created the image of her husband sitting in her car, an incident witnessed by her father. Asked how she produced these images, she said: 'I stop paying attention to everything around me. I decide whose apparition I want to make. I remember what the person looks like, as most people might with their eyes closed, except my eyes are open. And I produce the person.'

Modern Ghost Mysteries

When 17th century Englishwoman Anne Griffith died, she made a bizarre last request: that her head should remain in the house that was under construction at the time; if she could not occupy the house while alive, she wanted part of her to take up gruesome residence in death. Her wish was not fully complied with at first, and on each occasion that the skull was removed from Burton Agnes Manor House, in the north of England, horrible screaming was heard. It stopped only when the skull was returned. In order to ensure that Griffith's dying wish should be forever respected - and that the screaming should not come back - the skull was finally bricked up behind the wooden panelling of the house's Great Hall.

This story is a classic example of ghost mysteries of the modern era. Moreover, the apparent source of the strange manifestations does not even have to be human - there have also been reports of inanimate objects imbued with some kind of ghostly power.

Many mysteries are only judged to be so after the event, for they involve spectral visions in human form. The most common of these is the phantom hitchhiker, a phenomenon so prevalent that it has become an area of special research. It is certainly taken seriously in Norway, where unusual steps have been taken to counter the threat of one notorious hitchhiker. Giving this phantom lady a lift, it is said, will cause a person to have a terrible accident, and to alert drivers to that possibility, warning signs have been put up on the road - a red triangle containing a picture of a ghost.

'Timeslips' can also seem very real to the witness. This phenomenon occurs when a person appears to step through a doorway in time, seeing people and buildings that haven't existed for years, or providing glimpses of events yet to happen.

The ability to capture still and moving images on film has led to the incidence of a new kind of ghost: that seen by the camera but not the naked eye. Unlike anecdotal evidence, these images can be reprinted and re-examined, but definitive answers remain elusive as the argument merely shifts to one of interpretation. Are ghostly manifestations on film simply tricks of the light or quirks of the developing process? Or could it be that the camera is somehow more sensitive to a spirit presence?

The plethora of modern ghost mysteries, many on recurring themes, provokes a wider question: is this indicative, consciously or unconsciously, of a bandwagon effect? Or does it simply show a greater willingness on the part of witnesses to report their weird experiences?

Phantom Hitchhikers

The phantom hitchhiker is a phenomenon of the modern era which is so prevalent that it has become an area of research in its own right. Although one could envisage countless situations in which ghosts might wish to protect - or threaten - other individuals, nothing is reported so often as car crashes in which phantom hitchhikers have played a prominent part.

In 1981, at Quatrecanaux Bridge, near Montpellier in France, a woman hitched a lift and then warned the driver to slow down on some dangerous bends in the road. She then vanished from inside the vehicle, even though it was a two-door model and she had been sitting in the back seat between two other people.

One of the most famous ghostly appearances at the roadside is a young woman who frequents the area around the Blue Bell Hill in Kent, England. In November 1992, a Mr Sharpe described how a girl suddenly appeared and ran straight in front of his car. She looked straight at him at the moment of impact, and the driver was certain that he had run her over. Certain that she must have been killed, Sharpe pulled up and looked for the body, but there was no sign of her. He even examined the bushes on the side of the road, in case the collision had projected her some distance, but still he could find no trace. Eventually he drove to the police station to report what had happened. Officers went to the scene and made their own thorough search of the area, but they could find no body either. They had no option but to 'reassure' Mr Sharpe that he had seen a ghostly vision.

A similar phantom accident occurred on the same stretch of road some 20 years earlier. A Mr Goodenough was the unfortunate driver on that occasion, but in his case, he actually found the body of the person he believed he had struck. He carried the body to the roadside and covered it with a blanket while he went for the police. When they returned, they found the blanket but no body, no bloodstains and no tracks.

The Phantom Pillion Rider

In October 1972, a motorcyclist gave a lift to a male hitchhiker just south of the Blackwall Tunnel, which runs beneath the River Thames in London. From the pillion, the passenger managed to shout his address to the rider. Coming out of the tunnel, the rider glanced round to continue the conversation, but found that his passenger had vanished. Fearing that he had fallen off, the motorcyclist retraced the journey through the tunnel but found no sign of the missing man. The next day, he went to the address the man had given, only to be told that a person answering that description had died years before.

Many cases involving phantom hitchhikers are traced back to deceased individuals. In 1978, in Uniondale, South Africa, a motorcyclist gave a lift to a girl who also disappeared while they were riding. He said that he knew the moment when she had gone, for the change in weight distribution caused the bike to slew. In this case, the passenger was later identified as someone who had died 10 years earlier.

Recurring Hitchhikers

In the 1980s, an Englishman driving to work in Ipswich stopped at some traffic lights. As they changed and he began to pull away, the man heard someone whistling behind him. He looked in his mirror and saw a man in Royal Air Force uniform sitting in the back seat. When the driver asked him what he was doing, the figure ignored him. The man was badly shaken but said nothing to anyone when he got to work, fearing that he would be ridiculed. Before driving home later that day, he searched his car. But a short way into his return journey he again heard someone whistling: the pilot was back. The man drove on as far as the set of traffic lights where he had first become aware of the whistling that morning; at that point his mysterious passenger vanished.

In 1958, lorry driver Harry Unsworth was heading along the A38 in Somerset, England, at 3 o'clock in the morning, when he picked up a man wearing a grey overcoat and dripping with rain. The man told him stories of accidents that had occurred on that stretch of road. In the following weeks, Unsworth picked the same man up on several occasions. That might have been unusual enough in itself, but it was when Unsworth encountered the man twice in the same day that he became unnerved. Having dropped him off, Unsworth then saw the man again several miles further up the road. Unsworth did not see how the man could have got there ahead of him, and he sped off, terrified, leaving the man gesticulating wildly at the side of the road.

Opposite page: Snapped in the Queen's House, Greenwich, this photograph shows one, possibly two, figures walking up the Tulip Staircase

Below top and bottom: Maria Roux was killed in a road accident near Uniondale, South Africa in 1968. Since then a female hitchhiker has appeared at exactly the same spot several times

Ghosts on Film

The ability to capture first still and then moving images on film has been important to the world of the paranormal, as well as the world of art; for when films are developed, they sometimes reveal more than the photographer bargained for.

On December 5, 1891, a photograph of the library at Combermere Abbey in the north-west of England was taken. When it was developed, it revealed a ghostly figure sitting in an armchair. It looked remarkably like Lord Combermere, whose funeral was taking place at the time. A more prosaic explanation of the spectral image would point to the fact the picture was taken on an hour-long exposure. The photographer set up the camera, but was not present for all of this time. Perhaps someone else entered the room - a servant, possibly - sat down in the armchair, then left hurriedly after noticing the camera.

Ghostly presences seem no less likely in the age of video. In September 1993, the treasurer of the East Ardsley Conservative Club, in the north of England, saw a figure outside the door of the club on the security monitor. He went to investigate but no one was there. He returned to his office, where he saw the same figure on the monitor. This apparition was recorded on film for several minutes on that occasion, and made another appearance a month later. No explanation has ever been found.

Haunted Objects

In 1972, 11-year-old Colin Robson found two small, crudely-carved stone heads in Hexham, England. When he took them home, a series of terrifying events befell the family, including showers of glass crashing down onto Colin's sister's bed, and shadowy, werewolf-like figures being seen by both members of the family and also neighbours. The Robsons eventually had to be rehoused, and the heads were moved to a museum.

When an expert, Dr Anne Ross, took the heads home to study them, the mysterious figures that dogged the Robson family seem to have followed: both she and her daughter reported seeing a wolf-like man in the house.

One theory regarding the strange powers that appeared to emanate from the heads centred on the material from which they were carved. They were made largely from quartz, a substance which has long been associated with storing energy. But the mystery did deepen somewhat when a local man, Desmond Craigie, claimed that he had carved the heads for his daughter in around 1956. Up to that point, the pieces were thought to have been Celtic, around 2,000 years old. No one believed Craigie, but he did manage to make an identical carving. Whether they were ancient or modern, the stone heads seem to have been the source of some extraordinary incidents in the lives of those who possessed them.

In 1982, an American woman brought home a pottery model cottage, a souvenir from a trip to England. As soon as she arrived back with the ornament, she began to see shadowy figures lurking around her Las Vegas bungalow. Convinced that the model was responsible for these terrifying manifestations, she gave it to her daughter, Billie. She had exactly the same experiences, but these strangely ceased when the ornament was no longer used as a receptacle for storing odds and ends.

Opposite page: Photograph taken at Alton church, Staffordshire, England

Below left: These carved heads are linked to the appearance of a shadowy wolf-like figure in homes of those who possessed them

An Adventure in Time

The most famous timeslip - and the one which first caught the public imagination - was experienced by two principals of an Oxford college during a visit to Versailles on August 10, 1901. As Charlotte Moberly and Eleanor Jourdain walked around the grounds of the famous palace there, the atmosphere became eerie and strangely unreal. They noticed that everyone was wearing 18th century costume. There were dignified officials, servants - even a man and a woman who resembled King Louis XVI and Queen Marie Antoinette.

Ten years later, after a great deal of research, the two women published a book entitled An Adventure, in which they concluded that they had somehow slipped back in time to the 1780s, seeing Versailles as it was just before the French Revolution. The mundane explanation is that they witnessed nothing more bizarre than a fancy-dress party. Several such events are known to have been staged in the grounds of the palace, although there is no record of one being held there in August 1901.

Prisons and Chapels

The most common form of timeslip is a vision of the past. In the Tower of London, a building renowned for its mysterious occurrences, a Yeoman of the Guard told how he entered a room one day to see several other Yeomen, but all dressed in the style of a much earlier period. They were seated around a log fire, smoking pipes. The Yeoman left the room briefly, and when he returned, the men had vanished.

In his book The Candle of Vision, George Russell describes how he was once sitting in a ruined chapel, waiting for a friend. Suddenly, the scenery changed, the building was restored and he found himself a member of a small congregation attending a service.

Alice Pollock described how she had a similar experience when she was a child. It happened during a visit to Leeds Castle, in England. Alice was sitting in a comfortable, well-furnished room, when it suddenly became cold and bare. Even the geography of the room had altered - the fireplace had moved to a different position. A figure was also now present in the room, a tall woman dressed in white, and whose expression appeared to Alice to show great anguish. She wondered later if she had seen Queen Joan of Navarre, who had been imprisoned in the room centuries earlier, accused of witchcraft.

A Timeslip within a Timeslip?

In 1954, a South African named Searle visited Olympia, in southern Greece, along with a friend called Robert. During their stay, the pair climbed the local mountain, only to find the valley obscured by mist. Suddenly, the mist parted and the two men could see deep into the valley below. Searle describes the sight which met their eyes: 'Both Robert and I heard voices as if children were chanting. We thought it was coming from this wooden building, which looked like a school or church. Outside this large sandy area there were houses and rows of flat-topped mud huts with roads between. In several places smoke was going up in perfect spirals from these mud huts. We watched this scene for about five minutes.'

Above: At the Tower of London a Yeoman of the Guard witnessed the appearance of a group of Yeomen from a much earlier time period

Right: In Dickens' A Christmas Carol Ebenezer Scrooge is visited by a series of ghosts

Back at their hotel, Searle asked what the village was called. The astonished proprietor said there was no such place. The following day, Robert went to the site they had looked down on from the mountain top, but there was no trace of what they had seen.

This story is especially odd, for, as Searle himself pointed out: 'The wood-built structure that may have been a school was of a different period in time to the mud-built dwellings.' Had the two men witnessed a timeslip within a timeslip?

Living in the Past
In some timeslips interaction between the people of the different worlds takes place. In Norway in the 1950s, a party of skiers encountered a woman who insisted they were trespassing on her land. A row ensued, then suddenly, the woman vanished into the open landscape. Later enquiries revealed that no such woman had lived there for over 40 years.

In the 1930s, a young girl was cycling to a friend's house near Swindon, in England, when a storm broke. She saw a thatched cottage with smoke rising from the chimney, and decided to ask for shelter. An old, grey-bearded man opened the door and ushered her in. She later recalled many details of the visit, including the room's low ceilings and a brightly-burning fire. She also remembered how she heard no sound in the house at all - neither the man's voice, nor the noise of the storm outside. She then suddenly found herself back on the road again. The storm had blown over and she was completely dry. She returned to the spot where the cottage had been some time later, only to find a derelict dwelling. She was told that it had been unoccupied for 50 years.

Visions of the Future
It would seem that timeslips can involve a leap forward in time, as well as a step back. In 1934, Air Marshal Sir Victor Goddard was flying through mist and rain over Scotland. As he flew lower in search of a landmark, he saw a disused airfield at Drem. It was now bathed in sunlight and he had a clear view of yellow aircraft on the runway and technicians dressed in blue overalls. Goddard continued his journey, thinking no more about what he had seen until 1938, when the airfield was back in use as a flight training station. The aircraft were indeed painted yellow and the ground crew had been issued with blue uniforms - but for the very first time. Air Marshal Goddard had seen a vision of how the airfield would look when reopened four years later.

Above: This photograph, taken in 1891, seems to show the ghostly figure of Lord Combermere whose funeral was taking place at the time

Below: Air Marshal Sir Victor Goddard saw a vision of the future from the cockpit of his plane

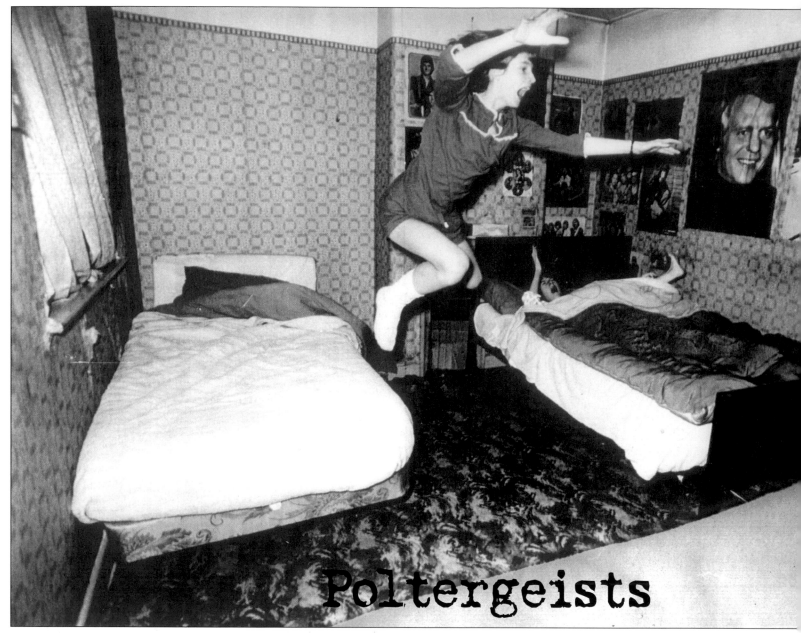

Poltergeists

'Cruel, purposeless and spiteful' - such are the adjectives British ghost-hunter Harry Price ascribed to what are regarded as the most destructive and terrifying of paranormal phenomena: poltergeists.

Price cannot be accused of basing his opinion on hearsay. Rather, it was the result of his own investigations, such as that which he conducted into the case of a Romanian girl in 1926. Eleonore Zugun was 12 years old when a poltergeist started attacking her. She was regularly bitten and scratched, resulting in strange indentations and swellings on her face, arms and hands. Price himself witnessed scratches and bite marks appear on Eleonore, even as he was observing her. On one occasion when teeth marks appeared on her skin, saliva was found. Examination showed that it was not Eleonore's.

Poltergeists have long been a favourite subject for films, because their manifestations can be so much more dramatic than the silent appearance of a misty spectre. Unusually, the content of such productions has not required exaggeration for cinematic effect; case histories involving poltergeists contain more than enough drama in their own right. As well as physical attacks, they have been deemed responsible for outbreaks of fire, cars and houses being pelted with objects, even buildings oozing blood.

The word 'poltergeist' is derived from the German language and literally translates as 'noisy spirit', though this barely seems adequate to describe the malevolent forces that appear to be at work. As Harry Price himself put it: 'A ghost haunts; a poltergeist infests.'

Above: This girl has been thrown across the room by some unknown force

The Human Focus

In most poltergeist cases, activity often centres on one individual, with girls around the age of puberty seeming to be particularly susceptible.

In 1889, the Dagg family in Quebec, Canada, were plagued by a disruptive spirit. Dinah, the Daggs' 11-year-old adopted daughter, was attacked by the spirit, and claimed that she had heard it speak. On one occasion, Dinah said she had seen something in the woodshed, and went to investigate, accompanied by a visitor. 'You there, Mister?' the girl asked. The voice which replied was that of an old man. 'I am the devil. Get out or I'll break your neck!' It also issued a string of obscenities. News of this incident quickly spread, and a large number arrived on the scene the following day. They too heard the voice of the poltergeist.

An 11-year-old girl was also the focus of a poltergeist which plagued a family in Enfield, near London, in 1977. The girl, named Janet, was levitated above her bed, subjected to attacks, and even became the 'voice' of the poltergeist. It was a loud, rasping male voice, and amid the many abuses it hurled, claimed to be that of a dead man.

A feature of this year-long poltergeist episode, the most famous in modern times, was the way in which objects were moved around. Apart from the levitation incident, a chest of drawers was seen to slide across the floor, books flew off shelves, drawers opened and closed. When the police were called in, they witnessed some of these amazing manifestations for themselves: WPC Carolyn Heeps, for example, described how she saw a chair moving round the room. The distraught family also sought the help of special investigators, one of whom was Maurice Grosse. Grosse listened to the voice for lengthy periods and was convinced of its authenticity. The investigators also positioned sealed cameras which captured some of the remarkable occurrences on film.

By the time the Enfield poltergeist ceased its activity, a large bank of compelling evidence had been accumulated. When it finally went, after more than a year, it was with more of a whimper than a bang, however. For as is the case with most poltergeists, it simply faded away.

The Murderous Witch

A 19th century poltergeist which became known as the 'Bell Witch' centred on a child, too; it is also one of the few recorded cases where poltergeist activity has resulted in a fatality.

John and Lucy Bell lived with their children on a farm in Tennessee, USA. In 1817, one of the children, Elizabeth, became the focus of poltergeist activity. The early incidents were of a minor nature - noises and scrapings - but this soon turned into bedclothes and furniture being thrown around. Elizabeth was subjected to physical attacks, and these persisted even when she went to stay with a neighbour. The poltergeist was also responsible for Elizabeth's engagement being short-lived. She was to marry a man named Joshua Gardner, but the engagement was broken off after the poltergeist started revealing her intimate secrets.

It was John Bell, however, who fared worst in the whole episode, which lasted more than two years. He became ill, his tongue swelling to such an extent that he was unable to eat. The poltergeist was blamed for this, and it responded by promising that Bell would be tormented for the rest of his life. The rest did not amount to very long; for Bell died on December 20, 1820, with the poltergeist triumphantly claiming responsibility.

Below left: Psychic investigator, William G Roll noticed that poltergeist activity in a Miami warehouse centred on a disaffected 19-year-old employee. When he was arrested for theft the disturbances stopped

Below right: Pillow filmed moving across the room

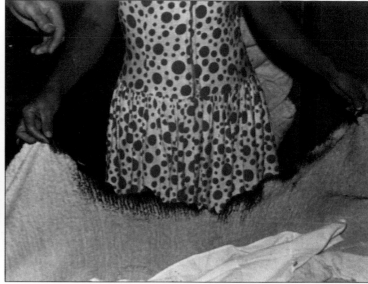

Spontaneous Fires

Spontaneous fires are often associated with poltergeists. In 1959, a family from Alabama fled their home after falling victim to 22 fires within the space of a few days. They quickly found out that the problem did not lie in the fabric of their home, for the phenomenon accompanied them. The matter was investigated by the police, and at the very time when they were interviewing the family, yet another incident occurred: a quilt hanging outside caught fire. An officer later tried to light a piece of the same material using matches, but could not do so.

The family moved on twice more, each time hoping that they would escape the terrible blight that was dogging them. The story then took a strange final twist. The family's 9-year-old son confessed that he had been responsible for starting all the fires. One might have thought that all parties would have been relieved that the mystery had finally been solved; but the fire marshal refused to believe the boy's story.

A family from Sheffield, England, suffered only one blaze, but it was one that so easily could have cost them their lives. The fact that it didn't the Newmans put down to a helpful intervention by a poltergeist.

The family had been experiencing noisy disturbances for over a year when, in January 1982, Derek Newman was awoken in the middle of the night. He later described what he heard as 'like someone running round the lounge with a hammer'. Opening the bedroom door, he found that the house was full of smoke. Derek roused his sleeping family, the fire brigade was called and a tragedy averted. Derek Newman firmly believes that the family owe their lives to the noisy hammering of a poltergeist. The question of how the fire started in the first place, however, was not resolved.

Hot Rocks

Bombardments of missiles, particularly rocks and stones, are also commonly associated with the poltergeist phenomenon. In 1962, showers of stones started falling onto a bungalow in Big Bear City, California. As is often the case in such incidents, the stones were warm to the touch. More unusual was the fact that they did not clatter onto the roof of the building as might have been expected, but gently floated down instead.

In 1960, a few miles from Brasilia, a group of people were standing by the roadside when stones rained down on them from an apparently empty landscape. They reported the incident at a police station and persuaded an officer to return with them to the place where it had happened; the spontaneous showers of stones duly recommenced.

A suburban street in Birmingham, England, was subjected to regular bombardments of stones and rocks over a number of years. There was substantial damage to property in the area, and at last the police agreed to mount a long-term covert operation to try to get to the bottom of the mystery. Chief Inspector Turley arrived in Thornton Road with a team of experienced officers and the latest surveillance equipment. A year and 3,500 man-hours later, the bombardments were still occurring and the police were no nearer to finding a solution. Forensic experts could offer little help either. The stones were examined but no fingerprints or fibres were found. There weren't even any traces of soil; the stones appeared to have been washed.

Above left: Damage to a roof caused by poltergeist activity

Above right: This blanket was burned in a fire believed to have been started by a poltergeist

Shocks and Explosions

A surveillance operation that met with more success took place in Rosenheim, Germany, in 1966. A team of investigators was called in to a lawyer's office there after engineers had failed to find the cause of some strange electrical disturbances. All the staff were under suspicion until the investigating team, headed by Dr Hans Bender, identified 19-year-old Annemarie Schneider as the focus of the weird goings-on. They noticed that the trouble started at 7.30am each day, exactly the time of her arrival at work; they also saw lamps swinging as she walked past.

Just before Christmas that year, the activity reached a peak. In addition to the continuing problem with the electricity supply, which was now reaching alarming proportions, lightbulbs exploded, pictures crashed to the floor, and drawers shot out of desks. Annemarie herself was by now becoming increasingly tense and upset at the situation.

The manifestations ceased over the Christmas and New Year period, but when Annemarie returned to work on 9 January, 1967, the problem resurfaced. Other staff began receiving electric shocks, and, in one particularly baffling incident, a heavy oak cabinet was found to have been moved; it took two burly policemen to return it to its proper position.

Annemarie's employers finally reached the point where they could no longer countenance the continual mayhem. She was dismissed, a decision that was soon vindicated in the respect that the workings of the office soon returned to normal. Unfortunately for Annemarie, the strange effects that she had on her surroundings followed her to a succession of jobs, and she was forced to leave each of them in turn.

Those investigating the case accepted that there was no wilful or malicious intent on Annemarie's part. The conclusion reached was that she 'seemed to instigate psychokinesis in response to emotional problems'. Annemarie certainly saw herself as the blameless victim in the whole affair: 'I never had influence over anything,' she said. 'I was very hurt indeed.'

Above left: Film poster
Above right: Drawings found in a sealed camera in France in 1977

Below left: Kitchen wrecked by poltergeist activity

Below middle: Poltergeist activity in Cheshire, England, 1985

Below right: Alleged messages between Marianne Foyster, wife of the rector of Borley, and a poltergeist

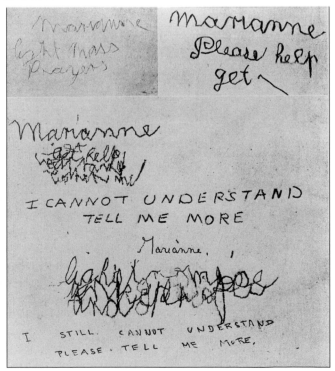

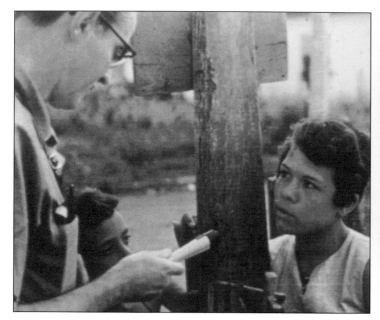

The Giles Sisters

One of the earliest recorded cases of poltergeist activity occurred in Bristol, England, in the mid-18th century. The focus of the unwelcome attention was the Giles family, who simply heard a variety of strange noises at first, but the manifestations soon escalated to the contents of their house being turned upside down.

There were two girls in the family, Molly and Dobby, both of whom suffered repeated attacks from the poltergeist. Some of these were witnessed by one of the first investigators of the phenomenon, Henry Durbin, who made an extensive study of the Giles family in 1762. On one occasion, 8-year-old Dobby claimed that a hand was at her sister's throat. Durbin was present at the time and reported seeing 'the flesh at the side of her throat pushed in, whitish, as if done with fingers, though I saw none. Her face grew red and blackish presently, as if she was strangled.'

On another occasion, Durbin described how he had witnessed Dobby being attacked: 'I was talking to her (when)...she was bitten in the neck. I looked and saw the mark of teeth...wet with spittle. It was in the top part of her shoulders, close by the neck; therefore it was impossible for her to do it herself, as I was looking on all the time, and nobody was near her but myself.'

During his investigation, Durbin set up a bizarre experiment involving the elder daughter, Molly. He marked some pins and placed them one by one into a pin cushion. Almost immediately, Molly cried out in pain, as Durbin observed: 'The identical pin that I marked was run through the neck of her shift and stuck in her skin, crooked very curiously. It was not a minute from the time I put the pin in.'

Scalded and Strangled

Two more recent cases illustrate the same degree of malicious intent. In July 1972, a Brazilian family living near Sao Paulo became the focus of poltergeist activity. They simply heard strange knocking noises at first, but soon they were witnessing furniture being flung around the room.

The poltergeist became increasingly aggressive. A concrete water tank that needed three men to lift it was hurled into the family's back yard; the mother was struck on the head by a flying brick; and one of the daughters was scalded by boiling water from a kettle that was 'wrenched from her hands'. The terrified family had already moved out of the house temporarily to stay with relatives. That had proved unsuccessful, for the poltergeist had followed. With the situation becoming ever more dangerous, they fled the area for good.

The second case involved a family living in southern Norway, who also experienced the characteristic escalation from minor irritation to violent assault. First, banging noises were heard. It was as if the walls were being hammered from the outside, but the family could see there was no one there. Then the poltergeist began to make its presence felt inside the house. On one occasion, the zips on the sofa cushions started to open and close. The children were naturally confused, and their mother, Sophie, explained the incident away by suggesting that mice were probably responsible.

Above left: Poltergeist investigator, Hernani Guimaraes interviews a victim in Brazil, 1970

Above right: The furniture in a house in Brazil was damaged by poltergeist activity

Then, one day, Sophie found that she could not open the children's bedroom door, even though it was not locked. The children screamed as she desperately tried to force her way in. As she pushed she let out a volley of threats directed at the poltergeist, at which point the door gave way. The distraught mother burst into the room, whereupon she immediately felt hands grabbing at her neck as if to strangle her. The family managed to escape and fled to the home of Sophie's ex-husband, who immediately asked what had happened to her throat. Sophie looked in a mirror and saw red fingermarks around her neck.

The family finally left the house for good in December 1989, but not, it seems, without a parting gift. For as they drove away, the flagpole shattered into pieces as though struck by lightning. It was a beautifully clear day.

Spirits at Work
Poltergeists have been known to blight the workplace as well as the domestic environment. In 1967, the manager of a firm of wholesalers in Miami, Florida, called in the police and reported that a ghost was damaging his goods. The officers even witnessed the problem for themselves - items mysteriously falling from the warehouse shelves.

Psychic investigators W G Roll and J Gaither Pratt were brought in to assist, and they noticed that the phenomena centred on a 19-year-old disaffected employee. He admitted to feeling happy when any stock was damaged, but denied all responsibility for it. Nevertheless, the problem ended when the same man was arrested for stealing cash from the warehouse later that month.

The sceptic might regard the simultaneous disappearance from the scene of the poltergeist and the employee as conclusive; others have suggested another scenario that is consistent with the facts. Pent up energy, frustration and stress can precipitate poltergeist activity, it has been claimed. If that is so, then the removal of those tensions - in this case, in the form of the removal of the employee - would also bring about the same outcome.

Whether or not one finds that idea persuasive, it seems to have little bearing on the case of two brothers-in-law who set up an engineering business in Cardiff, Wales, in 1987. For there was neither a disgruntled employee on the scene, nor any pent up stresses to contend with; and yet, soon after the two men occupied their new business premises, poltergeist activity began. Stones and coins began to fly around the room; tools went missing and turned up in strange places; and when one of the partners decided to keep a record of the bizarre events, a pen and notepad landed beside him.

The invisible cause of all the disturbances became known as 'Pete', and it was discovered that Pete would respond to requests. As well as the pen and notepad arriving on demand, coins started appearing after the men had jokingly asked for money. They also found that when they threw stones into a certain corner of the room, they would be flung back straightaway.

One evening, the poltergeist was challenged to move a carburettor float that had been placed on a gas fire. Later, the object in question appeared on the counter at a petrol station. Carburettor floats subsequently appeared at the homes of both men, ricocheting off walls and becoming impaled in the ceiling.

Above: Pan balanced on a door, Cheshire, 1985

Below left: Caught in the act - evidence of poltergeist activity in France

Below right: A poltergeist in Cardiff, Wales responded to requests for money

Spirits and
Mediums

A stone memorial outside a wooden house in Hydeville, New York State, boldly declares: 'There is no death...There are no dead'. It was in this building 150 years ago that two sisters, Kate and Margaret Fox, claimed that they possessed the ability to receive messages from the spirit world. The Fox sisters went on to give displays of their powers throughout the United States and enjoyed celebrity status. At the same time, the idea that communication with spirits was possible quickly took hold. For some it was no more than a parlour game, an amusing distraction; others took the subject much more seriously and spiritualism soon had many adherents.

In the same way, the techniques through which messages from the spirit world were received were employed by the serious medium and the casual party-goer alike. Table-tilting and Ouija boards became a feature of spiritualist meetings, but also readily lent themselves to fun gatherings. Any trickery employed during the latter was generally harmless; but vulnerable people desperate to contact their loved ones and pay handsomely for the privilege attracted those practising more cynical forms of deception.

Ironically, the very fact that spiritualism was all but an open invitation to the charlatan inspired researchers to set up more sophisticated experiments aimed at eliminating trickery. One of these took the form of a private arrangement between the two great psychologists William James and J H Hyslop. They promised each other that whoever died first would try to return and contact the other. In 1910, James died. Hyslop waited, but the years went by and he slowly lost hope. Then one day he received a letter from a couple in Ireland, saying that their seances had been plagued by persistent messages from 'a certain William James', nagging them to contact 'a Professor Hyslop'. In a desperate effort to rid themselves of this unwanted spirit, they had decided to track Hyslop down.

Above: An ouija board is often used to communicate with the spirit world

The Fox Sisters In December 1847, James Fox and his family took up residence in a wooden house in Hydeville, New York State. The previous occupant, Michael Weekman, had moved out after hearing loud rapping noises, and these soon began to plague the Fox family too. By March 1848, the banging sounds were keeping them awake; but on March 31, it was discovered that they were not totally indiscriminate. The children, 14-year-old Margaret and 12-year-old Kate, found that the rapping sounds were responsive to simple stimuli: when Kate snapped her fingers, and Margaret clapped her hands, there appeared to be a corresponding knock in reply.

The children then devised a code, through which they learned that the noises were coming from a peddler who had been murdered and buried in the house five years earlier. Although no evidence to support this story was found when the cellar was subsequently dug up, the Fox sisters soon became widely feted for their powers. The family moved across state to Rochester, where the first spiritualist meeting was held on November 14, 1848. Kate and Margaret Fox are credited with creating the international interest in spiritualism that continues to the present day.

The sisters' own later life, however, was not such a glittering tale. They both became alcoholics, and Margaret even confessed to having faked the noises in the house which set them on the road to stardom. But in a strange postscript to the Fox sisters' story, a cellar wall in that Hydeville property collapsed in 1904, revealing another wall behind. In the space between the two was found the skeleton of a man along with a peddler's box.

Types of Medium There are a variety of types of medium, each having a different method of contacting the spirit world:

- Physical mediums claim to be able to turn spirits into solid form. The materialisation process involves a jelly-like substance called ectoplasm oozing from various parts of the medium's body.

- Transfiguration mediums allow spirits to possess their body and talk through them. They adopt the verbal and physical mannerisms of the spirit, sometimes with a remarkable degree of accuracy.

- Clairaudient mediums hear messages from the spirit world. Some hear the voices inside their heads, others hear them externally.

- Clairvoyant mediums receive visions from the spirit world. The images are not always literal representations and may require interpretation.

Spirit Guides Mediums often use particular spirits known as spirit guides to introduce them to those in the spirit world. The spirit guide provides a link between the medium and spirits being contacted, assuming a role akin to a master of ceremonies in the proceedings.

The American psychic Leonore Piper worked through a spirit guide named Dr Phinuit. In 1893, she was trying to contact the spirit of a young girl, Katherine Sutton, on behalf of her grieving parents. Suddenly, Dr Phinuit announced: 'A little child is coming through'. Then, through Mrs Piper, he started speaking in the girl's voice: 'I want this, I want to bite it. Quick, I want to put them in my mouth.'

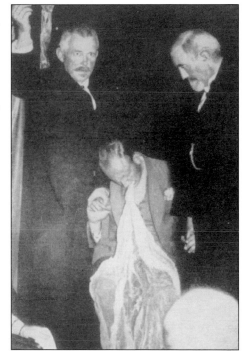

Above: Physical medium, Einer Nielsen produces ectoplasm from his mouth

Left and far left: Mediums Kate and Margaret Fox stimulated an international interest in spiritualism

Mrs Sutton was stunned both by what was said and the manner in which it was delivered. She revealed that Katherine had had a habit of biting her buttons, even though she had been forbidden to do so. Also, Mrs Piper had arched her mouth exactly as her daughter had done.

The spirit guide's role as an intermediary suggests an entity quite distinct from the medium - as in the case of Mrs Piper and Dr Phinuit - but many believe that the spirit guide is a sub-personality of the medium's own mind. One celebrated medium who subscribed to this view was Eileen Garrett.

Eileen Garrett

When Eileen Garrett attended a seance shortly after the end of World War I, she was singled out by a spirit guide named Uvani, who believed she possessed the ability to communicate with the spirit world. Garrett, who had been labelled 'unbalanced' as a child, went on to become a famous medium in her own right, with Uvani as her first spirit guide.

One of Eileen Garrett's contacts was a Captain Hinchcliffe, who had died trying to fly across the Atlantic. Through Mrs Garrett, Hinchcliffe contacted his widow, Emily; he also gave warnings about the airship R101, which was then under construction. The R101 crashed on its maiden voyage and 47 people were killed.

Among those who lost their lives was Captain Irwin, who also made contact with Mrs Garrett. Through her, Irwin spoke to Major Villiers of the Air Ministry Intelligence about the problems the R101 had encountered. In doing so, she displayed detailed technical knowledge of a kind that Villiers was certain she could not have known.

Eileen Garrett dissented from the view of her first spirit guide, Uvani, who said his purpose was to prove that the human personality continued beyond death as a free and conscious entity. Mrs Garrett believed her spirit guides might come from her own mind 'but raised to a level where they operate outside the laws of cause and effect that dominate daily existence.'

Getting Through

One of the earliest methods for receiving messages from the dead was table-tilting. This involved the participants gathering round a table and resting their hands on its surface. The spirits are asked questions, the answers to which are rapped out by movements in the table, the number of taps corresponding to letters of the alphabet. Whether the messages come from the spirit world or are generated by the sitters themselves, table-tilting is certainly a laborious way of receiving them. It has largely been replaced by the Ouija board and automatic writing.

On the Ouija board, numbers, letters and usually the words 'yes' and 'no' are arranged in a circle. In the centre of the board there is an object called a planchette, though an upturned glass is sometimes used. Each sitter rests one finger on the planchette, and when a spirit is asked a question, it responds by moving the planchette around the board. As with table-tilting, the sitters themselves can easily influence the outcome, and for this reason, Ouija boards have long been used as an entertaining diversion.

Opposite page: Photograph taken at a seance in Bristol, England in 1872

Above right: Medium Eileen Garrett received a warning of the crash of the R101 airship

Below: Mrs Leonore Piper worked through a spirit guide named Dr Phinuit

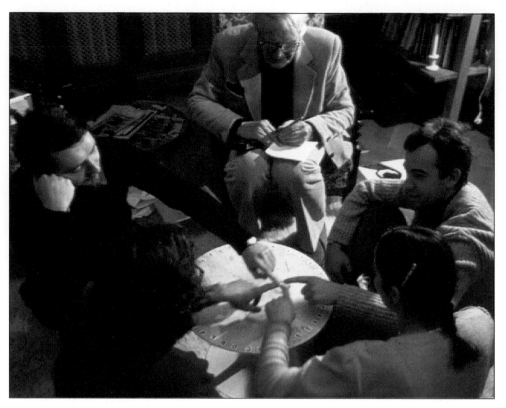

Something worthy of more serious attention, perhaps, is the practice of automatic writing. Here, the medium enters a trance-like state while lightly holding a pen, which then moves spontaneously across the page. Not only is this much quicker than table-tilting or Ouija, but it can produce impressive results. Whole books have been written in this way, and there have even been occasions when different messages have been transcribed by each hand simultaneously.

There is disagreement about the provenance of the messages received in this way. Some attribute them to the spirits of the dead, but psychiatrists and psychologists are more inclined to believe that the source lies within the sitter's own mind. This is because many of the messages seem to reflect what the recipient is wanting to hear. Automatic writing is thus often used as a tool to explore the realms of the subconscious.

Electronic Voice Phenomena   In 1957, the Russian-born film producer Friedrich Jurgenson was listening to some birdsong he had recorded, when he heard the unexpected sound of a man's voice. At first he thought that it was just a coincidence, that he had perhaps picked up a radio broadcast. But when he made further recordings - this time ensuring that no human voices were audible - he was amazed to discover that they, too, contained messages. Even more bizarre was the fact that the messages were directed at Jurgenson himself, urging him to continue with his experiments.

Jurgenson had stumbled upon a method of contact which is a product of the modern era - electronic voice phenomena, or EVP. While it may be true that EVP is worlds apart from mainstream science, it is also certainly the case that figures of the stature of Edison and Marconi both attempted to develop devices that would register the voices of departed spirits.

Above right: A glass tilting during a seance

Below: Do the messages communicated by mediums come from the spirit world or do recipients simply hear what they want to hear?

Someone who conducted many experiments on the subject of EVP was the psychic Matthew Manning. He tried to contact Adolf Hitler using this method, believing that it was easier to 'attract a power of evil than a power of good.' Manning left a tape running and invited Hitler to speak. Afterwards, he was astonished at what he had recorded: 'It began with distant rumbling gunfire, which soon gave way to regimented marching...as though the microphone was placed near to soldiers as they marched past it. Then, behind this noise a sound like a brass band could be heard playing a marching tune....later identified as one of the German

Nazi songs. The marching feet began running as gunfire could be heard more clearly in the background. Still the music kept playing over it all and incoherent shouting was audible.'

Some people claim that voices recorded in this way are from the spirit world; indeed, there have been cases when the voices have proclaimed themselves to be from beyond the grave. Another theory is they are from the experimenter's subconscious, which somehow influences the magnetic tape psychokinetically. These two theories are not mutually exclusive; the latter scenario would still admit the possibility that the messages originated in the spirit world.

Not all messages received via EVP are so mysterious, however. The Latvian psychologist Konstantin Raudive met Friedrich Jurgenson and became interested in the subject. He made many recordings of his own, his technique being to link his tape recorder to a radio tuned between stations. Often the messages Raudive received were personal and relevant only to him. On one occasion, a message ended with the sinister words: 'I follow you tonight'. Raudive had little cause to worry, however; the voice was later identified as a disc-jockey, plugging his show with the words: 'It's all for you tonight'.

More eerily, on June 18, 1974, Raudive's name featured in a message received by another researcher into EVP. Raymond Cass recorded a voice saying: 'Raudive, man of oak, towards the tomb'. Three months later, Raudive died.

Matthew Manning

Matthew Manning's experiments with EVP represent just one avenue for his renowned psychic abilities. He discovered his powers while still at school, when he became the focus of a poltergeist; he also found he was able to receive messages from the spirit world.

In 1971, Matthew discovered automatic writing while trying to compose an essay for school. He described the experience in his book The Link: 'I watched, startled, as I wrote words in a handwriting different from my own. Then, becoming momentarily frightened, I pulled my hand away and looked at what I had written. The words were incomprehensible and sprawled across half the page. I tore up the page almost immediately, and it was not until later that I realised that I must have written "automatically", and that my hand had been used and controlled by an outside influence.'

Matthew went on to use automatic writing extensively as a means of contacting the spirit world. The writing would come in a variety of styles and languages, many of which he could not understand. He also found that although he had 'never possessed any ability to draw or paint', he was able to use the same automatic process to reproduce the style of many dead artists, including Henri Matisse and Pablo Picasso.

Above: Table levitating during a psychokinesis experiment

Left: A table tilting during a seance in New York, 1937

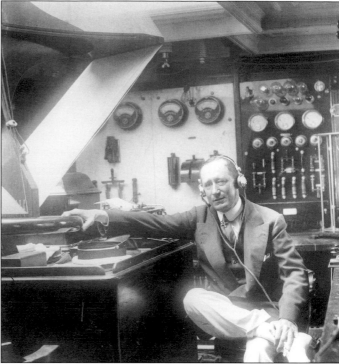

Cross-Correspondences

One of the methods aimed at eliminating the risk of trickery on the part of mediums is cross-correspondence. This is where unconnected mediums in different locations receive the same message.

An impressive example of cross-correspondence occurred around 1905, involving the Society for Psychical Research itself. A number of mediums reported receiving messages from Frederic Myers and other deceased founder members of the Society. Many of these said that the number 7 was in some way significant. An expert in the field, J D Piddington, was consulted, and he was stunned at this particular reference.

Four years earlier, he had given the Society a sealed letter with instructions that it should not be opened until after his death. Piddington asked for it back and revealed the secret it contained: 'If I am ever in spirit and if I can communicate, I shall endeavour to transmit in some form or other the number 7.' It seemed that not only had others had the opportunity of putting the idea to the test before Piddington, but they had even used his own coded message.

The Psychic Excavator

Glastonbury Abbey, in the south-west of England, dates back to the 5th century, and is reputed to contain the tombs of King Arthur and Queen Guinevere. A thousand years later, during the reign of Henry VIII, the Abbey was looted and destroyed. In 1907, the ruins were bought by the nation for £30,000, and the Church of England engaged an architect named Frederick Bligh Bond to plan the excavation.

Along with a friend, John Alan Bartlett, Bond tried to contact the spirits of the Abbey through automatic writing. The pair asked questions about Glastonbury, and answers came back in Old English and Latin. These responses contained information not available at the time; an outline of the building was also received, signed 'Gulielmus Monachus' - William the Monk.

When the excavations began in 1908, Bond was able to tell the workmen exactly where to dig. The spirits of the monks had given details of two chapels and two towers, which proved to be completely accurate. The Church authorities were initially delighted and amazed at Bond's success. They were rather less pleased, however, when he described what had guided him. The revelation resulted in the excavations being halted, while Bond himself was banned from the site.

Above left: Rosemary Brown composing a mazurka inspired by Chopin

Above right: Wireless pioneer Marconi spent the last 16 years of his life secretly working on a device to receive voices from the past

Daniel Douglas Home

Daniel Douglas Home was one of the most successful mediums of the 19th century. His seances were said to be spectacular events: dead people communicated with those present sometimes by taking possession of Home's body, sometimes by materialising in person.

Scandal brought about Home's downfall. It began when a wealthy widow named Mrs Lyon asked him to contact her dead husband. Home did so and over a period of time produced a series of messages that he claimed had come from the deceased. The contents of these were greatly to the advantage of Home himself: first he was to be given an income of £700 per annum, then he was to be treated as her son. Mrs Lyon eventually handed over £60,000, but then had a change of heart and had Home arrested. He was ordered to return the money, and support for him dwindled in the wake of the scandal. His abilities did not appear to desert him, however. One of the leading scientists of the day, Sir William Crookes, investigated Home's powers and stated that he could find no trace of deception.

Phone Call from the Dead

The message received by Mr and Mrs MacConnell one evening in 1971 came via an inanimate medium - the telephone - yet it proved to be as dramatic as the most sensational seance.

The call was from a friend of the MacConnells, Enid Johlson, who informed them that she was staying at the Handmaker Jewish Nursing Home. While they were speaking, Mrs MacConnell realised that it was nearly Enid's birthday and promised her a bottle of wine. 'I don't need it now,' Enid replied, adding that she had never been happier.

Five days later, Mrs MacConnell called the nursing home to speak to her friend. She was informed that Enid had died five days earlier, the day of the telephone call; but Enid had passed away in the morning, several hours before the MacConnells had spoken to her.

Blind Proof?

Mediums face a particular difficulty in trying to prove that messages do come from the spirits of the dead. A Catch 22 situation exists: if the information cannot be verified by a living person, then there are no grounds for believing in the medium's powers; but if verification is forthcoming, then there is always the possibility that the living person could be the source of the medium's information. In the latter case, this could be the result of a conspiracy, while some have suggested that the medium might even obtain information telepathically.

One way in which this problem could be overcome would be a 'blind' test, where the medium produces information of which even the verifying witness is unaware. This is precisely what happened during a seance in England in the 1980s. A woman was impressed by the information the medium was receiving from her dead father, including details she had almost forgotten herself. But then the medium spoke of her having a sister, which was not the case. This blatant inaccuracy made her sceptical of the medium's powers; but later, in a distressing family confrontation, her mother admitted that she had indeed had a sister who had been given away at birth.

Above top and bottom: Psychologists, William James and James H Hyslop, promised each other that whoever died first would contact the other. James died first and Hyslop waited for years in vain for contact, until a pair of Irish mediums wrote to tell them that their seances had been plagued by a William James seeking a Professor Hyslop

Left: Seances developed from a parlour game to become part of the ritual of Spiritualism

Acknowledgements

This book has been developed with a great deal of help
from the following people:
John Dunne; Christine Hoy; Tim Hill;
John Williams; Cliff Salter; Deborah Adams;
Charlie Allen; Nick Croydon; David Crane;
Rebecca Hedland-Thomas and Jo Chiles.

Picture Credits

The illustrations are reproduced courtesy of:

AKG London
Andrew Joly
British Library Newspapers
Charles Walker Collection/Images Colour Library
Comstock Inc 1997
Corbis UK
Don Whillans
Fortean Picture Library
Hulton Getty
Jo Chiles
John & Anne Spencer
Mary Evans Picture Library
Maurice Gosse
MUFON
Panos Pictures
The Imperial War Museum
The John Frost Newspaper Archive
The Marsden Collection
The Natural Law Party
The Roland Grant Archive
Tim Furniss/Genesis Space Photo Library
Tony Morrison/South American Pictures, Woodbridge, England
TRH Pictures
TRIP Photographic Library